THE ARTHURIAN LEGEND

THE
ARTHURIAN LEGEND

COMPARISON OF TREATMENT IN MODERN AND MEDIÆVAL LITERATURE

A STUDY IN THE LITERARY VALUE OF MYTH AND LEGEND

BY

MARGARET J. C. REID, M.A., Ph.D.

BARNES & NOBLE, Inc., NEW YORK

Publishers · Booksellers · Since 1873

Published in Great Britain by
OLIVER AND BOYD LTD.
Tweeddale Court, Edinburgh
39a Welbeck Street, London, W.1

FIRST PUBLISHED 1938
REPRINTED 1961

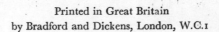

Printed in Great Britain
by Bradford and Dickens, London, W.C.1

AUTHOR'S PREFACE

An apology is perhaps required for adding yet another volume
to the extensive and scholarly work already done on the
subject of the "Arthurian Legend." The bibliography
compiled at the end of J. D. Bruce's *Evolution of Arthurian
Romance* (1923) is sufficient evidence to its extent and
thoroughness. To these studies on origins I do not claim
to have contributed anything. But in my studies, occupying
four years, in which I completed an annotated bibliography
of the Arthurian Legend, I found little connected literary
criticism on the modern poets, who have used as subject-
matter the traditional material of this legend. The chief
treatise is by H. Maynadier, *The Arthur of the English Poets*
(1907), to whom I have made reference throughout, in my
own work. However, in my argument in this monograph,
I have followed the logical and philosophical method of
criticism rather than his chronological one. Also, as I have
written at a later date, I have included modern poets and
playwrights up to the neo-moderns. Thus I have attempted
to throw fresh light on the interesting question of the use of
legendary material (in particular that of the Arthurian
Legend), by modern poets and playwrights. On this subject
I have found Sir H. J. C. Grierson's essay, "The Background
of English Literature," [1] most inspiring and illuminating.

I wish to acknowledge my deep sense of gratitude to
Dr E. A. Baker, late Director of the School of Librarianship,
for his unfailing encouragement and help.

The initiation, completion and publication [2] of this Study
would have been impossible without the generous financial
aid of the Carnegie Trust to whom my gratitude is due.

---

[1] In volume of same name.

[2] I held a Scholarship 1921-3, Fellowship 1923-5 and also a Grant for
publication 1937.

I am also indebted to Miss A. Rudmose Brown, Principal of Dudley Training College, Professor A. A. Jack and Professor Oliver Elton for their stimulating, constructive and detailed criticism ; and for help in typing and arranging the manuscript I wish to thank my sister, Miss C. E. C. Reid.

This thesis was accepted for the Ph.D. Degree by the University of Aberdeen, July 1937.

MARGARET J. C. REID.

September 1938.

CONTENTS

CHAP.   PAGE

I. INTRODUCTORY   1

What is meant by the term " modern " ? Courtly love expressed
by Marie of France, Chrétien de Troies and Malory. General
comparison of mediæval with modern treatment in Literature.

II. ARTHUR IN THE CHRONICLES AND IN MALORY . . 14

King Arthur in early history, twelfth and thirteenth centuries,
in Nennius, Geoffrey of Monmouth, Wace, Layamon. " Morte
d'Arthur " (Alliterative and Stanzaic) ; In Malory.

III. ARTHUR IN THE SIXTEENTH, SEVENTEENTH AND EIGHTEENTH
CENTURIES : SPENSER, MILTON, DRYDEN . . . 30

Warner ; Hughes. In Spenser's *Færie Queene*. Milton ; and
Dryden's *King Arthur* ; Blackmore's *King Arthur*. Arthur, in
chap-books and popular miscellanies. Percy's *Reliques*.
Warton's *Grave of King Arthur*. Lytton.

IV. ARTHUR IN MODERN TIMES : SCOTT, TENNYSON, MASEFIELD 42

Scott's " Bridal of Triermain." Tennyson : early life of King
Arthur in the " Coming of Arthur," Arthur as a type of perfect
kingship, plan and argument of the *Idylls*, with criticism.
Westwood. Laurence Binyon's *King Arthur*. Comyns Carr.
John Masefield, " Badon Hill," " Birth of Arthur," " Sailing of
Hell Race."

V. GAWAIN 59

Early English Gawain ; Chrétien de Troies ; Lord Lytton ;
Tennyson's " Pelleas and Etarre."

VI. MERLIN 70

In Geoffrey of Monmouth : in sixteenth, seventeenth and
eighteenth centuries ; in Wordsworth ; in Tennyson's " Merlin
and Vivien " and " Merlin and the Gleam " ; in Swinburne's
Tristram of Lyonesse ; in Gordon Bottomley's *Merlin's Grave* ; in
Edwin Arlington Robinson.

VII. LANCELOT 87

Early origins ; in Chrétien de Troies and Malory ; in Tennyson.
Morris and the Pre-Raphaelites ; Richard Hovey ; in John
Davidson ; John Masefield and Laurence Binyon.

VIII. THE WELSH TRADITION 108

Thomas Love Peacock, *The Misfortunes of Elphin*. The *Mabinogion*.
Malory and Spenser. Tennyson's " Geraint and Enid."

vii

CHAP.   PAGE

IX. THE HOLY GRAIL : EARLIER VERSIONS 128
Origins. The *Queste* Version. Wolfram von Aeschenbach's *Parzival*. Malory.

X. THE HOLY GRAIL : MODERN VERSIONS 136
Tennyson ; R. S. Hawker ; Westwood ; Lowell. Neo-modern Versions : T. S. Eliot and J. C. Powys.

XI. BALIN AND BALAN 159
In Tennyson and Swinburne.

XII. WAGNER : PARSIFAL, LOHENGRIN, TRISTAN . . . 165

XIII. TRISTAN : SOURCES AND MALORY 191
Two sources which have affected modern literature. Version of Gottfried von Strassburg and Eilhart von Oberg compared to the Prose Romance and Malory in several incidents.

XIV. TRISTAN : TENNYSON AND SWINBURNE 204
"The Last Tournament." Swinburne, his purpose. Earlier work, *Queen Iseult* and later *Tristram of Lyonesse*, described and compared with the Sources poet used. Prelude.

XV. TRISTAN : OTHER MODERN VERSIONS 220
First Group—showing influence of tradition. L. Binyon : Comyns Carr : Arthur Symons : Michael Field. Second Group—in which tradition is adapted and changed freely. Thomas Hardy : John Masefield : Matthew Arnold : Edwin Arlington Robinson.

XVI. THE ARTHURIAN LEGEND IN SATIRE 244
Dinadan in Malory. Satire of Romances in *Don Quixote*. John Hookham Frere's Burlesque. Mark Twain's *A Yankee at the Court of King Arthur*.

XVII. SUMMARY AND CONCLUSION 250
Value of Myth as exemplified in Plato, Wagner and Shakespeare. Difficulty of the modern poet. Lack of traditional background. Study of W. B. Yeats and Irish Renaissance, and comparison with literary history of the Arthurian Legend. Final summing up of value.

APPENDIX A 264
Chronological Summary of Original Poems, Plays and Prose Works after 1485 which have Arthurian Subjects.

APPENDIX B 266
The Arthurian Legend in the Decorative Arts.

APPENDIX C 266
List of Important Reference Books including Texts.

INDEX 271

CHAPTER I

INTRODUCTION

IN the study of the Arthurian legend, the first problem before us is to determine what is meant by the term " modern," and in this special instance, what date is to be fixed for the division between " mediæval " and " modern."

" Modern " is a term which, for the sake of convenience, may be determined chronologically. But reasons must be given why this special date is chosen and is at least approximately suitable. In the history of the Arthurian legend this is not a difficult task. The year 1485, the date of the first edition of Malory, printed by Caxton, has been chosen. Though Malory wrote when the age of chivalry was declining in morals and ideals, the material of his compilation embodies the various conceptions of the chivalric age.

The two main factors which went to form the chivalric ideal, whose best period was in the twelfth and thirteenth centuries, both originated in an actual feudal society.[1] The first was the relationship between inferior and superior, vassal and lord, based on mutual agreement. The possession of land held by the vassal from the lord was assumed, for which the vassal gave in return loyalty and service. In romance, however, this factor was not stressed. In Geoffrey of Monmouth,[2] Arthur, as a great feudal lord, gave lands to his lords, among whom were Bedevere and Kay. But in Malory this aspect had fallen into the background. The military relationship, the tie between knight and lord, held more glamour for the romanticist. The Holy Wars of the Crusades had brought this special set of relations into the

---

[1] For full description see Osborne Taylor, *The Mediæval Mind*, 1911, vol. i., Book IV.

[2] Book IX, ch. 14, " Everyman " Edition.

service of Christianity and thus idealised it, at any rate in theory. The second factor was the relationship purported to exist between knight and his lady, the well-known *amour courtois* or courtly love.

Malory's work, though written when the finest flowering of the chivalric age was past, is yet one of the classic representations in English literature of those two factors, the relationship between knight and lord, and that of knight and lady. The former is shown forth in the depiction of Gawain and Arthur, Lancelot and Arthur, and the latter in the story of Lancelot and Guinevere,[1] though in the handling of the latter there is more natural emotion portrayed than in the tabulated poems of courtly love. This " courtly love " had been developed first in the south of France and in the aristocratic and pleasure-loving centres of Languedoc and in the great feudal courts of the north, Aquitaine, Champagne and also Flanders. Actual courts of love were held and a series of so-called " laws " invented for the proper conduct of the lovers.[2] The close connection of the courts of France and England at this time made England also a partaker in this most formal tradition. It will be remembered that Eleanor of Poitou, the wife of Henry II, had as her first husband Louis VII, and had had by him a daughter, Marie of Champagne. Both Eleanor and Marie encouraged at their courts this literary convention.

Amidst the various and somewhat machine-made products of the courtly tradition, the names of Marie de France and Chrétien de Troies stand out, clearly deciphered in the Temple of Fame. Both have made outstanding contributions to French and to Arthurian literature.

Little is known of the life and circumstances of Marie of France.[3] She dedicated her *Lays* to a " nobles reis " who was probably Henry II of England, and the poems have

---

[1] For a fuller study see below, Chap. VII.

[2] For a full account of these see W. A. Neilson, *Origins and Sources of the Court of Love* (Harvard Studies and Notes in Philology and Literature, VI).

[3] The *Lais* are edited by K. Warnke, 1900 ; and E. Hopffner, 1921 ; translated by E. Rickert (1901).

been dated from 1165-7.   Thus she lived at the very zenith
of the courtly period.   An attempt has been made to identify
her with Countess Marie of Champagne herself.   Scholars
inform us that from the dialectical peculiarities in her works
she belonged to the Norman border of the " Ile de France."
She probably visited England.   She herself tells us that she
took her subjects from the Celtic *contes,* either what she
heard herself or what " li Bretun " [1] had made known.   The
exact form of the latter is disputed.   It is suggested that, like
the early epic of the Welsh bards, the *contes* may have
been partly narrative and partly lyrical sung to a musical
accompaniment. [2]

Two of these poems, " Lanval " and " Chèvrefeuille,"
both written in octosyllabic couplets, are Arthurian in subject.
They are of extreme interest in that they form a link between
the simpler folk-tale and the more sophisticated poems, such
as those of Chrétien de Troies.   They conform in certain
details to the conventions of courtly love.   For example,
the epithets attached to Lanval, "*preux,*" "*courtois,*" etc.,
are the usual stock ones.   Lanval, as a knight and kinsman
of Arthur's, is attached to his court, and has some expectations
of land, which are not, however, fulfilled.   On the other
hand, the emotions are more natural than many of those
described in the " courtly poems."   Guinevere, whose offered
favours are rejected by Lanval, already in possession of a
most charming fairy mistress, shows quite strong human
jealousy and anger.   In " Chèvrefeuille," Tristan is pictured
as a dweller in the woods and beside a stream, by means of
which he communicates with Iseult.   He loves his lady
undauntedly through rain and shine and comforts his love-
longing by composing a lay in her honour.   In both poems
there is a straightforwardness in action and a sincerity and
naïveté of emotion, which has been lost in the later more
elaborate poems.

Chrétien de Troies, much more than Marie of France, is
to be considered the poet of courtly and chivalric love.   He

---

[1] E. K. Chambers considers this to mean " of Brittany."   See *Arthur
of Britain,* p. 148.   A bitter dispute has raged round this point.

[2] E. K. Chambers, *op. cit.,* p. 147.

composed six poems on Arthurian subjects. The dates are variously given between 1160 and 1180, but their order is fairly certain. They include " Erec et Enide " (Geraint and Enid) ; " Cliges " (only slightly Arthurian) ; " Lancelot " or " Le Chevalier de la Charette " ; " Yvain " or " Le Chevalier au Lion " ; and " Perceval le Gallois " or " Conte del Graal." An early poem on Tristan is lost. The first four were written in the service of Marie of Champagne. In the beginning of " Lancelot," Chrétien tells us the poem was written at her request, who gave him " matière " (subject-matter) and " san " (manner of treatment). Marie, daughter of Louis VII and Eleanor of Aquitaine, married in 1164 Henri of Champagne, and their court was one of the centres of this *amour courtois*. Of Chrétien's life and circumstances little is known, though it has been suggested that he may have been a herald.

Of the two forms of relationship which sprang from the conditions of feudal society and feudal ideals, Chrétien in his poems laid stress on the second, the code which ruled the conduct of the knight towards the lady he had vowed to serve. With the fealty which the knight owed his supreme lord, Chrétien was not so much concerned. Arthur, in his romances, is represented chiefly as the head of the court, which is the centre of various knightly adventures. He is also made the arbiter of all matters of courtesy and etiquette. Indeed, in such a poem as " Lancelot de la Charette " the poet was wise not to insist on this point of loyalty. For in the conventional ruling of the " Courts of Love " a knight ought by preference to love and serve as his lady, a married lady of higher station than himself. If the wife of his feudal lord was chosen, this choice was difficult to reconcile with his duty and loyalty. It must be remembered, however, that in Chrétien's earlier poems, " Erec " and " Yvain," the love between the hero and the heroine is morally irreproachable.

But all Chrétien's poems, except the " Perceval le Gallois," are built round the concepts of this chivalric love, and the incidents and characters are adapted to illustrate these. These conceptions—as has already been observed—had hardened into a code held by a leisured and aristocratic society and expressed in their literary productions. But where Chrétien excels in comparison with the majority of the poets of these courtly traditions is in his manifest gifts as story-teller combined with an analytic talent for character-drawing. A modern critic may find he fails in plot-construction and unity of design and is guilty of diffuseness. Yet his skill in romantic narrative and versatile description, his fluency and ease of style, charmed a worldly and luxurious society which preferred surface qualities and polish to solidity and fineness of substance.

The question of Chrétien's actual originality in plot and construction can hardly be solved without documentary proof of the work of his predecessors, which does not exist. Whatever the actual debt he owed these, there is no doubt that he was handling a good deal of mythical and legendary material alien in substance and spirit to the aim he had in view. Scholars have analysed many of his incidents, adapted superficially by him as knightly adventures, and traced them back to mythical origins. To give one example among many, the description of the fountain in " Yvain " and the sprinkling of the water on the stone and its results, evidently referred originally to some magic-compelling rite to bring rain.[1]

But the important fact in regard to the literary evolution of Arthurian tradition is that Chrétien welded together and gave substance and form to a series of stories, each of which circles round a hero connected with the court of Arthur : Yvain, Erec, Lancelot. And each of these heroes exemplifies by his conduct, his adherence to the precepts of chivalric love. These narrations were to be translated [2] into many European languages—English, German, Italian, Spanish, Dutch—gaining many accretions in their transit. These were formed into Cycles in prose with many interpolations and elaborations. Certain names were attached to these, such as those of Robert de Borron and Walter Map, though many of

[1] See W. A. Nitze, " The Fountain Defended," *Mod. Phil.*, vii., pp. 145-164.

[2] Translated not in an exact sense—for often other incidents native to the various traditions of the countries became attached to the hero in question.

them were anonymous.[1]   It was Malory, compiler and author, who fell heir to this tradition contained in the manuscripts which provided his sources.[2]   In his work are set forth the chief virtues of the knight, bravery, loyalty and generosity. There is also illustrated the conception of courtly love between knight and lady.   Both are somewhat modified to suit Malory's own conception and the more realistic and less fantastic English temperament.   The ideal knight and lover is Lancelot.   Thus Malory's book stands out as the great landmark between mediæval and modern in the history of the legend.   The general trend and qualities of Arthurian literature after the fifteenth century cannot be followed or used for comparison with the period before that date, unless his various books are studied with their sources and some knowledge is possessed of the conditions of society which went to produce those sources.[2]

In surveying the literature of Arthurian legend after this date, there will be differences in attitude and treatment, arising out of the fact of a different state of society, with other morals and ideals.   However much a later author, for example Tennyson, tries to enter into the spirit of the chivalric age, yet unwittingly he brings the judgment of another century and code of ideals to bear on his subject-matter.

There will be also a different relation between the author and his readers.   The conditions under which literature was produced before the time of printing with its cheap and accessible books, must always be kept in mind.   Before legends and stories were ever written down, there was a mass of floating traditions handed down, at one time from mother to child, at another recited by the minstrel.[3]   It is easy to imagine how welcome in the feudal castles, during the long winter evenings, the minstrel or the band of minstrels must have been.   The minstrel galleries in some of the old keeps

[1] For full account and bibliography, see J. D. Bruce, *Evolution of Arthurian Romance*, 1923.

[2] One of the best studies of Malory and his sources is by E. Vinaver, *Malory*, 1929.

[3] In bardic literature it was recited to the harp.   See E. K. Chambers, *Arthur of Britain*, p. 59.

still testify to this fact. And in the bowers and pleasure-grounds, the ladies, whose husbands and sons may have been absent in the Crusades, would be glad to listen to the tales of fighting and love.

Even when the stories became more conventionalised and literary and were reproduced more formally by poets and prose-writers in manuscript copies, there must have been a good deal of story-telling by word of mouth, because the manuscripts were costly and difficult to obtain. Whether or not there was such a book as Geoffrey of Monmouth's " liber," [1] which he announced as the source of his history, he must also have gathered together much matter from oral sources.

Thus this common tradition, oral and written, in courtly circles in France and England, and in more rustic ones (as the *fabliaux* and ballads witness), created a relation between singer or teller and audience or between author and reader, which has never been recovered. The modern author or poet, writing in his study for an educated audience, has lost this intimate bond. John Masefield, in his lecture on Poetry,[2] regretted that the speaking of verse had given way to the reading of it in the study. He himself has done something to renew the closer relationship of poet and audience by reciting his own verse.

From the conditions of mediæval society there sprang also what might be termed the impersonality (often joined to anonymity) of a great part of this literature, founded on Arthurian story. The earlier audiences may have been like children, more interested in the tale than in the teller. And when the stories began to be written down, copied and re-copied, the author or transcriber did not trouble to record his name or obtrude his personality. Certain names became attached to the various Cycles, Robert de Borron and Walter Map, but these were probably affixed later. Even when the author did give his name, as in the case of Geoffrey of

[1] For discussion see R. H. Fletcher, *The Arthurian Material in the Chronicles* (Harvard Studies and Notes, X), Boston, 1906.

[2] Given at the inaugural meeting of the Scottish Association for the speaking of Verse, Edinburgh, 24th October 1924, " With the Living Voice."

Monmouth, he referred to his source, real or assumed. The later romancers copied manuscript after manuscript with interpolations and additions, without affixing their names, or any personal matter. Of course there are great exceptions such as the case of Chrétien de Troies, whose polished style and psychological insight into character might almost be termed " modern."

It is interesting also to compare the form and style used in mediæval and modern times. Before Malory, the stories of Arthur were related in history-chronicle and in long romances, many of them in French, without much form or proportion at all. One knight sets out on an adventure and is crossed and re-crossed by others. Often the story of a second is begun before the first is finished. By the time the second is completed, the reader has forgotten the details of the first. Sometimes the first adventure is never finished at all. Thus the work resembles a maze rather than a highroad leading to a definite goal. The "Tristan" as compiled by Malory shows these defects, although Malory's rhythmic and balanced prose makes the reader often forget this fault.

In verse-tales, as in such romances as " Sir Gawain " and " Sir Tristrem," the metre is rude and halting. The metrical romances and ballads of Gawain which Dr Weston believes were native to England and part of a Gawain cycle, partake of the same rough and forceful nature. Chaucer, who had learned his metres and story-telling from the French, only once used Arthurian matter, namely, in " The Wife of Bath's Tale," which is closely connected with the " Marriage of Geraint." [1] In Marie of France and Chrétien de Troies the verse is more polished.

Thus the Renaissance and later ages had qualities to give literature in regard to the sense of form both in the construction of a story and in metrical form. These qualities affected the handling of Arthurian as well as other matter. In this case,

---

[1] See G. H. Maynadier, *The Wife of Bath's Tale ; its Sources and Analogues*, 1901. He discusses fully the connection of these two tales, also *Dame Ragnell*. He himself thinks Chaucer may have used an earlier source. Though the scene is laid in Arthur's court, the connection in Chaucer is not very close.

the mediæval writers provided the storehouse which the later writers rifled, choosing a story here and there, moulding it and lavishing on it all their skill in craftsmanship. Thus Tennyson has celebrated the death of Arthur in his masterly blank verse, and Swinburne, the story of Tristram and Iseult in his rich flowing cadences. In the latter tale, the dramatic progression with the culminating point in the drink, with its fateful consequences, has appealed to modern playwrights of the twentieth century who have made a choice of scenes for their own purposes. The time for the epic or long narrative poem seems past. What Milton, with his architectonic skill would have made of the subject is a matter for conjecture. Tennyson comes nearest to the epic in his *Idylls*.

After Malory, that is, after the fifteenth century, these main differences which have been indicated,[1] will be found. There will be on the part of the artist a different attitude to his public. The minstrel or poet is no longer reciting a tale to an audience with the knowledge of a certain tradition. He is writing in his own domain, removed from his readers, and thus able at leisure to polish his style. He is a more self-conscious artist, aware of his own personality and his task.

Thus Spenser writes in the Invocation to the *Faerie Queene* :—

> Lo, I the man whose Muse whilome did maske,
> As time her taught, in lowly Shepheard's weeds,
> Am now enforst a far unfitter task,
> For trumpets sterne to chaunge mine Oaten reeds,
> And sing of Knights and Ladies gentle deeds.[2]

THE NINETEENTH AND TWENTIETH CENTURIES

The strongest searchlight is, in the following chapters, to be thrown on the Arthurian literature of the nineteenth and twentieth centuries, to which the term " modern " is especially to be applied. This period is to be the main subject of analysis

---

[1] Of the deeper religious and mystical spirit in the Middle Ages, see *Holy Grail*, Chap. IX.

[2] See Spenser's *Faerie Queene*, ed. J. C. Smith, 1909, p. 2.

and discussion. The history of literature often proceeds in
circles rather than straight lines. Thus the relations between
the fifteenth century, with its great representative in Malory
and the nineteenth (including the later eighteenth) and
twentieth centuries are closer than the time chart indicates.
The " Romantic Revival " includes among other things a
revival of interest in the " Middle Ages," often rather
inaccurately termed the " Gothic Revival." There was an
eager study of Malory and Spenser. But the interest proved
a creative one and did not issue merely in a slavish copy of
the mediæval.

A literature must be studied in the society which produces
it and thus a very general comparison between the Chivalrous
Ages and the Romantic Revival is not useless.

Both the periods in question had their ideals of love ;
in the earlier age, of " Courtly Love " and in the later, of
" Romantic Love." This ideal of love had in both cases
its root in a spirit of revolt,¹ the one against a constant pre-
occupation with things of the soul and the next world, which
the Middle Ages showed, the other against the limited and
formal art and culture of the eighteenth century. Each had
its revolt against marriage.² In the Age of Chivalry, the
relationship was ignored in the romantic relationship between
knight and lady, often a married lady of higher birth than
her lover. In the Romantic Revival, the legal bond of
marriage was considered too narrow a vessel for the seething
potion of romantic passion. Yet no marriage could have
contained more restricting rules than the chivalric code.
This is perhaps why the representative poets of the Romantic
Revival — Shelley, Keats, Byron — found more appropriate
subjects for their poems, passionate in love and revolt, in
the myths and legends of Greece and Italy. Chivalric love,
especially as represented in Malory, is too conventional and
literary a theme. It was the poets of the early nineteenth
century—Tennyson, Morris, Swinburne—who found in the

---

¹ Dr H. J. C. Grierson expands this idea in his essay on " Classic and
Romantic " in his *Background of English Literature*, 1925.

² The great exception is in the *Parzival* of Wolfram von
Eschenbach in which there is a depiction of ideal married love.

subjects of Arthurian legend what they considered inspiring themes for their poems.   Tennyson, of course, was a Victorian in sentiment and an upholder of the religious sanctity of the institution of marriage.   Therefore his attempt to fit Arthurian stories into the moral framework was not altogether successful, however much beauty may be found in his detailed workmanship.   Morris, again, as a Pre-Raphaelite, was attracted by the picturesqueness of the mediæval setting and a certain beauty and sentimental fervour which accompanies the aftermath of illegal passion, as typified in Lancelot and Guinevere. Swinburne revolted against Tennyson's moral rigidity and extolled natural passion.   The religious background of his poem on Tristan might be called romantic pantheism.   The more virile hero suited his purposes better than the chivalric Arthur.

From a general point of view,[1] those qualities of mediæval literature (mentioned in the last chapter) which arise from the impersonal and often anonymous element within it, and also from the closer and more informal relation of the teller of the tale to his audience, will have changed still more in the nineteenth and twentieth centuries.   On the total disappearance of an oral tradition, whose last traces are seen in the collections of eighteenth-century ballads, the subject-matter of the Arthurian legends will have become more and more literary, and further removed from the lore of the people.

Of the anonymous element, much is found even in Malory, who must be looked upon as a compiler as well as an author. After Malory, the literary artist is no longer dealing with a tradition behind which he humbly conceals his personality and even his opinions.   The age of authority on the field of pseudo-history and romance is past.   Malory's work may, in a certain sense, be termed the Bible of Arthurian tradition, though it never had the literal authority the Bible possessed. It has rather been a storehouse into which the modern poet or dramatist has delved, choosing what has suited his purposes. The poets of the later nineteenth and twentieth centuries have also taken their material from renderings and versions

---

[1] The treatment in this introductory section is, of course, of the briefest, and will be carried out throughout the following chapters in this treatise.

of Arthurian story, prepared by scholars ; for example, the fine English translation by Lady Charlotte Guest, of the *Mabinogion*,[1] Joseph Bédier's translation of the *Tristan*,[2] made from various existing versions, and the translations of Geoffrey of Monmouth, such as is found in Giles' *Six English Chronicles*.[3] From these, poets and dramatists took their stories and moulded them according to their desire.

In modern times also, the distance between writer—no longer teller—and reader has been increased. The cheapness and accessibility of books in the nineteenth and twentieth centuries is one of the prime causes of this. The poet or dramatist composes his plays in the study and often, even in the case of a play, his work is read instead of being acted, or heard. Thus it will be found that many of the plays on Tristan, written in the twentieth century, are of merely academic interest. Perhaps the main exception to this is Thomas Hardy's *Queen of Cornwall*, which possesses more vitality than the others, and has been actually represented on the stage. It is this cutting off of literature from the living voice, the writer from his public, and the subject-matter from the tradition of the common people, which causes atrophy.[4]

The living link between the eighteenth and nineteenth century is the Ballad. In the case of Arthurian legend, there have been a good number of ballads preserved on Arthur and Gawain. Dr Weston considers Gawain primarily an English hero. That the story of Arthur was once common property in the taverns, is witnessed by Shakespeare, who made Falstaff sing the ditty " When Arthur first in Court began " in the Eastcheap tavern.[5] The only remnant of this popularity seems to have come down to the later centuries in nursery rhymes and songs. Tom Thumb is a late descendant of Sir Lancelot.

---

[1] *The Mabinogion*, translated by Lady Charlotte Guest, 3 vols., 1838-49.

[2] Thomas, *Le Roman de Tristan*, ed. J. Bédier, 1902-5.

[3] J. A. Giles, *Six Old English Chronicles*, 1841. The best critical text of Geoffrey of Monmouth's *Historia* is in E. Faral, *La Legende Arthurienne*, 1929.

[4] The invention of " wireless " may bring back the power of the living voice to some extent.

[5] Second part of *King Henry IV*, Act II, Scene 4.

If the Arthurian legend has lost in popularity and traditional worth, it has gained in one respect, in respect of form, at least in poetry. Among the poetic forms, epic, lyric or dramatic, the drama and the narrative poem, short and long, have been the most employed in the last two centuries. The Tristan legend, by the very nature of the story, lends itself to the dramatic form and has produced many plays in the twentieth century. The narrative poem, short or comparatively short in comparison with the epic, enables the modern poet to choose one theme and make of it an artistic unity, as Tennyson's " Lady of Shalott " and John Masefield's " Sir Bors." Tennyson has chosen a more complex form in his series of *Idylls* with their blank verse stanza. These *Idylls* are strung together like beads on a string, logically held together, yet not so organically composite as the epic.

CHAPTER II

ARTHUR IN THE CHRONICLES AND MALORY

THE Arthurian legend, which later had so many branches, had its main roots in the story of King Arthur, told in the pseudo-histories of Nennius, Geoffrey of Monmouth, Wace and Layamon. Later in the romances, the adventures of the Knights of the Round Table obscured those of the King, and he became a mere figure-head, and his court a centre from which knights sallied out on their various quests and returned with their trophies.

The two strands, interwoven in the stories which have Arthur as a hero, are the two which are found in most legends, the mythical [1] and the historical or pseudo-historical, treating Arthur as a human being, though of heroic stature.

The twelfth-century historians, of course, had little idea of history as a relation of fact ; they wove together probable incidents and quite improbable ones, many of the latter being derived from oral legends. The mythical element is also strongly represented in the *Mabinogion*, translated by Lady Charlotte Guest from a fourteenth-century manuscript, the "Red Book of Hergest." These tales are, however, considerably older [2] than the manuscript and the two oldest which contain Arthurian matter, " Kilhwch and Olwen " [3] and the " Dream of Rhonabwy " [4] show no traces, as the later stories do, of the Normanised world of Geoffrey of Monmouth. They show Arthur as a kind of superman, towering above his underlings in a world of magic. This magic communicated

---

[1] Using myth in sense as a story referring to a god.

[2] See discussion, *Mabinogion*, ed. Nutt, p. 345 ; also Loth, introduction to *Les Mabinogion*, 1913, pp. 33-34.

[3] Probably not later than 1175. For fuller treatment see below, p. 115 ff.

[4] Between 1159 and 1165.

14

itself to all which Arthur possesses.[1] The importance of Geoffrey of Monmouth in the history and development of Arthurian legend can hardly be exaggerated. What were his sources, the authenticity of the " liber " of which he makes mention, how much or how little he took from his sources, in what manner he adapted, transformed and added to them, what legends were current in his own day—all these questions over which scholars have laboured [2] are of interest. But from the wider point of view of Arthurian literature, and English literature in particular, there is one chief fact to be emphasised and remembered. This is that Geoffrey was the first to give in eloquent and rhetorical Latin a detailed account of Arthur, his barons and knights, an account which, written as history, appealed to the imagination of the future poets and prose writers who were to elaborate still further the various incidents.

The researches of scholars have brought to notice certain passages in the contemporary and Pre-Galfridian chronicles which go to prove that Arthur held a certain place as a character in history (or pseudo-history) round which legendary stories had begun to gather. The first mention of him is in an entry in the ninth-century Chronicle of Nennius.[3] Arthur in this entry [4] is mentioned as fighting against the Saxons as " dux bellorum." Twelve battles are here given, including the twelfth, Mount Badon, when Arthur " alone in one day killed nine hundred and sixty men " [5] and in which he was victor.[5] In the eighth battle at the fortress Guinnion, it is

---

[1] For Welsh Arthur see below, Chap. VIII.

[2] These questions are treated fully—amongst other treatises—in E. K. Chambers's *Arthur of Britain*, 1927, and R. H. Fletcher's *Arthurian Material in the Chronicles* (Harvard Studies and Notes, No. 10), 1905. I am indebted to both of these for facts and references.

[3] Harleian MS. 3859 is the most typical MS. E. K. Chambers dates the MS. eleventh and early twelfth century, but asserts the Chronicle was written in the ninth century, arguing from the mention in it of the historical Elfodd, Bishop of Bangor, who died about 811 (see his *Arthur of Britain*, p. 6).

[4] *Historia Britonum*, ch. 56, ed. T. Mommsen in *Chronica minora Saeculorum*, iv.-vii. (*M. G. H.*, iii. 111).

[5] William of Malmesbury more judiciously reports nine hundred (J. A. Giles, *Six Old English Chronicles*, 1841, ed. Bohn, p. xi).

stated that he "bore the image of the Virgin Mary on his shoulders (*super humeros suos*)." As regards his rank, the Vatican [1] manuscript adds ."although many were nobler by birth (*nobliores*) than he."

This description speaks for itself, but it is interesting to note that Arthur has already been made a Christian warrior. The tenth-century "Annales Cambriæ" gives two entries relating that Arthur, in the Battle of Badon, carried the cross of our Lord Jesus Christ for three days and three nights on his shoulders. The chronicle also mentions the battle of "Camlann" in which Arthur and Medraut fell. [2]

Of especial interest in regard to the legendary Arthur, are the passages in the Appendix to the *Historia* of Nennius, the Mirabilia [3] which relate marvels of the South Country.

" In the region of Buelt is a heap of stones and on the top is one stone bearing the print of a dog's foot." This mark was made by Cabal—so the document goes on to relate— and he was the dog of Arthur the warrior when he hunted the boar Troynt. The cairn was called Carn Cabal.

Another passage tells of the wonders of the tomb Anir in the region of Erfing (Hereford), [4] who was the son of Arthur (Arthur *militis*) and killed by him and buried here.

The story of the hunting of the boar Troynt is of especial interest as it appears again in the story of " Kilhwch and Olwen." [5]

There is, before Geoffrey, still another important witness to the fame of Arthur, namely, William of Malmesbury, a contemporary of Geoffrey and a historian of considerable critical discernment for his times, and a worthy follower of

---

[1] E. K. Chambers dates this MS. eleventh or early twelfth century, but R. H. Fletcher assigns it to the tenth century (*Arthurian Material in the Chronicles*, note, p. 15).

[2] E. K. Chambers quotes for this passage the Harleian MS. 3859 (eleventh and twelfth centuries) ed. by E. Phillimore in *Y Cymmrodor*, ix. 141, and J. Loth, *Les Mabinogion*, xi. 370. (See *Arthur of Britain*, Appendix, p. 240.)

[3] From ninth-century *Historia Britonum*, ed. T. Mommsen in *Chronica minora Saeculorum*, IV-VII (*M. G. H.*, iii. 111).

[4] See *Mabinogion*, ed. Lady C. Guest (" Everyman " Edition, p. 325).

[5] See below, pp. 116 ff.

Bede. In his *Gesta Anglorum*, of which the first version was finished about 1125, he makes an important statement concerning Arthur : " This is that Arthur of whom the trifling of the Britons talks such nonsense even to-day ; a man clearly worthy not to be dreamed of in fallacious fables, but to be proclaimed in veracious histories, as one who long sustained his tottering country, and gave the shattered minds of his fellow-citizens an edge for war." [1]

From the above excerpts it will be seen that there is enough written evidence from the Chronicles to show that Arthur was already known as a successful British chief and that legends were collecting round his name.

Besides this, the students of comparative mythology have examined Geoffrey's characters and names and have in many instances attempted to trace the origin of these to mythological sources. Even although there is much disagreement concerning these, nevertheless there is a general consensus of opinion that there is in his *History* a considerable foundation of legend. Among the figures concerning whom there was probably a more or less established tradition, are Kei and Bedwyr, known in the *Mabinogion* and the " Triads " and in the *Vita of Cadoc*.[2]

Geoffrey has created them great lords and followers of Arthur. Bedevere the butler is made Duke of Normandy, and Kay the Seneschal, Duke of Anjou.[3] In the final battle against Mordred, both were killed and Arthur had them embalmed and buried. Bedevere the butler was carried into Bayeux and Kay buried near Chinon.[4]

Arthur's weapons, his shield Pridwen, his sword Caliburnus and his lance Ron, are mentioned in the tale of " Kilhwch and Olwen," although Prydwen (so spelt) is a ship, not a shield. The lance Ron has, in the Welsh tale, the form Rhongomyant, and the sword Caledvwich ; the latter has been equated with

---

[1] Translated by E. K. Chambers, *op. cit.*, pp. 16 and 17.

[2] In the *Vita of Cadoc* (c. 1075) printed from Cotton MS. Vesp. A XIV (early thirteenth century) by W. J. Rees, *Lives of the Cambro-British Saints*, p. 22. The forms of the names are Chei et Bedguur.

[3] Latin form, Beducrus and Caius.

[4] Book X, ch. 13, of Geoffrey's *History* (" Everyman " Edition).

the Irish Caladbolg, the fairy sword of the hero Cuchulain and the Excalibur of the romances. The ship Prydwen is also mentioned in a Taliessin poem " Preiddeu Annwfn," [1] the Harryings of Hades, which may belong to an earlier nucleus of Welsh tales than " Kilhwch and Olwen." [2]

The main interest in Geoffrey's picture of Arthur up to and including the eighteenth century was a patriotic one. Geoffrey was regarded as a skilful portrait-painter and the likeness to his original was not too closely examined. The later chroniclers, poets and romancers, only elaborated the detail. To them Arthur was the type of a successful British king whose conquests reached far and wide.

In the ninth book of the *History* [3] there is a magnificent and eloquent description of Arthur's crowning at " Urbs Legionum " (Caerleon) on the Usk, at Whitsuntide. He had had a previous ceremony at York. A long list is given of the vassals who were invited to attend the court at Caerleon, including four kings of Scotland. The scene is one of great pomp and grandeur, such as would have accompanied the crowning of a great Norman king, like William the Conqueror. Geoffrey relates that after Arthur had been invested with the " ensigns of the kingship " he went in procession to the " Church of the Metropolitan See." He was supported on either side by two archbishops, and four kings of Albany, Cornwall, North and South Wales, marched before him bearing four golden swords, while marvellously sweet music was being chanted by the clerics. The Queen also went in royal state to the " Church of the Virgins dedicate " and was attended likewise by four queens, bearing four white doves. The whole day was given up to national celebration and the streets were thronged by the populace. After the divine service the courtiers entered the palace and the meats and

[1] So called by Professor Rhys. An English note in Lady Charlotte Guest's edition spells it " Preidden Annwn," translating it " The Spoils of Hell." See "Everyman" Edition of the *Mabinogion*, p. 308. Lady Guest gives the spelling " Taliesin."

[2] Relegated by Welsh scholars to the late eleventh or early twelfth century. Spelt by Loth " Kulwch."

[3] Geoffrey's *History*, Book IX, chs. 13 and 14 (" Everyman " Edition), translated by San Marte.

the drinks were served to them by a thousand youths and pages in livery. The master of the food ceremonies was Kay the Seneschal, clothed in a "doublet, furred of ermines." He is a very different figure from the Kei in "Kilhwch and Olwen" reproved by Arthur for discourtesy, and possessing many mythological characteristics. Bedevere the butler presided over the drinks. Meanwhile the women feasted in another palace. Then after the banquet, both men and women adjourned to view the tournament and sports which lasted for three days. On the fourth day, Arthur, as a great feudal lord, dispersed honours and offices, "unto each was made grant of the honour of the office he held, in possession, earldom, to wit, of city or castle, archbishopric, bishopric, abbacy, or whatsoever else it might be."

There are one or two details not Norman, such as the separation of the men and women, and, at the sports, the game of flinging heavy stones seems native in origin. But in the main, the account is that of a great Norman king or great feudal lord with his court.

Among the many translations and adaptations of Geoffrey,[1] two stand out and may be classed as original works. The first of these is Wace's *Brut*, a French metrical romance, and the second, Layamon's *Brut*. Wace's *Brut* was finished in 1155 and the *Brut* of Layamon is approximately dated at the end of the twelfth century.

Little is known of Wace's life except a few facts which, however, are significant. He was born in the Island of Jersey, educated in part in Paris and lived at Caen in Normandy, holding a regular position at the court. Layamon mentions that a dedication of Wace's *Brut* was addressed to Queen Eleanor, wife of Henry II, but it is lacking in the extant manuscripts.

Although Wace's poem is, in general, a translation of Geoffrey, yet it is distinctive and vivid in style and shows the influence of the French chivalric ideals then permeating the mediæval court. Probably, too, Wace was acquainted with

---

[1] For list and for facts in these two sections on Wace and Layamon, see R. H. Fletcher, *Arthurian Material in the Chronicles* (Harvard Studies and Notes, X), a very full and able study.

some of the actual French romances. In the portrait, for
example, which he draws of Gawain, he introduces the
romance conception of this hero. He makes him praise
peace even in the Council of War, and say that the pleasures
of love are good and that for the sake of his *amie* a young
man performs feats of chivalry. Geoffrey gives no account
of a speech of Gawain. Again, Wace, all through his work,
minimises the details of barbarity and cruelty which he found
in his source to suit the more civilised conception of his
audience. The conception of Arthur as the centre of a court
of knight-errantry, instead of a world-conquering hero, is
beginning to appear in his poetic chronicle. The circumstances
of his own age of feudalism are portrayed : fortresses become
feudal castles ; senators, barons ; and consuls, contes. And
not only in his matter, but in his manner and style Wace
has, for the most part, the characteristics of the romantic
poet, conscious of his audience and taking the delight of an
artist in dwelling on picturesque details.

Layamon, in his epic the *Brut*,[1] gives a stirring account of
Arthur's deeds and paints a different portrait of the heroic
and warlike king from that of Wace.[2] In Wace, Arthur is
a chivalric hero of romance with his mediæval court, but in
Layamon's poem, which partakes of the nature of a saga,
he is more of an actual English monarch winning victories
over his enemies. True, his exploits and qualities are
magnified and represent Layamon's own idea of what an
English king should be—brave beyond dispute, stern to his
followers, unbending and often cruel and revengeful towards
his foes. Thus Layamon gives in greater detail than Wace
the number of his hostages, and evidently delights in portraying
the submission of the conquerors, Gillomar and others.[3] This
exultant patriotic feeling probably causes the poet to expand
such a triumphant scene as Arthur's elevation to the throne.

[1] There is only one edition, ed. Sir F. Madden, 3 vols., 1847, with
translation.

[2] Layamon names three sources which scholars have traced to be
(1) Wace's *Brut* on which his own work is in fact almost directly based,
(2) Bede's *Ecclesiastical History*, and (3) a Latin translation of the same.

[3] For Gillomar's submission, see vv. 22,357 ff.

Layamon is not a mere dull chronicler, he is the poetic successor of the unknown author or authors of *Beowulf*, and in action and description his ringing words and phrases seem to have been hammered out in the glowing forge of his own exultant feeling.

In one or two passages in which he breaks away from his chief source,[1] he demonstrates his own dramatic power. For example, he gives a more detailed account than Wace of the circumstances in which Arthur received the evil tidings of the betrayal of Modred.[2] A young knight had come one evening to the court of Arthur. He had been deputed to bear the news of the rebellion of Arthur's nephew Modred and his abduction of Arthur's wife Guinevere (Wenhaver). Arthur welcomed him as a messenger of good news and he did not dare to tell the king the real truth. So the king went to bed in ignorance. During the night he was haunted by distressing dreams. He thought that he was in his hall and that Wenhaver and his knights were pulling down the roof and the pillars about his ears and that all was going to destruction. On awaking, he felt ill and calling for the messenger related his terrifying dream. When he finished, the knight turned and said " Lord, if it had happened, and may God forbid, that Modred had taken thy Queen and thy land, yet thou mightest avenge thee and stay all thine enemies."

Arthur replied that he never supposed that Modred and Wenhaver would betray him and then, at this dramatic point, the knight stated the facts bluntly.

One of the most important elaborations is the account of the making the Round Table, mentioned also by Wace. There is a most realistic description [3] of the preliminary brawl which arose at the Yuletide feast where seven kings with seven hundred knights began to quarrel about precedence.

[1] For a list of the passages in which Layamon differs from his source, see R. H. Fletcher, *Arthurian Material in the Chronicles*, pp. 131-3, also the introduction to Sir F. Madden's text.

[2] See vv. 27,992 ff. Compare a similar dream in the *Morte' Arthur* (alliter) below, p. 25.

[3] See vv. 22,737.

The fight raged hotter and hotter to the shedding of blood until Arthur arrived and quelled it in an equally savage manner. After this, Layamon relates, the King went to Cornwall, where a carpenter informed him that he could make a table where sixteen hundred men and more could sit without one being more exalted in place than the other. This convenient table Arthur could carry wherever he went. Timber was bought and the work completed in four weeks.

Celticists [1] maintain that the table is of fairy and Celtic origin. Whether this be so or not, other original passages show that Layamon, in spite of his realistic Anglo-Saxon outlook, used legendary material in this poetic chronicle. For example, he describes how Arthur armed himself with burnie, shield and sword. The burnie, the poet informs us, was the work of Wygar, an elfish smith, his spear, of the smith Griffin. This seems to have reference to the Wayland legend. His shield " Pridwen" and his sword " Ron " is also mentioned, and a special name " Goswhit " is given to his helm, which may be British or from Teutonic saga.

Layamon also gives a graphic account of the fight with the monster at Mont St Michel, with details of his own. [2]

The most famous of his descriptions [3] is that of Arthur's death and the coming of Argante, the Courteous, who with another woman, wondrously fair, bore him in a small boat to Avalon to be healed of his wounds. This incident, the poet remarks in a former passage, [4] was foreseen by Arthur himself and his own return prophesied.

The Morte Arthure, [5] a northern alliterative poem [6] named from the scrivener Thornton, calls for attention both for its subject-matter and its fine literary qualities. The author is

[1] See A. C. L. Brown, Studies and Notes, VII, pp. 184 ff.
[2] vv. 25,720 ff.
[3] vv. 28,610 ff.
[4] vv. 23,061 ff.
[5] Ed. J. O. Halliwell, 1847 ; ed. G. G. Perry, Early English Text Society, 8, 1865 ; reprinted with revised text, E. Brock, 1871 ; ed. M. M. Banks, 1900.
[6] L. A. Paton, in Introduction to " Everyman " Edition, says N. West.

unknown, though it has been ascribed to Huchown of the Awle Ryale. It [1] gives a vivid and detailed account of Arthur's campaign against Rome, after the spurning of Lucius the Roman ambassador, and the submission of Rome. Written about the middle or end of the fourteenth century,[2] the writer handles the subject-matter in a way to glorify the English people. Many of the details are evidently taken from the campaigns and accoutrements of the warlike Edward III and his soldiers who fought in France.

Underneath the portrait of Arthur, the conquering British king, can be discovered an earlier representation of a more mythical Arthur, the slayer of the monster of St Michel's Mount who " sups on seven children of the commons, chopped up on a charger of pure white silver with pickles and finely ground spices and wines of Portugal mixed with honey." [3] This monster also has a mantle made of the beards of kings and demands the beard of Arthur. This trait has been copied from the King Ritho of Welsh legend.[4]

But the writer's chief interest and enthusiasm is for the heroic and chivalrous Arthur. He waxes eloquent in describing the glittering armour and trappings of warfare, showing a technical knowledge of heraldic symbols. He takes a delight in colour wherever displayed, either in the moving mass of warriors and steeds or in the details of the ladies' dresses. And what is more remarkable in a mediæval poem of battle, is the writer's appreciation of the sweet sounds and peaceful scenes of Nature :

> Thane they roode by θat ryver, θat rynnyd so swythe,
> θare θe ryndez overrechez with realle bowghez ;
> The roo and the rayne-dere reklesse thare rounene,·
> In ranez and in rosers to ryotte thame selvene ;
> The frithez ware floreschte with flourez fulle many,
> With fawcouns and fesantez of ferlyche hewez ;

---

[1] For discussion, see Sir I. Gollancz, *Pearl*, pp. xliii-v, and G. Neilson, *Huchown of the Awle Ryale*, 1902. In this case it would be Scottish.

[2] See L. A. Paton, introduction to *Morte Arthur* ; two early English romances (" Everyman " Edition).

[3] Quoted from modernisation in " Everyman " Edition.

[4] See below, p. 120.

All θe feulez thare fleschez, that flyex with wengez,
ffore thare galede the gowke one grevez fulle lowde,
Wyth alkyne gladchipe θay gladdene theme selvene ;
Of θe nyghtgale notez θe noisez was swette,
They threpide wyth the throstills thre-hundreth at ones.
θat whate swowynge of watyr, and syngnynge of byrdez,
It myghte salve hyme of sore, that sounde was nevere ! [1]

[Then they rode by that river that runneth so swift where
the trees overstretch with fair boughs, the roe and the reindeer
run recklessly there in thickets and rose-gardens to feast
themselves.   The thickets were in blossom with may-flowers,
with falcons and pheasants of fair hues—all the birds there
which fly with wings, for there sang the cuckoo full loud on
the bushes, with all birds of merriment they gladden themselves ;   the voice of the nightingale's note was sweet, they
strove with the throstles three hundred at once, that this
murmur of water and singing of birds might cure him of ill
who never was whole.]

This narrative partakes of the qualities of the chronicle
and the romance and has borrowed from both.   The substance
of the story of Arthur's wars against Lucius, the author takes
from Geoffrey of Monmouth's *Chronicle*, but his work shows
the influence of Layamon's *Brut* and he must also have known
one or more of the Romances.   On the other hand, the chief
motif is that of a Chanson de Geste rather than a Romance,
for it is the virile one of the glory of wars and victories, nor
does the writer spare his audience the realistic details of
carnage.   The fights are not, as so often in Malory, mere
tournaments for the sake of prowess, but often life-and-death
duels, as in the case of Sir Priamus and Sir Gawain, or fierce
struggles between the hosts of Arthur and the Roman barons
and knights or between Arthur's men and Modred's.   Again
the tragedy of the final act is not that of conflict between
passionate love and loyalty as in the " Stanzaic Morte " and
Malory.   The treachery of Lancelot whose " honour rooted
in dishonour stood " is not a theme of the " Thornton Morte."

[1] Ll. 920-932—edition by G. G. Perry, translated from " Everyman "
Edition.

It is Modred, not Lancelot, who is the betrayer of Arthur and who carries Gaynor off, evidently considered only as part of the booty. The tragedy mourned is one of costly victory in battle with its consequent slaying of the finest flower of Arthur's knights. One of the most poignant and eloquent of speeches is that of Arthur's lament over the fallen Gawain, the noblest of friends and the bravest and most chivalrous of foes.

This heroic poem reaches its highest level when the disastrous end is sighted. It is foreshadowed, in true mediæval fashion, by a dream of Arthur's in which he beholds fickle Dame Fortune spinning her wheel. In the vision he is shown six kings of the earth, including Alexander the Great and Julius Cæsar, who have mounted to its highest rung and been ignominiously hurled down. Arthur himself is placed on the wheel and whirled under until all parts of his body are smashed to pieces. He awakes trembling, and on demanding from his magician the interpretation of the dream, learns that it is his turn to be cast down to the lowest rung, he who has ascended so high as a brave conqueror of the world !

Almost immediately Sir Cradock arrives in breathless haste as the bearer of evil tidings. In the King's absence Modred has seized the kingdom and his wife Gaynor, made common cause with the Danes, and awaits him at Southampton. King Arthur must summon his followers and embark for England. The naval battle is described in a stirring fashion with details evidently taken from contemporary fighting. Arthur is to the foremost; as in the Chronicles, his chief banner " bears a ' chalk-white maiden with a Child in her arms ' who is Lord of Heaven " [1] : and the chief hero is the good Gawain. The grappling together of the ships, the inrush of the men on to the vessels, the falling of the masts, the fierce hand-to-hand fighting on board until the hatches are filled with dead Danish men (allies of Modred), the swift and sure havoc of the famous archers of England—all are described in vigorous phraseology. These convey to the mind the mortal conflict, the deadly blows, the noise and confusion of a great

[1] This is an elaboration from Nennius.

struggle in a small space. Even the few lines quoted below give some idea of the effect of the packed style :—

Thane was hede-rapys hewene θat helde upe θe mastes :
Thare was conteke fulle kene, and crachynge of chippys !
Grett cogges of kampe crasseches in sondyre !
Mony kabane clevede, cabilles destroyede !
Knyghtes and kene men killide the braynes !
Kidd castelles were corvene with alle theire kene wapene,
Castelles fulle comliche that coloured ware faire !

    .   .   .   .   .   .

Thus they dalte that daye thire dubbide knyghtes,
Tille alle θe Danes ware dede, and in θe depe throwene.[1]

[The modernisation runs :—Then were the stays hewn down that hold up the masts : there was a furious collision and the cracking of ships could be heard : great battleships burst asunder, many a cabin was broken and the cables destroyed ; knights and keen men killed the enemy—fine castles were cleft asunder with their keen weapons—full fair castles that were beautifully coloured.[2]

    .   .   .   .   .   .

Thus they dealt blows that day, these dubbed knights, till all the Danes were dead and thrown into the deep.[2]]

The narrative now moves on with dramatic swiftness. Genuine and heart-stirring is Arthur's grief on losing his battle-lords, especially Gawain, who is buried with all the honours of war. Modred is finally slain in a hand-to-hand encounter with the King, but in his death-struggle he inflicts a mortal wound on his foe, who is conveyed to a manor of the Isle of Aveloyne (Avalon). Here Arthur dies, bequeathing his kingdom to Constantine. The royal monarch is buried at Glastonbury according to this chronicler, who gives a dignified account of his end.

[1] From text, ed. G. G. Perry (Early Eng. Text Soc.), ll. 3669-3675 also 3694-3695.
[2] From the translation in the " Everyman " Edition of the Morte Arthure.

The " Stanzaic Morte " [1] has not the same descriptive excellence as the " Thornton Morte Arthure." At the best, it has a certain naïve sincerity and pathos which make up for its unpolished form. Its subject-matter is, however, of great interest, as the poem contains a version of the story of the Maid of Ascolat and of Arthur's death. The question of the sources of the poem and its relation to Malory's *Morte Darthur*, Books XVIII, XX and XXI, have been the subject of keen controversy. [2] Suffice it to say here that it is agreed that this *Morte* and Malory have for common source a lost redaction or redactions of the French prose Lancelot. Thus it is clear that the relation between the *Morte* and Malory is a close one. For example, in the now famous story in which King Arthur commands Bedivere to throw his sword into the lake, which command the knight does not obey till the third time, there is great similarity in incident and in phraseology.

Scholars have established the following facts concerning the " Stanzaic Morte." It is contained in a unique MS. written in two hands. Its dialect is Midland, although whether East or North-West Midland is disputed. Linguists show evidence that it belongs to the latter half of the fourteenth century. The author, probably belonging to the minstrel class, is unknown. Recurring phrases such as " bright as blossom on brere," " hende and free," its crude form (stanzas in eight lines of four accents, with alternate rhymes) as well as its plain unvarnished story, place it in the category of the ballad.

Even if Malory had not, with his more sophisticated art, immortalised the romantic story, this ballad-poem would have been worthy of note. There is a certain directness about the simple and human emotions which impress the reader. The true love which Lancelot's fellow-knights show towards him, their delight in his prowess, and grief at his absence, make a sincere appeal. The pathos of the story

---

[1] Has been edited several times—in the Roxburghe Club by F. J. Furnivall, 1864 ; ed. J. D. Bruce, Early Eng. Text Soc., No. 88 ; S. B. Hemingway, 1912.

[2] For bibliography of texts and discussion, see " Everyman " Edition, p. xviii. See also in E. Vinaver's *Malory* : Sources.

of the maid who dies for love of Lancelot has been finely
transmitted in Malory's rendering. And surely never has a
fight been more sorrowfully waged than that of the unwilling
Lancelot with Gawain, revengeful of his brother's death !
Full of poignancy is Arthur's lament for his fallen comrades.
The passionate attachment of Lancelot and Guinevere and
the havoc it threatens to bring about is succinctly summed
up by the bishop, the ambassador for peace, in his appeal to
Lancelot, " Wemen are frele of hyr entayle. Syr lettes not
ynglande go to noght." [1]

In the chronicles of Wace, Layamon and the two
" Mortes," there has been an interpenetration and development of the romantic outlook. The " Alliterative " or
" Thornton Morte " which has been shown by scholars [2]
to be a near parallel to Book V of Malory's *Morte Darthur*
forms thus a link between the chronicle and the romance
in English literature. The other sources of the first four
books of Malory have been found to be the " Ordinary "
or " Vulgate " Merlin, the " Continuation " and the " Huth "
Merlin. The first four books of Malory tell of the doings of
Arthur and Merlin, including the story of Arthur's birth, and
the incident of the sword fast embedded in the stone at
Westminster, which would only yield to the foreordained
hero, Arthur. There are other legendary and pseudo-
historical narrations. Book V shows Arthur to be the hero-
king of England waging war both against giants and against
Rome.

Drawn from so many sources, the picture of Arthur in
Malory is not altogether unified. At one time he is king
in a fairy land, over which Merlin presides as the king's
helper, overcoming all difficulties by means of his magic
wiles. At another, he is a truly English king with his loyal
followers Gawain and Lancelot, all concerned in bringing
England glory with their swords, and refusing to submit
even to that great world-conqueror, Rome. In the later
books, the king is somewhat overshadowed by his knights, but
comes to his own again in the poignant narrative of his death.

[1] From " Everyman " Edition, p. 155.
[2] See E. Vinaver, *Malory*, Appendix : Sources.

The sources from which the picture of Arthur is drawn in English literature in the next four or five centuries, are Geoffrey of Monmouth's *Chronicle* and Malory's *Morte Darthur*. The more prosaic eighteenth century, in depicting the historical Arthur, drew mainly from the *Chronicle*, and Spenser and the romantic poets of the nineteenth and twentieth centuries from Malory.

The five editions of Malory,[1] published from 1485 to 1634, show his popularity. Indeed, Roger Ascham would not have condemned the *Morte Darthur* so thoroughly, if it had not had such a wide influence and been such a favourite in the sixteenth century.

[1] The respective dates are 1485, 1498, 1529, 1557, 1585, 1634.

ARTHUR IN THE SIXTEENTH, SEVENTEENTH AND EIGHTEENTH CENTURIES

No great romantic work introducing Arthur was composed till Spenser wrote his *Faerie Queene*, the first three books of which appeared in print in 1590. William Warner published his metrical history, *Albion's England*, in 1586, in English ballad metres of fourteen-syllable lines, which relates, besides tales from various sources, the more prosaic parts of Geoffrey's *Chronicle*.

Thomas Hughes is of more interest historically, in that he attempted the first play on Arthurian matter in England (1587).[1] It was a five-act drama of the Senecan type, in smooth blank verse, with long dull speeches, a chorus, and all violent action off the stage. It has the merit of having a unified plot dealing with the rise and fall of Arthur, and the conflicts, within himself and within his kingdom. It is curious that none of the greater Elizabethan dramatists have chosen an Arthurian subject. Shakespeare has only a reference or two to Arthur and Merlin.[2] The later nineteenth and twentieth centuries were to return to the dramatic form, which requires a more concentrated plot and logical development than the epic.

Spenser was the first important English poet after Malory to make use of the Arthurian legend for his own romantic purposes. In order to ornament his dignified and pillared Renaissance palace he ransacked the treasure-houses of many lands. His spoils were displayed in every niche of its walls, without regard to their origin and period. The whole gives an effect of luxuriant richness and splendour rather than

[1] *The Misfortunes of Arthur*, 1587.
[2] In *King Lear*, Act III, Scene 2, the Fool says : "This prophecy Merlin shall make for I live before his time."

unity of design. Spenser, as the successor of Geoffrey of Monmouth, was the first English poet to show the picturesqueness of the Arthurian stories.   He realised the romantic appeal of knights and tournaments, of distressed damsels and of quests.   Such a realisation means a certain detachment in time and space. Spenser was far enough from the Middle Ages to possess this. His point of view was removed from that of Caxton's preface to the first edition of Malory.[1] In it, the famous printer answers the sceptics of his time as to the evidence of Arthur's birth and death. Spenser's point of view, on the contrary, was that of the romantic poet, not the chronicler. The chivalric world which he describes, is seen through the veil of illusion which a distant view gives. Thus the revival of romance in the Romantic Revival was accompanied by a new study of Spenser, " the poet's poet."

In Spenser's *Faerie Queene*, Prince Arthur is the central figure. Having seen the Faerie Queene in a vision, he sets forth to seek her. He appears first—in Book I—to aid Una, who is searching for her Red Cross knight. At various times the Prince comes to the rescue of the principal personages at a critical moment. He stands for Magnificence. Thus he has stepped out of the pseudo-historical domain and become a prince of romance. He is an inhabitant of that magic nowhere of the poet's world, and is no longer a doughty feudal chief.

Spenser used the old traditions rather as suggestions for his descriptions than as a foundation for them. Arthur's armour and sword are pictured with considerable detail, in the scene where he meets Una.

> Athwart his brest a bauldrick braue he (Arthur) ware
> That shynd, like twinkling stars, with stons most pretious rare.
> And in the midst thereof one pretious stone
> Of wondrous worth, and eke of wondrous mights,
> Shapt like a Ladies head, exceeding shone,
> Like Hesperus amongst the lesser lights,
> And stroue for to amaze the weaker sights ;

---

[1] 1485.

Thereby his mortall blade full comely hong
In yuory sheath ycaru'd with curious slights ;
Whose hilts were burnisht gold, and handle strong
Of mother pearls, and buckled with a golden tong.[1]

His helmet and shield are described in the same elaborate
way.   Maynadier [2] suggests that the precious stone, shaped
like a lady's head in the midst of his baldric, may be a
reminiscence of the image of the Virgin on Arthur's shield
or banner in the Chronicles.   Likewise, the crest of his helmet
in the form of a dragon, may be taken from the account of
a similar dragon in Geoffrey's account.[3]   But his sword
Morddure differs from Excalibur in that it will not harm its
owner and his shield is unlike any Arthurian tradition of a
shield.

Later on in the same book, Prince Arthur tells as much of
the story of his life as he knows to Una, as also his love for the
Faerie Queene.   He relates that he was brought up by
Timon (not Sir Ector as in Malory) and educated in warlike
feats.   Merlin (as in Geoffrey and Malory) became the
guardian of the king and was a man of mystery.

Thither the great Magicien Merlin came,
As was his vse, ofttimes to visit me ;
For he had charge my discipline to frame,
And Tutours nouriture to ouersee,
Him oft and oft I askt in priuitie
Of what loines and what lignage I did spring :
Whose aunswere bad me still assured bee
That I was sonne and heire vnto a king,
As time in her iust terme the truth to light should bring.[4]

That Spenser knew Geoffrey of Monmouth's *Chronicle* is also
shown in the second book, where Arthur meets Sir Guyon,
and where the poet evidently has made use of Geoffrey.   In
the third book also, when Merlin is revealing to Britomart

[1] Quoted from Spenser's *Faerie Queene*, ed. J. C. Smith, 1909, p. 88,
Book I, Canto 7.
[2] Maynadier, *The Arthur of the English Poets*, p. 266.
[3] See *History* (" Everyman " Edition), Book IX, Chap. 4 ; *cf.* Spenser,
Book I, Canto 7, Stanza 31.
[4] Spenser's *Faerie Queene*, ed. J. C. Smith, Book I, Canto 9, p. 109.

that she is destined to meet and marry Artegal, the genealogy, somewhat altered, is taken from Geoffrey. It is used as an occasion to glorify Queen Elizabeth by tracing her descent from the ancient British kings.

But except for these genealogies, which attempt to give Arthur a historic background, Prince Arthur is merely a romantic figure, somewhat of an abstraction, conforming to the perfect pattern of what a knight should be.

Milton, at one time, had purposed to write an Arthurian poem. He has referred to it in his poem to Mansus (1638-9),[1] in an autobiographical discursion and more fully in " Epitaphium Damonis " (1639-40). The lines in both poems suggest that Milton, at least, would have made the names of Geoffrey's *History* ring in sonorous chime. He refers in the " Epitaphium Damonis " to the story of the deception, aided by Merlin, which proved the cause of Arthur's birth

> mendaces vultus, assumptaque Gorlois arma
> Merlini dolus.

This Latin poem, written on the death of his Italian friend Diodati, shows that at this age of thirty-one he was ambitious to become famous as the singer of his own native woods and streams, in his own native tongue. But alas ! patriotic claims intervened, and in the epic of his later life, *Paradise Lost*, and in *Paradise Regained*, there are only two references to the Arthurian legend.

In the first he refers to

> what resounds
> In fable or romance of Uther's son,
> Begirt with British and " Armoric knights." [2]

And in the second he speaks of

> Faery damsels met in forestwide
> By knights of Logres, or of Lyones
> Lancelot, or Pelleas, or Pellenore.[2]

---

[1] See *Poetical Works*, ed. Masson, 1882, vol. i., p. 300, ll. 78-88, also p. 306, ll. 161-171.

[2] *Paradise Lost*, Book I, ll. 579 ff. ; Book II, ll. 359 ff.

Lovers of the earlier Milton of *Comus* cannot help regretting that he did not take the fairy element in the first part of the life of Arthur, as found in Malory, and treat it after the fashion of that exquisite poem. Whether the subject would have made a great epic poem in the manner of *Paradise Lost* is a matter of conjecture.

The treatment of Arthur in Dryden's play *King Arthur*, performed in 1691, is typical of the seventeenth century. The material, interspersed with much that is alien both to the spirit and matter of the Arthurian legend, was taken from Geoffrey. The history, with King Arthur as hero, was made use of for political purposes. Unfortunately for Dryden, it was written at the end of Charles II's reign, but was not performed till the Revolution, so the references had to be changed. It is not altogether a success, although Sir Walter Scott admired it. Purcell's music must have made the songs acceptable. The author tried to make a good political play and, at the same time, a fantasy, and to modern tastes he has succeeded in neither aim.

In Dryden's play, Arthur is a British hero, descended from Aeneas, who fights the Saxons, who, in their turn, are led by Oswald. The former is brave and war-like, but not subtly drawn by the dramatist.

> Arthur is all that's excellent in Oswald,
> And void of all his faults. In battle brave,
> But still serene in all the stormy war,
> Like heaven above the clouds : and after fight,
> As merciful and kind to vanquished foes,
> As a forgiving God. But, see ! he's here,
> And praise is dumb before him.

He loves the blind Emmeline, who is cured of her blindness by Merlin and captured by Arthur's Saxon enemy Oswald and finally rescued.

Dryden's supernatural agents are reminiscent of Shakespeare's *Tempest* and of Milton's angels and devils. Yet Philidel, the ethereal spirit, lacks the charm of Ariel. She is employed by Merlin, in the same way as Ariel is by Prospero. Merlin is depicted as a mere wonder-worker.

The supernatural agents, grouped in two opposing camps, are rather mechanical. Shakespeare seems to have called his fairies and elves out of the woods, but Dryden seems to have taken them out of a box and to have placed them on wires, like marionettes, on his stage. The romantic atmosphere around the figure of King Arthur which Malory creates is absent. He is merely a successful warrior.

Sir Richard Blackmore wrote in heroic couplets two long dull epics, which were political allegories. These are called *Prince Arthur* (1695) and *King Arthur* (1697). The former recalls *Paradise Lost* in that there are good angels, Uriel and Raphael, who aid Arthur, and evil ones such as Lucifer, who hinder him. The latter, invoking the aid of the god of the winds, drives him on to the coast of Armorica. Here Arthur relates to his converted enemy Hoel, long portions of Bible history, including the Fall and Redemption of Man. In this epic, Arthur is meant to stand for the Prince of Orange ; and Arthur's enemy, the Saxon tyrant, for James II, the opposer of the Protestants.

Thus Blackmore, in typical seventeenth-century style, exploited the historical Arthur. He was unable to enter into the spirit of Malory's early books, but looked upon Arthur as a mere lay figure round which to group other characters of interest to his own day, though concealed under the drapery of personages taken from various sources.

Of great importance in the literary history of Arthurian legend is the appearance of the ballad collections which both signified and increased interest in this form of literature. The first general collection of ballads in England was in 1723, followed three years after by a second and followed in 1727 by a third. A year after the first English collection, came Allan Ramsay's *Evergreen*, a Scotch miscellany. Interest in Welsh literature was shown in the publishing of *Specimens of the Poetry of Ancient Welsh Bards* (1764) by Evan Evans, forerunner of the *Myvyrian Archaiology*, 1801-7. The most famous of these productions was Bishop Percy's *Reliques of Ancient Poetry*, the first edition of which appeared in 1765. Bishop Percy had been fortunate enough to find in an old folio MS. (damaged by fire and a housemaid's predatory fingers), a collection of ballads and songs made by some old county gentleman, probably of the north-west of England, about the middle of the seventeenth century. From these, Bishop Percy selected the most complete and the ones which interested him the most. Actually he made use of only one-fourth of the pieces in the *Folio*. These he edited and amended, and according to the precise and irritable Joseph Ritson, made a " patched-up publication " to suit the more refined entertainment of his readers. The acrid controversy between Bishop Percy and Ritson must have advertised his book. Though in some measure Ritson's attack had some grounds,[1] yet Bishop Percy's publication came at the psychological moment for his public and was hailed with all the interest and joy which a new discovery brings. The many learned and more accurate editors who succeeded him did not receive the same acclamation from the literary world.

The Arthurian poems in the *Reliques* consist of six pieces, five of which were taken from the *Folio* and " edited." These are " King Arthur's Death," " Legend of King Arthur," " Sir Lancelot du Lake," " The Boy and the Mantle," " The Marriage of Sir Gawain," [2] and a sixth, " King Ryence," not in the *Folio*.

" King Arthur's Death " and the " Legend of King Arthur " are taken from the old Chronicles, especially that of Gerard de Leew (1493), with the addition of some events from Malory. They are written in doggerel metre of four lines. One incident tells [3] how in the last battle there was a parley and how an adder stung a knight which caused him to draw his sword in alarm. The armies, mistaking the signal, joined battle with dire consequences to Arthur's side. He lost all his men but three. His grief is described with a simple poignancy sometimes lost in more polished verse :

> And when the king beheld his Knightes,
> All dead and scattered on the molde ;
> The teares that trickled down his face
> That manly face in fight so bolde.

---

[1] See Ritson's Preface to *Select Collection of English Songs*, 1783.
[2] See below, p. 60 *note*.   [3] In " King Arthur's Death," p. 17.

> Now reste yee all, brave knights, he said,
> Soe true and faithful to your trust :
> And must yee then ye valiant hearts,
> Be lefte to moulder into dust !
>
> Most loyal have yee been to mee
> Most true and faithful unto deathe,
> And oh to rayse yee up againe
> How freelye could I yield my breath ! [1]

"Sir Lancelot du Lake" is of literary interest, because Shakespeare put the first lines into Falstaff's mouth, "When Arthur first in court began." [2] The ballad is attributed to Thomas Deloney.

"The Boy and the Mantle" is a tale of chastity tests, the Mantle and the Horn, applied with amusing and embarrassing results to the husbands and wives in King Arthur's court, including King Arthur and Guinevere. The incident is also told in Malory, but in this ballad the story is more clearly told and the humour broader. [3]

"King Ryence's Challenge" is not in the *Folio MS*. Bishop Percy informs us it was sung before Queen Elizabeth at Kenilworth in 1575. It is the same story as in Malory, of King Ryence's haughty request that King Arthur should furnish him with his beard to ornament his cloak, which was to have a trimming of the beards of twelve kings, Arthur to be the twelfth. Naturally, Arthur refused with equal hauteur. [4]

An Arthur story which seems to be more in the nature of a *fabliau* and not merely taken from the Chronicles or romances, is "King Arthur and the King of Cornwall," in the *Folio MS*. [5] but not in the *Reliques*.

It is a tale of a boast. Queen Guinevere says to King Arthur that she knows of a better Round Table than the King's. So, in order to prove the contrary, Arthur Gawain and Tristeran (so spelt) and Sir Bredbeddle set off

---

[1] In the *Reliques*, vol. ii., "King Arthur's Death."
[2] *King Henry IV* (Second Part), Act II, Scene 4.
[3] See below for story in Welsh and other forms, p. 120.
[4] For story in Welsh, see below, p. 120.   [5] Vol. i., p. 59.

to go to the King of Cornwall disguised as palmers. They arrive, and on asking the King of Cornwall if he knows one King Arthur, the King of Cornwall boasts he has a daughter by Guinevere, and also that he possesses a steed finer than any Arthur has. The visitors retire to bed and a fiend is set to watch them secretly. Arthur boasts that he will prove the bane of the King of Cornwall and Gawain reproves him. Sir Bredbeddle manages to gain power over the fiend, makes him appear and disappear at will and perform his behests by means of a holy book. Thus Arthur gains possession of the fiery steed and of the wand which will subdue his mettlesome nature, so that he can mount him at will. He also obtains the King of Cornwall's sword and cuts off the boaster's head.

The fact that Arthur is here depicted as a companion of his followers—especially Gawain—and almost on a basis of equality, not as a mere figure-head round which the knights revolve, seems to point to an earlier stratum of legend, and to a popular origin instead of a literary one.

The revival of the study of Malory and Spenser was to result in a desire to perfect the form in which the old tales were to be retold. Warton holds an interesting place in this revival. In his *Observations on the Faerie Queene* [1] of Spenser, he discusses Spenser's indebtedness to Arthurian romances, and himself shows considerable knowledge of mediæval Arthurian romances.

His poem the " Grave of King Arthur " [2] has the triumphant and patriotic eloquence of one of Dryden's Odes, and shows also a good deal of feeling for Arthurian romance and topography. It takes the form of a dispute between two bards. One maintains that there is a tradition that Arthur, after his mortal wound, was carried to Avalon.

> For when he fell, an elfin queen,
> All in secret, and unseen,
> O'er the fainting hero threw
> Her mantle of ambrosial blue ;
> And bade her spirits bear him far,
> In Merlin's agate-axled car,

---

[1] Published 1754 (First Edition, B.M.).   [2] Published 1777.

> To her green isles enamel'd steep
> In the navel of the deep.
> O'er his wounds she sprinkled dew
> From flowers that in Arabia grew :
> On a rich, inchanted bed,
> She pillowed his majestic head :
> O'er his brow, with whispers bland,
> Thrice she wav'd an opiate wand ;
> And to soft music's airy sound
> Her magic curtains clos'd around.

But from Fairyland he is to return to Britain.

> Once more, in old heroic pride,
> His barbèd courser to bestride ;
> His knightly table to restore
> And the brave tournaments of yore.

But the other bard replies that this is not the case.   The truth is that,

> When he fell, with wingèd speed
> His champions, on a milk-white steed
> From the battle's hurricane
> Bore him to Joseph's towered fane,[1]
> In the fair vale of Avalon :
> There, with chantèd orison,
> And the long blaze of tapers clear,
> The stolèd fathers met the bier :
> Through the dim iles, in order dread
> Of martial woe, the chief they led,
> And deep intomb'd in holy ground
> Before the altar's solemn bound.

Warton's diction and style are still of the rhetorical eighteenth century and yet there is true feeling for romance and Welsh scenery in the poem.   Warton also wrote two Sonnets, one on Stonehenge, which is connected with Merlin, and the other on King Arthur's Round Table.   Both show the same romantic interest in places connected with this legend.

King Arthur, by Lord Lytton (Edward Bulwer Lytton),[2] an epic poem, though written in 1848, has many characteristics

---

[1] Glastonbury Abbey.   [2] See also under Gawain below, pp. 64 ff.

of the eighteenth century. Lord Lytton, like Spenser, of whom he was a great admirer, draws from various mythologies, in especial the Norse. Though his poem shows imagination in conception, it lacks the sensuous charm of Spenser. It is long-winded and moralising with conventional descriptions of Nature. The first three verses, quoted below, proclaim its subject and illustrate the descriptive style :

Our land's first legends, love and knightly deeds,
    And wonderous Merlin and his wandering King,
The triple labour, and the glorious meeds
    Won from the world of Fable-land I sing.
    Go forth, O Song, amidst the banks of old,
    And glide translucent o'er their sands of gold.

Now is the month when, after sparkling showers,
    Her starry wreaths the virgin jasmine weaves
Now lure the bee wild thyme and sunny hours ;
    And light wings rustle thro' the glinting leaves ;
    Music in every bough ; on mead and lawn
    May lifts her fragrant altars to the dawn.

Now joyous lives with every moment, start
    In air, in wave, on earth ; above, below ;
And o'er her new-born children, Nature's heart
    Heaves with the gladness mothers only know,
    Fair time yet floating before haunted eyes
    King Arthur reigns and song is in the skies.[1]

The first labour which was set for Arthur, was to gain the sword forged from a diamond from the possession of the Lady of the Lake under the water, the second to obtain the silver shield of Thor, the third to visit the Fate, entrenched in a cave, who spun the thread of life. To accomplish these, Arthur had to visit the icy North. In the keeping of the Esquimaux was the shield of Thor. When Arthur had accomplished his labours successfully and returned to fight the Saxons, he did not altogether overcome them. However, he learned from a prophecy of Merlin that one of his race, Henry Tudor, should restore the ancient line. Lord Lytton

[1] *King Arthur*—an epic poem.

here copies Spenser and the prediction of Merlin to Britomart in the *Faerie Queene*.

Lytton's poem is not of great intrinsic value as a poem, nor is it even a stirring tale. The poem, and especially the preface, is, however, of interest to students of the literature of the time as showing the interest awakened in legends of all kinds, especially the Norse and the Welsh. But a deeper and more academic study was to make such a mixture of legendary material as Lord Lytton makes in his poem, unpleasing. It would require a much finer quality of poetry or a much more stirring story to disarm the critical faculty of his later readers on this point.

CHAPTER IV

ARTHUR IN MODERN TIMES

Scott : Tennyson : Masefield

In the previous chapter it has been shown that the way was being prepared for the great lover of chivalry, Sir Walter Scott. He had become a reader of Percy's *Reliques* at twelve, and he and his antiquarian friend, Dr Leyden, had together prepared the *Minstrelsy of the Scottish Border*. The latter antiquarian, in his poem, the " Scenes of Infancy," has two long Arthurian references, and places the Avalon of Arthur in the Eildon Hills.[1]

Sir Walter Scott's Arthurian poem, the "Bridal of Triermain " (1813), combines a legend of the " Sleeping Beauty " variety with an invented tale of Arthur. It is in pleasant, easy-flowing verse, which, like a shallow murmuring streamlet, glittering in the sun, seems to know from whence it has come and whither it is going. It has none of the wide and rhythmic flow or sudden deeps of Tennyson's blank verse.

Scott tells first of a love adventure of Arthur, who turned aside from the responsibilities of his court and kingdom, to dally with a lady, half-human, half-fairy, called Gwendolen. Three months she kept him with her, making use of all her wiles and charms to lure him into forgetfulness. But suddenly he remembered his court and his knights and tore himself reluctantly away. Before he went, he promised Gwendolen that if the child she was to bear him happened to be a boy, he would be heir to the kingdom ; if a girl, he would provide her with the bravest knight he could find, whose prowess would be tested in the lists.

Years passed, and, as was the custom, Arthur was holding

---

[1] It was probably this tradition Masefield used in " Midsummer Night."

solemn feast at Whitsuntide. When all were assembled, a maiden on a white horse, arrayed as a huntress, appeared at the head of a band of maidens. This was Gyneth, the daughter of Arthur and Gwendolen, as proud and cruel as she was fair, who had come to claim the promise. Arthur naturally glanced at his Queen to see how she would take this living proof of his dalliance, but the morals of the story are lightly handled by the poet :

> But she, unruffled at the scene
> Of human frailty, construed mild,
> Looked upon Lancelot and smiled.

So, in accordance with Arthur's promise, a tournament was announced by the heralds to discover the best and bravest knight for Gyneth. But, alas, that which began as a game of tilting ended in baleful slaughter. For Gyneth, who had had bitterness implanted in her heart by her betrayed mother, would give no sign to stay the carnage. At last, a youth of Merlin's kin fell dead at her feet. Merlin, the sage, suddenly appeared in wrath to bring the struggle to an end. For penance he meted out to Gyneth the fate of the Sleeping Beauty, " punishment blent with grace " :

> Sleep, until a knight shall wake thee
> For feats of arms as far renowned,
> As warrior of the Table Round.

Thus the second part of the story is a romance of the Sleeping Beauty, waiting to be kissed, awakened and made a bride. The knight who performed the daring deed was Sir Roland de Vaux. He won his bride, after overcoming many temptations, lured by seductive maidens and by visions of wealth and power. His quest was carried out amidst the conventional scenery of romance, lonely mountains, Gothic battlements and enchanted castles. Scott's descriptions, however, show the sincere lover of the Scottish wilds. Finally, in an enchanted bower, under a rock, was discovered the lovely maiden, smiling in her sleep, with " doubt, anger and dismay " dispelled from her brow. Wondering and trembling, Sir Roland de Vaux gazed upon the girl, half fearful to destroy the long-enduring spell. But Gyneth raised her dark-fringed lids, and the warrior dared to kiss her hand. Suddenly the lightning flashed, the thunder rolled, and the Castle disappeared. The bold de Vaux was left, astonished, with the princess safe in his arms.

It is a pretty fairy tale in verse, somewhat lengthy, but with the different strands woven skilfully together. It shows that, in spite of the growing popularity at this time of the prose novel and tale, verse is a fit instrument for the imaginative story.

Though Scott, like Spenser, did not to a great extent use the subject-matter of the Arthurian romances, yet, like that other romanticist, by his poems (and in Scott's case his prose novels), he prepared the way for a study and interest in what were termed the " chivalric " ages. Even Wordsworth, whose temper was not romantic in the sense of idealising the historic past, attempted an Arthurian poem, the " Egyptian Maid." [1]

Scott—as the above narration shows—has treated freely the story of Arthur, combining it with another fairy tale as it pleased him. But at this time and a few years later, there were one or two events in the publishing and literary world, in connection with the Arthurian tales, which were to lead to a more scholarly study of Malory, especially among the poets. One of these, in 1804, was the editing and concluding of the romance of *Sir Tristrem* by Sir Walter Scott himself. Though he had not the textual knowledge which modern scholars now possess, his emendations and conclusions are very ingenious. Three editions of Malory appeared from 1816-1817 after a lapse of a hundred years. Sir Frederick Madden had gathered together the English stories about Gawain and edited them in *Syr Gawayne* in 1847. Of great importance is the publication of Lady Guest's *Mabinogion* in 1838, which pleased both scholars and poets. Tennyson found the story of Geraint and Enid, not related in Malory, in this volume.

Tennyson and the Pre-Raphaelites both took Malory as their text-book. The latter, who inherited the aftermath

[1] For fuller reference, see pp. 77 ff.

of the emotional fervour of the Romantic Revival, were chiefly interested in King Arthur as a foil to Lancelot. The King was the legal lord of Guinevere, and thus by his mere existence, in making the passion between Lancelot and Guinevere forbidden, he made it romantically interesting, especially in its latter stages.

Tennyson's conception of King Arthur and the Arthurian legends was certainly wider than this. It involved a good deal of preparation both from the point of view of subject-matter and form. He had already written shorter narrative poems, dealing with Lancelot and King Arthur, published in the 1832 volume, namely, the " Lady of Shalott " (published in 1832) ; " Sir Launcelot and Queen Guinevere " and the " Morte d'Arthur " (published in 1842).[1] The latter was transported bodily into his later *Idylls* (1869) and shows in its perfection his melodious and highly rhythmic blank verse.

Tennyson was a serious and scholarly student of Malory, but he had not the knowledge of European literature and romance which Swinburne possessed, and was thus more tied to this source than the latter poet. In the case of the Tristan legend, this limitation was not for the best, but in the case of Arthur's early life in the first five books of Malory, he was more fortunate. He has contrived to make an imaginative and unified poetical version of diverse matter. If the poet is read with his source, it will be allowed that he shows great skill in the manner in which he has chosen the incidents and woven them into a logical tale. " The Coming of Arthur " is a clear and coloured narrative, written in blank verse, which moves in a dignified and harmonious manner to the required close of the section. Two or three characters emerge from a misty background of shifting scenes. These are Merlin, King Arthur, King Leodogrance and Guinevere. The poet makes King Leodogrance ask who Arthur is, as he (Arthur) wishes to marry his daughter Guinevere. And so, as a natural sequence, the riddle of Arthur's birth is discussed and the parentage of Uther and Ygerne confirmed by Merlin's story. Arthur's birth is surrounded by mystery and the sense of dimness and uncertainty is communicated to us with

---

[1] For fuller study of these, see below, pp. 91-92

all the art which Tennyson has at command. The magic elements in the tale shift before our eyes like a garment, spun of gossamer, and every now and then we have a glimpse of elemental truth beneath, which legend ever symbolizes. The whole riddle of man's destiny in general, and Arthur's in particular, is in the now far-famed story of the sword Excalibur, given him by the Lady of the Lake :

> There, likewise I beheld Excalibur
> Before him at his crowning borne, the sword
> That rose from out the bosom of the lake
> And Arthur row'd across and took it—rich
> With jewels, elfin Urim, on the hilt,
> Bewildering heart and eye—the blade so bright
> That men are blinded by it : on one side,
> Graven in the oldest tongue of all this world,
> " Take me " but turn the blade and ye shall see,
> And written in the speech ye speak yourself
> " Cast me away."   And sad was Arthur's face
> Taking it, but old Merlin counsell'd him,
> " Take thou and strike ! the time to cast away
> Is yet far off."   So this great brand the King
> Took, and by this will beat his foeman down.

The early freshness of the dawn is on the verse which describes the meeting of Arthur and Guinevere and their betrothal. Lancelot, Arthur's beloved warrior, is ordered by the King to ride and bring forth the Queen. And so, in May, when blossoms are white, Arthur and Guinevere are made man and wife, with solemn vows made by both. Arthur's knights stand round him, rejoicing.

Thus begins one of the greatest stories of romance. But Tennyson has not been content to use his art to tell a romantic story. In the *Idylls of the King*, looked upon as a complete poem, he has attempted to build up a logical and ethical argument. He shows how the sin of Lancelot and Guinevere, beginning as a small canker, infects at last the life-long creation of Arthur, the ideals embodied in the Round Table and its knights. The poet does not only suggest this miasma, which is felt like a pestilential fever in the air ; he points it out like a moralist, " Thou ailest here and here."

And to accentuate his moral lesson, he has tried to draw in Arthur the type of perfect kingship, justice and sexual purity, which according to the Victorian ideal and Tennyson's own was to be found in married life. To create a perfect character is a difficult task, and the material Tennyson found in Malory made his task even more difficult. For in this source, Arthur is at one time a fairy changeling, at another a chief of lawless times, and at another a magnificent feudal chieftain. Tennyson has allowed Arthur at times to be seen through the mists of fairy enchantment, but at others he has modernised him, modelling him after the type of Albert the Good.

The ideals and sentiments of married love which are put into Arthur's mouth in his interview with Guinevere, are Tennyson's own. For the ideals of chivalry, it must be remembered, which glorified love and the faithfulness and service of the lover, did not necessarily imply the love of husband and wife. The lover must find a worthy mistress and great lady to which he could attach himself, and from this attachment must spring his brave and knightly deeds, as flowers from rich soil. Sometimes, as in Wolfram's *Parzival*, the marriage ideal is upheld, for Parzival, even though he goes on the Grail Quest, and is successful, is passionately devoted to his wife, and becomes the founder of the family who guard the Grail. But more often, in chivalric tales, the lady adored is already married to a lord, and is high in station above her humble worshipper.

When this love implies guilty relations, Malory does not commit himself to stringent moral judgment. On the one side there is the extremely barbarous practice of " trial by ordeal " from which Lancelot saves Guinevere, and by which a cruel society showed their condemnation of adultery. On the other hand, even after the havoc Guinevere has caused in the kingdom has been shown, she is praised in Malory as a " good lover." And Lancelot's virtue consists not only in being a good knight and a loyal and great-hearted friend, but in being a noble and chivalrous lover. And even though Mordred is legally justified in accusing Lancelot, the scales are weighted against him by the way in which he tries to entrap Lancelot in the tower, alone and unarmed.

This very inconsistency of Malory gives a modern poet a right to choose his point of view ; he may either take the purely romantic and neutral one of telling a story and letting it speak for itself ; or he may assume a definite position, as Tennyson wished to do, in upholding the ideals of marriage. But suggestion and subtle persuasion is a stronger influence in poetry than the didactic method which is apt to arouse anti-suggestion and produce the opposite effect to what is intended. This is what has happened.

Consequently, Tennyson has not drawn the champion of the ideals he wished to uphold, in a way to gain the sympathies of modern readers. The fact that Arthur is so much more and so much less than a man, alienates sympathy. Arthur's portrait stands out in a high bright light, but Lancelot's is sketched in with light and shade, and as we gaze on his scarred yet noble features, our sympathy goes with him, even though, or perhaps because, he is earth-stained. It is the case of Milton's Satan once again. The artist in the poet has betrayed the moralist.

The unfortunate thing is, that the whole of the plan and argument of the *Idylls of the King* is sketched around the perfect King and the ideals he has created in his court by making knights, in order to raise men out of the beast. In the earlier *Idylls*, the sin of Lancelot and Guinevere has not yet begun to cast its shadow on the pure and shining purpose. But gradually, from the tale of Balin and Balan and onwards, the noxious stain begins to spread over the canvas. The rumour, whispered mockingly by Garlion and echoed by Vivien, that the Queen is not perfectly " pure," haunts Balin in his dream and sends him into the wolds again to give way to his old savagery. And in one of his ungovernable moods, he fights with and slays his disguised brother, Balan. This treatment of the story is quite different from that of Swinburne. In Swinburne, Balin is pursued by the dark malignity of Fate.

In the " Holy Grail " Lancelot fails to find the Holy Grail, though on the threshold of the discovery, because of ·his relations with Guinevere. Here Tennyson is in accord with Malory, who, in following and even in modifying his source the " Queste," is perforce more ascetic in his attitude than in the rest of the books of the *Morte Darthur*, [1]

The mockery of the lost ideal echoes through the " Last Tournament." Tristan exclaims, " The glory of our Round Table is no more."

In " Guinevere," the fact that sin has destroyed Arthur's court and its ideals could not be more strongly stressed. Guinevere has fled to a nunnery in Almesbury. When Arthur appears, pure, proud and cold, she throws herself at his feet. The King addresses her sternly from his great height of unwavering rectitude and tells her of the ruin she has brought about. In pronouncing finally words of forgiveness, he is made to take his stand by the side of Almighty God. But it is God the Judge rather than God the Father of the prodigal.

" Lo, I forgive thee as Eternal God forgives," he pronounces. He then goes on to tell her that when they meet before the high God, she will claim him as her husband, " not a smaller soul, not Lancelot, nor another."

Thus it must be allowed that Tennyson is not altogether successful in his modern presentation of Arthur, and so the *Idylls* in general suffer from the attempt to fit the whole into too rigid a frame. This criticism does not necessarily apply to the separate Idylls, which often form a unity in themselves.

In the *Sword of Kingship*, published in 1866, Thomas Westwood relates the story of King Arthur told in the first book of Malory. If an academic prize had been offered for an Arthurian poem in the style of Tennyson, this one would have carried off the palm. Fortunately, imitations of the Victorian poet do not seem to be desired, and Westwood's fame has been fugitive.

Laurence Binyon's play *Arthur* [2] centres in Lancelot and the acts of the last days. But Laurence Binyon's conception of Arthur and his working out of it is worthy of note here, and interesting to compare with Tennyson. Arthur, in Binyon also, is often more of a king than a man ; as

---

[1] For study of source, see E. Vinaver, *Malory*, 1929, Appendix 2-3.

[2] *Arthur*, a tragedy, 1923. See also below, p. 107.

Queen Guinevere puts it, he defends her " from afar with a palisade " like a city. He struggles to uphold justice, somewhat at the expense of his humanity.

> " I am the King,
>   And therefore justice : if I fail, that fails
>   Which is of costlier essence than a king
>   Which salts corruption."

This justice is hard to render because he is betrayed as a husband and a friend by Lancelot. When he is asked to forgive Guinevere, at first his point of view is the same as that of Tennyson's King.

The King replies to Lancelot, when he asks Arthur to forgive the Queen and take her back.

> " Take my Queen pardoned to my heart, you plead,
>   Ah Launcelot ! were it merely man and woman,
>   Love should be wide and infinite as air
>   To meet her at the world's end with my arms
>   Even at the farthest erring.   There's no help.
>   A man may pardon, but the King may not.
>   The King is justice or no more a King."

But when he has his last meeting with Guinevere in the cloister, he is less cold and self-righteous than in Tennyson, and indeed asks the forgiveness of Guinevere, who herself is remorseful for the evil she has wrought in the land.

The play of *King Arthur* by J. Comyns Carr is a well constructed drama, which moves naturally and swiftly to its tragic close.   Variety is introduced by a prologue, interspersed with lyrics, by prose scenes with a touch of the comic, and by the rustic episode in the woods at May time.   The dramatist changes the sequence of the events, as given in Malory, and one or two of the events themselves, but this departure from tradition is justified by the result, which speeds up the dramatic action.

In the proclamation which Merlin gives over Arthur's dead body, the poet gives expression to the idea of the immortality of King Arthur through the ages.

Guinevere. He's gone, the light of all the world lies dead.

Merlin.   Not so : he doth but pass who cannot die,
          The King that was, the King that yet shall be :
          Whose spirit, borne along from age to age,
          Is England's to the end.   Look where the dawn
          Sweeps through a wider heaven, and on its wings,
          By those three Queens of night his barge is borne
          To that sweet Isle of Avalon whose sleep
          Can heal all earthly wounds.

If Tennyson has idealised King Arthur and tended to modernise him, John Masefield has adopted the plan of going back to the more primitive representations of him. He has resurrected Arthur the British chief, in " Midsummer Night." [1]

According to one tradition, King Arthur and his knights lie buried under the Eildon Hills,[2] in a limestone cave.   They are awaiting the trumpet-call in order to arise and come forth once more.   The poet describes how, one Midsummer Night, when midnight chimed, they all came to life again, only to sink back to marble stillness when their hour was past.

At the critical hour on an exquisite midsummer night, when the moonlight made the earth radiant, the poet started off on his journey to the cave.

      So perfect was the beauty, that the air
      Was like immortal presence thrilling all
      The downland with deep life ;
      Presences communed in the white owl's call ;
      The rampart of the hill-top stood up bare,
      High on the windy hill, a brightness shone—
      I wondered whose, since shepherd-men had gone
      Homeward a long time since to food and wife,[3]
      Yet brightness shone, as from a lantern there.

---

[1] *Midsummer Night and Other Tales in Verse*, 1928.
[2] Leyden mentions this tradition in " Scenes of Infancy."
[3] " Midsummer Night," *op. cit.*, p. 78.

He entered the corridor hewn far within the hill. There he saw all the company.

> King Arthur, black and keen,
> Pale, eager, wise, intense ;
> Lime-blossom Guinevere, the red-gold queen,
> Ban's son, the kingly Lancelot, the bright
> Gawaine, Bors, Hector, all whom trumpets drew
> Up Badon at the falling of the dew.
> And over them brooded the immense,
> Helper or Spirit with immortal Sight.[1]

When the valley bells chimed midnight, Arthur spoke :—

> Midsummer Night permits us to declare
> How Nature's sickle cut us from the air
> And made the splendour of the summer fall.[1]

They all claimed in turn to have been the cause of the downfall of the kingdom. The truth is that they all contributed, including Arthur, Lancelot and Guinevere.

This central poem called " Midsummer Night " is in the middle of the volume, to which it gives its name. It is the thread on which the other tales are strung. The whole is a valuable modern contribution to the " Arthurian Legend." Masefield accomplishes less than Tennyson, for there is no attempt at organic unity, but the later poet succeeds in what he sets out to perform. He writes in a simple ballad style, for the most part, with many short descriptions and similes from Nature and wild animals, showing keen observation, and used with dramatic fitness.

Tennyson takes his traditions chiefly from Malory and often shares in his literary conventionality. Masefield, as in the central idea of his book of poems, takes them where he finds them, and is indifferent to verbal accuracy, especially in names. He imports a fable, like that of the Venus and the Ring in this volume,[2] and connects it with Arthur, although it has no connection at all with him. Yet the poet's dramatic talent—for in prose and poetry he is a first-rate story-teller— carries us along with him. He is akin to the minstrels, and

---

[1] *op. cit.*, p. 79.   [2] " Arthur and his Ring," *op. cit.*, p. 66.

he himself has told us that he has heard many of the stories he delights in from his old nurse.   Perhaps it is because he gives from time to time readings of his own poetry, that he keeps in touch with his audience.   His verse has the directness of the spoken word ; it is not only to be read in the study.   Certainly, his verse is often crude and rough and drops down suddenly to the prosaic, but often again it soars and sings.   The description of Midsummer Eve just quoted is an example.

In depicting the character of King Arthur, Masefield rejects the tradition of the feudal and courtly King and goes back to the earlier chieftain of Britain of the early chronicle. The story of the fairy gifts for the Baby Arthur, he owes to Layamon and Welsh legend.   For the rest he uses imagination, the keen practical type of the boy who has played at pirates or heard tales of early Scandinavian raids.   In such a description as follows, we recognise a man who has had actual experience of ships, and who can register in fit words each movement of these.   This passage also illustrates Masefield's direct dramatic power, and simple construction of his verse. The manner in which he adopts any suitably sounding names, whether in the orthodox Arthurian tradition or not, is worthy of remark.

In the poem " Badon Hill," Masefield describes how Kol, Loki and Wolf the Red Fang, landed on the western isles in their ships the " Dragons."   They moored their ships and marched onwards, hoping to raid the cattle.   But they saw no cattle nor any sign of life.   Drunken Kol diced, while his companion slept.   When they were thus off their guard, Lancelot and Arthur stole a march upon them.

> Arthur and Lancelot, the son of Ban,
> Took burning touchwood in an iron pan ;
>
> They slid into the water among reed,
> No pirate saw their coming, none gave heed.
>
> .   .   .   .   .   .
>
> The weather Dragon-ship rose overhead,
> Like a house—pale, sun-blistered, painted red.

Arthur and Lancelot together smeared
Tar to the leadings whence her hausers veered.

Then heaping twigs and pine-cones, they gave touch
And blew, until the little flames took clutch.

No watcher heard or saw them, no one came,
The little flame became a bigger flame.[1]

It spread along the seams and thrust its tongues
Out, till the straikings looked like ladder-rungs.

First, the wind bowed it down, then at a gust,
The flame that had been greedy, became lust ;

And like a wave that lifts against a rock
Up, into shattering shining at the shock,

So it upshattered into spangs of flame,
That writhelled red, and settled, and laid claim

And tore the Dragon's planking from her bones
Roaring ! the Dragon sighed with little moans,

Now swearing pirates ran to fight the flame
And Arthur's archers shot them as they came.

And Loki rising from his drunken sweven,
Saw all his longships blazing red to heaven

And Arthur's army coming with a will
Straight from the fire up the Badon Hill !

And so, in a rhymed page of old chronicle, come alive,
we are told that Arthur fought the pirates at Badon Hill,
cut them off from food and retreat, and now

Under the grasses, where the cattle browse,
King Loki's army keep eternal house

In Badon earth, for none escaped alive,
Thereafter Arthur's realm was free to thrive.

For many years no pirates had the will
To band against him, after Badon Hill.

---

[1] In " Midsummer Night," pp. 43-47.

The above lines illustrate the realistic manner in which Masefield treats the historical Arthur, so that he becomes a real fighting pirate-King.

How is the fairy element treated? It is treated very simply, after the manner of the Celtic lay and fairy tale. It will be remembered that in Layamon, it is related that at birth the elves attended Arthur's cradle.

In Masefield's poem "The Birth of Arthur," [1] Arthur was laid on the Dragon's stone chair at moonrise by Ygerna, his mother. The kings and the queens came to look upon him. Modred came amongst the rest, and prophesied that Arthur would have a son who would accomplish his father's ruin. Last came his helper, who prophesied that her beauty would stir him and that she would inspire his noble deeds. Another instance of the freedom with which Masefield uses tradition is given in the " Sailing of Hell Race " in the same volume. [2]

True, there is the precedent in many Celtic stories of a hero visiting the Other-World. Many of the sword-bridges, which, for example, occur in the Gawain and Lancelot tales, have their origin in bridges over to the Other-World.

The " Sailing of Hell Race " is written in a more elaborate stanza than the other tales and shows imaginative power in the descriptions of the dreary and the terrible. Even although Masefield, in diction and manner, is far removed from Spenser, yet this poem is reminiscent of the " Cave of Mammon " in the *Faerie Queene*. Horror is piled on horror, with no relief.

Arthur and his men set sail in their ship the *Britain*, westward, beyond familiar seas to a granite coast and into a bay of desolation. In a cairn a wooden box was seen, with a writing enclosed. It ran thus :—

> " Beyond this harbour are the granite rocks,
>   Which are the gates of Hell, where courage dies,
>   Brother, I call upon you to be wise ;
>   Return, before the Key turns in the locks.

---

[1] From *Midsummer Night*, 1928, pp. 16-23.
[2] From *Midsummer Night*, 1928, pp. 50-64.

> Return, and do not dare,
> Death beyond death, the Cities of despair.
> Return, to where the lark sings in the skies,
> And on the Down the shepherd keeps his flocks."

But Arthur replied that they had adventured far, and would adventure farther, for the " door of hell is dark until assailed."

So on they sailed until they came to a narrow cataract of foaming water. On either side sat two granite forms, who cackled with laughter as the ship passed into the " Race of toppling seas." But Arthur's ship was made of sacred wood and was not dashed to pieces. Further on, they came to a city of devils, dancing and shrieking and hurling crockery about.

> Within his vast and dirty temple sat
> Mammon, the god and monarch of that Hell,
> With sharp suspicion blinking through his fell,
> Toad-throated, hooft yet pinioned like a bat,
> Athwart the temple's span,
> Across the walls, a fire-writing ran,
> Blazing the prices of the souls to sell,
> For all to read, the devils yelled thereat
>
> .   .   .   .
>
> Yet more than Mammon, Lady Self was lord,
> Within that city of the lust for gold,
> The jewelled thing, bespiced, bepainted cold,
> Whom Mammon purchased for his bed and board.
> A varnisht shell was she,
> Exquisite emptiness of vanity,
> Unbodied and unminded and unsouled,
> The mirror Self, whom all who saw adored.[1]

Nine of Arthur's men gave way to the temptation of trying to gain some of the prizes of Mammon, " the chinking gold," and were lost for evermore. King Arthur cut his ropes and thrust to seaward, leaving his nine deserters to perish. They came to another city of Hell under the curse of war and rapine. The inhabitants of the city arose and tried to murder Arthur

---

[1] *Op. cit.*, p. 55.

and his crew, and some fell victims. But Arthur escaped and as he sailed away, he saw lightning run along the city's ramparts and a dreadful glare, which finally died down to blackness.

The next city they came to lay under an ominous quiet, for the inhabitants were overcome by pale fevers, palsies and madness.

The Queen of this rotting city thought she had Arthur in her power. Indeed a strange inertia came over him, against which he could not struggle. His seamen dropped, fever stricken ; they were too feeble to pull an oar.

Aloft on her throne, the City's cruel Queen sat in shining green armour, no thought in her eyes, gleaming with the knowledge of her victims' suffering. She addressed Arthur and his Britons, who were compelled to come before her. She told them that they stood in Nether Hell upon the sediments of Pride and Greed, and the dust of nations that had perished. She said she had slain the nations, one by one, and that she was the final death and the ender of all hardihood.

She addressed the adventurous King thus, " You, too, with your adventurers, are sealed as mine, already."

Then Arthur felt weariness attack him, nor could he rouse himself to effort. But, in his darkness, a sudden glory thrust on his senses and the immortal Queen, his helper, stood before him, and bade him cast off his prison bonds, take power from her touch and sail forth into life and freedom again. Then once again, " Spirit kindled Arthur " and at length

> It stirred his seamen from the malison
> Of that third monarchy of the unwise.

So they sailed homeward—the seven of the seamen who remained, and they beheld once more the hills of home and the country green with corn. They coasted past King Dyved's territory, beyond King Ryence's lands, past mountains and shining rivers.

Lo, a princess came to meet them in a golden chariot ! She was clad in green and had streaming red and gold hair.

She drove two white horses of her father King Ocvran's body-guard.

> The red-gold lady dear,
> Was Ocvran's daughter, princess Gwenivere,
> Whom Arthur worshippt then and evermore,
> As in the night, the traveller the star.[1]

In this poem, " The Sailing of Hell Race," Masefield has been daring enough to give Arthur a new adventure, yet not one out of the line of tradition altogether. It can be seen at a glance, that this is a very different portrait from that of the Head of the Court in Malory. And yet the imaginative force of the action and descriptions carry Masefield's readers on to the end of the tale, and make them forget the liberties he takes with the traditions. This poem has also something of the nature of an allegory, without losing its realistic nature.

[1] *Op. cit.*, p. 64.

CHAPTER V

GAWAIN

No character in Arthurian legend has received less justice at the hands of poets of the nineteenth and twentieth centuries than Gawain. Scholars, in particular Dr J. L. Weston,[1] have done much to restore him to his own, but not poets. For this state of things Malory is partly responsible. The portrait of Gawain in Malory is not consistent. The books which are based on the Chronicles, including the alliterative *Morte Arthure*, present him as Arthur's constant companion in his wars in France, brave, loyal and warlike, though revengeful, particularly where the honour of his own family is concerned. In Malory's later books, for the most part, he is brave, courteous and ready to do a lady a service. He is loyal to Lancelot almost to the end. When Lancelot's enemies propose to show up Lancelot and Guinevere to Arthur, he will have nothing to do with it and replies, " As for my part, I will never be against Sir Launcelot for one day's deed when he rescued me from King Carados of the Dolorous tower and slew him and saved my life. . . . Methinketh, brother, such kind deeds and kindness should be remembered." [2] It is not till Lancelot kills Gawain's brothers, Gareth and Gaheris, unwittingly, in a sudden confused fight, that he (Gawain) turns against him.

On the other hand, Gawain has many lady-loves and his conduct in regard to Etarre is exceedingly dishonourable, according to present-day standards. His many conquests, as Dr Weston has pointed out, are due to the fact that he was such a popular hero, that stories originally related

[1] See J. L. Weston, *The Legend of Gawain, Studies upon its Scope and Significance*, 1897 ; also J. L. Weston, *The Legend of Sir Perceval*, 1906- 1909, 2 vols.
[2] In Malory's *Morte Darthur*, " Everyman " Edition, vol. ii., p. 340.

concerning other heroes became attached to his name. Gawain was originally the typical English hero, brave, courteous and loyal.   Dr Weston has also maintained that the group of fourteenth and fifteenth century metrical romances which have as heroes Arthur and Gawain are indigenous.[1] These are particularly interesting as showing Gawain in a somewhat different light from that of Malory's conception. They place some of their scenes in the green forest, the famous Inglewood Forest near the town of Carlisle, which also figures largely in the romances.   A green knight plays an important part in one group ; some are stories of enchantment and of challenge, the performance of which breaks the spell, and one and all illustrate Gawain's perfect courtesy.

[1] Metrical romances celebrating Gawain, mainly with scenes in North-West England, in approximate order chronology :—

(a) " Sir Gawain and the Green Knight," probably of Western Midlands, about 1360.   Scene in Lancashire or Westmorland. " The Grene Knight " in *Percy Folio MS.* in a southern dialect, tells practically the same story as above.

(b) The " Auntres of Arthure " in dialect of North-West, fourteenth century (second half), scene in Cumberland.   1350 +

(c) The " Avowynge of Arthur " in same handwriting as dialect and manuscript as the " Auntres of Arthur " and probably of the same date.

(d) " Morte Arthure," Border dialect, possibly Scottish with some English forms.   Composed between 1350 and 1400.

(e) " Carle of Carlile," dialect North England, fifteenth century (early).   Scene chiefly in Cumberland, though Arthur holds court in Wales.   Same story with few variations in *Percy Folio MS.* of seventeenth century.

(f) " Golagros and Gawain," composed in Southern Scotland in fifteenth century (second half).   Story takes place on the Continent.   Arthur is on his way to the Holy Land.

(g) The " Weddynge of Sir Gawen and Dame Ragnell."   Mixed dialect.   Scene in Cumberland, date fifteenth century (late). Substantially same story as in ballad of *Percy Folio MS.*, " Marriage of Sir Gawaine."

(h) The " Turk and Gowin."   Dialect, North.   Fifteenth century (late).   Scene, North of England and Isle of Man.

For account of English Metrical romances, including Arthurian, see *Cambridge Literary History*, Vol. I., and Bibliography.   Also, A. H. Billings, *Middle English Metrical Romances.*

The definiteness of their topography is also noteworthy in comparison with the vagueness of certain of the French romances and of Malory. The incident of decapitation and the term " Green " in the " Green Knight " have led students of origin to surmise that the original form of the stories of this group pertained to a vegetation myth.[1] The attachment formed with the Arthur stories is no doubt much later in this case.

Three romances have for their subject a challenge ; two of these relate a decapitation incident. The " Grene Knight " [2] is an abbreviation and summary of the finer fourteenth-century " Sir Gawain and the Green Knight," [3] with its fresh and vigorous descriptions of the scenery of Lancashire and Westmorland. At the Yuletide feast, the Green Knight comes riding boldly into Arthur's hall to propose a grim jest, namely that he should himself bend his neck to the stroke of a huge battle-axe which he carried, to be wielded by any knight of the court, on the condition that the same knight would meet him a year hence at the Green Chapel and submit to a similar stroke. Gawain accepts the strange challenge, cuts off the knight's head, and to the horror of the spectators, the headless body rides away with its gory head in its hand. Then follows a severe testing time for Gawain. The last adventure and the most critical takes place at a Castle two miles from the Green Chapel, the appointed place of meeting, and three days before the set time. The Knight of the Castle, the host, for sport he says, makes a bargain that he and Gawain should each in the evening give to the other what he has received during the day. To this Gawain agrees. The wife of the host tries hard to tempt him to unchastity, but all he receives from her, very unwillingly, are kisses which he duly renders to her husband, as agreed. On the third day, however, she gives him from her waist a green and gold lace which she declares will save

[1] See J. L. Weston, *From Ritual to Romance*, 1929, p. 51.
[2] Ed. Hales and Furnival, vol. ii. 56.
[3] Ed. Sir F. Madden, 1839. Ed. Morris, 1864 (Early Eng. Text Soc.). Ed. J. R. R. Tolkien, 1925 ; modernised by J. L. Weston, *Romance, Vision and Satire*, 1912.

him from wounds. In view of his approaching ordeal next day, he resolves to be silent concerning it and to keep it.

On the appointed day he rides to the Green Chapel in the glen. The Green Knight duly appears, his head firmly on his shoulders. Gawain kneels and bows his head to the stroke. The first time he flinches, but the second time he bravely awaits the blow from the axe. But the Green Knight brings down the axe so gently that it only makes a skin wound. Up jumps Gawain, and explanations follow. The Green Knight and Gawain's host are one and the same person. All has been for Gawain's testing. He has stood firm on every occasion except on the matter of the lady's lace. This has been the cause of his flinching and the slight wound. The romance of the " Grene Knight " (*Folio MS.*) goes on to explain that this is why the Knights of the Bath wear a lace on their left shoulder until they have performed their first courageous deed when a lady removes it. The explanation is merely fictitious.[1]

The " Carle of Carlile " also illustrates Gawain's courtesy, even to the foal in the stable, over which he throws his mantle for warmth. All that the rude churl asks him to do, Gawain performs and thus releases the spell. Then the Carle, released from his compulsory savagery, becomes a gentle, courteous knight and marries his daughter to Gawain. King Arthur is invited to his table and makes him, the Carle, the Earl of Carlisle.

The short fifteenth-century romance entitled " The Weddynge of Sir Gawen and Dame Ragnell " gives virtually the same story as the ballad in the *Folio MS.* " edited " in the *Reliques.*[2] It takes place near Tearne-Wadling (or Tarn), a small lake or tarn near Hosketh in Cumberland on the road from Penrith to Carlisle. It relates how a huge giant with a club challenges Arthur and will have his life unless he

---

[1] See the interesting note on the Order of the Bath in Hales and Furnivall's edition, vol. ii. 57.

[2] ii. 195, " Everyman " Edition. The same story is told in Chaucer's *Wife of Bath's Tale*, in Gower's story of " Florent " in the *Confessio Amantis*, and in the Scottish ballad of " King Henry." For study of analogues and sources see G. H. Maynadier, *The Wife of Bath's Tale*, 1901.

can tell him the answer to the riddle, what women desire most. He is to have a year in which to solve the problem. After sending to the giant various wrong solutions, the King, when out riding, meets a hideous hag who says she will tell him the answer, if he promises to give her the boon she desires. The answer she provides him with is the correct one, for she is the sister of the giant who has challenged Arthur. It is " That all women will have their wille." Arthur thus escapes the penalty of death, but the hag demands as her price that he will marry her. However, the courteous Gawain hastens to the rescue and takes upon himself the dreadful task. Finally, all is well, for the ill-featured bride, disenchanted by the bridegroom's kiss, appears radiantly young and beautiful. In the original story, probably a simple fairy tale of a wicked spell, the hero would be the same throughout. But as Arthur is in tradition wed to Guinevere, Gawain is brought in and the tale adapted.

In the " Turke and Gowin " a curious little man, broad but not high, the " Turke " gives a similar challenge to Gawain as in the " Green Knight " to cut off his head. Gawain does so, and up stands a stalwart knight released of his enchantment. A point worthy of note is that in common with other Arthurian romances, the courtesy of Gawain has a foible in the rudeness and brusquerie of Kay. It will be remembered in the Welsh Romance " Kilhwch and Olwen," [1] Kei appears as the chief officer of the court and is rebuked by Arthur for discourtesy to Kilhwch on his arrival. Gawain also appears in the Welsh documents as Gwalchmei, the Walwain of William of Malmesbury. Another interesting fact in the " Turke and Gowin," is that the scene is laid in the Isle of Man, with its numerous legends of giants and its connections with Merlin.

Other metrical romances connected with Gawayne are " The Auntres of Arthure at the Terne Wathelyn," " Golagros and Gawaine," [2] and the " Avowynge of Arthur." In the " Auntres " (adventures) and " Avowynge "—both fourteenth-century romances—the story takes place by the small lake,

---

[1] In the *Mabinogion*.
[2] Ed. in *Syr Gawayne*, by Sir F. Madden, 1839.

the Tarn Wadling, in the centre of the forest of Inglewood. In the first romance, Gawain and Guinevere confront a grisly spectre and in the second Gawain takes a vow to watch all night by the same water.

All the tales have a racy, humorous and sometimes coarse smack of the soil about them, which allows us to place them among the *fabliaux*. And certain hints here and there, as has been shown, give likelihood to the conclusions of certain scholars [1] that Gawain's descent can be traced far back to an inhabitant of the solar world or to the seasonal myth. A vestige of a sun-myth seems to remain in the fact which is stated in Malory that his strength waxed greater at noonday and waned towards sundown.

From the point of view of English literature, it makes for variety to have these metrical romances and the later ballads, for they give their sturdier, convincing, though less refined picture of a hero which seems to have been regarded as an English type.

In Chrétien de Troies' *Perceval*, or rather in Wauchier de Denain's continuation, Dr Weston [2] points out the traces of this Old English Cycle, which she believes was anterior in origin to the French. Gawain, according to her, was the original hero of the Grail and was replaced by Perceval. When Lancelot became popular, he could not be made the chief Grail hero, because of his unlawful love of the Queen. So a compromise was reached. Galahad, Lancelot's son, was chosen as the Grail-Quester in the later romances.

Lord Lytton seems to be the only English author who has realised the true character of the English Gawain, " golden-

[1] J. Rhys in *Arthurian Legend*, 1891, and J. L. Weston in *From Ritual to Romance*, 1920.

[2] See *Legend of Sir Perceval*, 1906-9, vol. i., chaps. 6-9. She comes to the conclusion that the " majority of our vernacular Arthurian poems or sections of the *Perceval* and the prologue of the Mons MS., are all three remnants of a once popular and widely spread story group concerned with the deeds of Gawain and his kin." She thinks this group of tales was of insular origin known by the title " Jeaste (Geste) or Syr Gawayne " and popularly ascribed to " famosus ills fabulate Bledhericus." Professor Bruce, a representative of the opposing " Continental " school, criticises this severely (*Evolution of Arthurian Legend*, pp. 96 ff.).

tongued," humorous and sturdy. He has celebrated in his
verse his amusing encounters and racy wit. His adventures
are for the most part fabricated by Lytton, but his earlier
ones (in Book VI of *King Arthur*) are true to the spirit of what
might be called the Gawain *fabliaux*. This Gawain, as
represented in the metrical romances and in Bishop Percy's
Reliques, also finds himself in awkward predicaments and
with an unwanted marriage partner.

One of the most characteristic episodes as related by
Lytton runs thus :—

Merlin has bequeathed to Gawain his raven as a guide,
not altogether a welcome gift.

> " Please to call back this offspring of the skies !
> Unworthy I to be his earthly rest ! "
> " Methought," said Merlin, " that thy King's emprize
> Had found in thee a less reluctant breast ;
> Again his friendship granted to his side—
> Thee the bird summons, be the bird thy guide." [1]

Merlin commanded him to let the raven lead him to the coast.
The bird proved an erratic guide :

> Grave as a funeral mourner rode Gawaine—
> The bird went first in most indecent glee,
> Now soared from sight, now gambolled back again—
> Now munched a beetle, and now chaced a bee—
> Now plucked the wool from meditative lamb,
> Now picked a quarrel with a lusty ram. [2]

" Was he never going to stop for dinner ? "

At last he halted in a glade where knights and ladies
were feasting. Courteous as always, Gawain doffed his cap
and requested food for a famishing man. But his big broad-
shouldered host would allow him to eat his fill only on two
conditions. The first was that after the meal he should
fight him and if he conquered, should wed his daughter.
Gawain did not hesitate.

> " Sir Host," said Gawaine, as he stretched his platter,
> " I'll first the pie discuss and then the matter." [3]

---

[1] *King Arthur*, 1848, Book VI, Stanza 22 ; *ibid.*, Stanza 23.
[2] *King Arthur*, Book VI, Stanza 33.   [3] *Op. cit.*, Stanza 37.

After the feast, Gawain stood forth for his duel and gave his opponent many a quick blow:

> " They foined, they fenced, changed play, and hacked and
>   hewed—
> Paused, panted, eyed each other and renewed " ; [1]

At length by a " dexterous and back-handed blow," he drew his host to his knees.

But Gawain's bargain was not yet completed. He had still the second condition to fulfil. He had tackled the father, now the daughter ! He had still to embrace his wife. The worst was yet to come.

> " O cursëd bird," cried Gawain, with a groan,
> " Into what trap hast thou betrayed my life ;
> Happy the man to whom was given a stone
> When he asked bread ; I have received a wife.
> Take warning, youths, and never dine with hosts
> Who make their daughters adjuncts to their roasts." [2]

Gawain, however, was always ready to fulfil his vow. He led her to the bridal chamber and noted with brightening eyes that she was " tall and buxom, fresh and young." As he took her hand to kiss her, lo ! a sword flashed down from an unseen hand and struck him on the shoulder. The bride began to weep and Gawain, in attempting to kiss her tears away, nearly lost his nose. The sword had once again swept down ! Then his bride confessed that he was her eleventh husband and that the other ten had been doomed to destruction by her father from the fatal sword in the chamber. It was a trick to gain the swords and armour of the knight. So Gawain, taking heed of the warning, gave his bride a wide berth that night, creeping to the corner of the room and keeping a wary eye on the ceiling. The bride's father was astonished and chagrined to find him unhurt in the morning.

But the hero, escaping with his life, had to shoulder the burdens of life again, and without breakfast, he and his

---

[1] *Op. cit.*, Stanza 46.   [2] *Op. cit.*, Stanza 48.

unwished-for spouse set out for the open road, he on a steed, she on a palfrey by his side.

"The bride rode dauntless—daunted much Gawain."

In vain he tried to free himself of her company. She stuck to him as a faithful woman to her chosen mate.

But as she began to woo him with gentle words, she appeared so lovely that he leant forward to kiss her. Suddenly, the neck of her palfrey was jerked away by a strong hand. A "huge black-browed gigantic" churl had leapt from the thicket and was seizing the kiss "defrauded of the knight." In great wrath, Gawain sprang from his saddle and prepared to defend his rights (even though he had not seemed to appreciate them !). But the thief made use of the hapless lady as a shield and Gawain knew not where to strike so as not to injure her. In the pause, the churl proposed another bargain. "A word in time may often save a life," he said. "Why not let the lady choose between us ? I have a notion she prefers *me*." So it was determined.

The churl was homely and rough, Gawain courteous and winsome, but "ladies' hearts are hidden and occult." The lady looked and mused and chose the former.

The forsaken knight rubbed his eyes in astonishment, and rode away. But, as he was doing so, he heard behind him the deep tones of his successful rival. Gawain turned pale and groaned. Had the other changed his mind ? Did he wish to return the lady ? But no, it was but to ask for the lady's hound, which had remained behind. Gawain was quick to turn the tables on him. Let the dog also choose ! The dog showed better sense than the lady. It chose Gawain for its master !

Thus with courage and shrewd wit, Gawain won through his labours. He had other trials, such as being tormented by the fairies, but the one related above seems to be the one most akin to the conception of the older English hero. It certainly diverges from tradition in the actual events, but it shows Gawain true to type. It is refreshing to find some humour in the Arthurian legend, for Malory is almost devoid of it. But in these cantos of Lytton's *King Arthur*, Gawain as a humorous character is restored to his own.

Tennyson and Morris give an altogether different picture of Gawain. They degrade him to a greater extent than Malory. Morris makes him one of the chief accusers of Lancelot. In Tennyson he is shown as light of love and careless, and even, in " Pelleas and Etarre," as behaving dishonourably.

Tennyson takes the story of Pelleas and Etarre from Malory. He places it the fourth from the last of his *Idylls* [1] and thus the moral degeneracy shown in the tale is used as an example of the gradual deterioration of the Round Table and its ideals. It shows Gawain as a light-of-love and worse, a traitor. For he filches Etarre, Pelleas' lady love, from the trusting youth, after swearing loyalty to him by the Round Table itself.

The poet elaborates the tale by means of every kind of poetical device. The picture of the youthful and innocent Pelleas is at first attractive, but a masculine " Enid," who allows his lady-love to bind and trample on him, does not appeal to modern readers. Not that Pelleas is a physical coward, he is muscular and active and overthrows his jailers easily enough, three at a time. But he has no weapons of defence against a woman ; perhaps his training in the code of courtly love has bereft him of them. The episode of his finding the lovers Gawain and Etarre sleeping together in the arbour at his mercy, and his placing his sword between them without injuring them, is a repetition of that in the Tristan legend. But, in this case, the action seems to savour of irresolution on the part of the hero, not nobility. Here is no overwhelming fatal love, but only an intrigue.

The last part of the story is laboured. The description of Pelleas' disillusionment and despair is too long drawn out. As Arthur Symons puts it, " Tennyson is often lacking, through a too fastidious working upon too thin a surface." In the tale of Malory, Fate has her revenge, Pelleas is caught in the toils of the Lady of the Lake and falls a victim to her charms. Etarre now pines away for what she could not have —the love of Pelleas ! It is the comedy of *A Midsummer Night's Dream*, though Malory does not treat it humorously as Shakespeare does. Tennyson mentions this *revanche* as being in the old tale, but he has rejected it.

[1] Published 1869.

The narrative is one of the least pleasant incidents in his Arthurian tales, though it contains beautiful passages and similes such as the following, which illustrates also Tennyson's moral purpose in choosing the story.

When Pelleas springs, despairing, from the presence of Lancelot and Guinevere,

> The Queen
> Looked hard upon her lover, he on her ;
> And each foresaw the dolorous day to be :
> And all talk died, as in a grove all song
> Beneath the shadow of some bird of prey ;
> Then a long silence came upon the hall,
> And Modred thought " The time is hard at hand."

CHAPTER VI

MERLIN

THE Arthurian legends would lose much of their charm if
the figure of Merlin were blotted out, or the story of his
miraculous deeds untold. Indeed, it would be impossible,
for he is the guardian of Arthur and, like Prospero in the
Tempest, uses his magic arts to aid those he is protecting.
Again, he is the very embodiment of legend itself, in his
transformations, taking the form of a child or an old man,
now giving good practical advice and again uttering riddles
and presaging woe. He is ageless and selfless, he cannot die,
he can only be enchanted for ever and ever. It is fitting that
when he takes a mistress, who encompasses his ruin, she
should be of fairy origin.[1]

The manner in which writers and poets in the various
centuries have regarded Merlin is characteristic of their
attitude to legend. He is a kind of touchstone. Geoffrey
of Monmouth invented or adapted him to suit his so-called
History. Later, the Romancers, French and English, elaborated
the incidents relating to him and fabricated others, working
his figure into the loosely-woven texture of their romances.
The eighteenth century used his name as a sign-board for
their political prophecies. To Tennyson he signified the
glamour and kingly power which surrounded Arthur, and
he chose the incident of his ensnaring for one of the most
romantic poems of the *Idylls of the King*. To Swinburne he
was the symbol of the beauty and power of Nature.

As far as literary origins are concerned, Geoffrey of
Monmouth was his originator. He gives, however, two very
different portraits in the *History* and in the *Vita Merlini*." [2]

---

[1] In Malory, Book IV, chap. 1.

[2] See edition by J. J. Parry (Illinois Studies in Language and Literature,
X, No. 3, 1925). Now definitely ascribed to Geoffrey.

Around the question what material Geoffrey used, a fierce conflict has ensued which has brought some interesting material to light but which has issued in no very clear issue. The shape-shifting Merlin, lost in the mists of time, seems to elude the grasp of those who would discover his origin! The Romancers solved it by giving him the devil for his father and a mortal for his mother!

First of all there are the Celticists whose views are summed up clearly by Mr Chadwick, who has examined the material in detail.[1] He shows the similarities and differences in the account of the Welsh Merlin (Myrddin) in the Welsh poems, especially three, two in the *Black Book of Carmarthen* (I and XVII), "Dialogue between Myrddin and Taliesin" and the "Afallenau," and one in the *Red Book of Hergest*, the "Cyvoesi," dialogue between Myrddin and his sister Gwenddydd.[2] These, this critic maintains, Geoffrey must have known. Also, he examines what he calls the Glasgow Records of the Life of Saint Kentigern and agrees with the identification [3] of a certain Lailoken, a mad prophet who goes mad after the battle of Arderydd (573), with Myrddin. Then he makes an examination of the incidents in the *Vita Merlini* and maintains that Geoffrey in this poem took his traditions, though altered in details, from the Welsh poems and the Glasgow Records, not vice-versa.

The second group is more cautious and with W. E. Mead [4] is of the opinion that Geoffrey may not have known the actual Welsh poems extant, but that " a set of parallel traditions based in part on the same events referred to in the Welsh poems may have formed the groundwork of those portions of the Latin poem which tell of Merlin's madness and of his discourse with Taliessin." Dr Chambers [5] states his opinion more strongly " that Merlin is a creation of Geoffrey's

---

[1] *Growth of Literature*, 1932, vol. i., pp. 123 ff.
[2] This is the most doubtful of three and rejected by Skene, *Four Ancient Books*, vol. i. 234-241.
[3] First made by Ward, in *Rom.* xxii., pp. 50 ff.
[4] Introduction to English *Merlin*, ed. Wheatley (Early Eng. Text Society, 1899, p. cxxii.)
[5] In *Arthur of Britain*, 1927, p. 98.

active brain." He admits, however, that in the *Vita* he draws "upon Northern stories and makes a wholesale transfer to Merlin of adventures which really belong to one Lailocen." [1] This is, in fact, a more extreme form of the second view.

Whatever opinion be adopted, it is safe to say that Merlin in the greater part was a literary invention of Geoffrey, and that the Merlin of the *History* and in some measure the *Vita* is the forerunner of the Merlin in the Romances, in Malory and in English literature through Malory.

Geoffrey's history crystallised into literary form many of the stories and oral traditions handed down in Armorica and Great Britain. In the *Lays* of Marie of France, however, which formed a kind of intermediary between the songs and popular poems and the more sophisticated romances, Merlin does not appear. The earliest date known for a French translation of Geoffrey's *History* is that of Geoffrey Gaimer's in 1145 which is lost. In 1155, however, Wace translated the *Historia* into octosyllabic rhyming verse. As far as Merlin was concerned, however, he added little of importance. The popularity of his *Brut* was shown by the transcription into prose and countless copies and imitations.[2] A new realm was opened for the Romancers.

The first French romance of "Merlin" was probably written early in the last decade of the twelfth century. It was composed by Robert de Borron [3] in verse and was intended to serve as a link between two other poems, the "Joseph of Arimathea" and the "Perceval." It was reduced into prose and thus formed the shorter romance of "Merlin," part of the shorter "De Borron" Cycle, though it was not necessarily his own transcription. This shorter Cycle was elaborated and

---

[1] In the "Notes on the Sources," p. ccxxix. in Wheatley's edition of the English *Merlin*, for example, the three strange laughs of Merlin are compared with that in the *Vita Merlini*, when Merlin laughs at a leaf caught in the Queen's hair, and, asked for the reason, answers that it is a sign of her unfaithfulness to the King. (Presumably she has betrayed her assignation with her lover in the woods.) For discussion of the incident in different forms in the *Life of St Kentigern* (Glasgow Records) see Chadwick, *Growth of Literature*, vol. i., pp. 109 ff.

[2] For these consult R. H. Fletcher, *Arthurian Material in the Chronicles*, 1906.   [3] Another spelling is "Boron."

lengthened interminably and became part of the " Cyclic Romances," known as the *Vulgate Cycle*.

In the case of Merlin and the development of the stories connected with him, there seems a wide gap from Geoffrey to the Romances. So much has disappeared that it can be bridged only by conjecture which has been somewhat steadied by modern research, but not changed in many cases into certainty. The Romancers, especially in France, cast a wide net and brought in strange products which have suffered a " sea change." Let us take one example [1] which has been chosen because it has come into English literature through Tennyson, namely, the imprisonment of Merlin in an enchanted circle. This may have some reference to a late Triad [2] in which Merlin enters the Glass House in Bardsey with his nine bards, bearing with him the thirteen treasures of Britain, and is never heard of afterwards. In the French Romance, and its English translation, the story of Merlin and Nimiane is a pleasant one, in spite of the maiden's final betrayal of her counsellor and teacher. The lovers lie together in the shady grove and have many talks of marvels before she weaves the final spell Merlin himself has taught her. She is not in this Romance so revengeful as in Tennyson. She is a lady of charm as well as of charms. In Malory she is connected with one of the Ladies of the Lake.

In the sixteenth and seventeenth century, the name of Merlin as a magician was kept alive by the poets, dramatists and chroniclers.

Spenser gave him an important place in his *Faerie Queene* as a magician and protector of Arthur. He lives at King Ryence's court and has constructed a wonderful looking-glass in which all can see what is happening in the world. In this mirror Britomart sees her future husband Artegal and goes in disguise, which Merlin soon penetrates, to ask further information of the sage. [3] The poet also relates how

[1] From Rhys, *Studies in Arthurian Legend*, p. 354.

[2] Considered by Mr Phillimore as late and spurious. For discussion see *Merlin*, ed. Wheatley (Early Eng. Text Soc.), vol. i., pp. xcviii.-c.

[3] The first three books were published in 1595. The passage mentioned is in Book III, Canto 2, ll. 18 ff.

Merlin surrounded Carmarthen with walls of brass before he was lured to his own prison in the rock by his seductress.[1]

In 1641, Merlin's *Life* was written by Thomas Heywood.[2] It is an attempt to interpret English history in the light of prophecy, from the beginning to the time of Elizabeth, that time when shall a phoenix rise whose

> . . . bright and glorious Sun-beams shall expell
> The vain clouds of the Castle, Booke and Bell.[3]

Most of the prophecies are ascribed to Merlin the Soothsayer, but the sceptic is inclined to suspect these are prophecies after the event. The whole is a marvellous tangled web with a strand here and there of historical fact. Here is told,[4] in greater detail than in Geoffrey of Monmouth,[5] by what miraculous accident young Merlin came to be known to King Vortigern, of the combat between the red and the white dragon and his prophecy thereof." This is the story of a castle in Wales, Generon (in Geoffrey a tower in Wales, on Mount Eryri) (Snowdon), which mysteriously fell down as soon as it was built up. The seers on being consulted said the stones would never be cemented until it was done " with the blood of a man child, who was born of a mother but had no man to his father." This turned out to be Merlin, whose mother, a nun—so the story goes—was daughter to King Demetrus,[6] but whose father was a spirit who assumed the shape of a beautiful young man.[7]

---

[1] Book III, Canto 3, ll. 10 ff.

[2] *Life of Merlin, surnamed Ambrosius,* by Thomas Heywood, first edition, 1641 ; second edition 1831, quoted here.

[3] *Op. cit.,* p. 272.   [4] Chap. 3.

[5] Book VI, chap. xvii of the *History,* " Everyman " Edition.

[6] In Geoffrey, Demetia, " Everyman " Edition.

[7] These spirits were supposed to be of diabolical origin and in conjunction with their female victim were said to produce monsters. An example is given in the *Gesta Romanorum* (ed. Bohn, 1877, p. 306) of a lady who, while at mass, was borne off by one along with part of the chapel. That extraordinary collection of superstitions, *The Hierarchie of Angels* (1631), gives some examples (viii. 542). Heywood in it quotes a story similar to the Lohengrin story, the version which has no connection with the Grail in which the husband disappeared after a long married life. The interpretation is interesting, " Now who can judge this to be other than one of those spirits that are named Incubi."

Luckily for Merlin, the King Vortigern considered it more politic to consult the wonderful young enchanter, rather than to cement the stones of the castle with his blood. Merlin thereupon informed him of the existence of two horrible dragons enclosed in the rocks at the foundation of the hill on which the castle was being erected. It was these fiery creatures who were causing the disturbance. And surely, when the rocks were opened, there issued forth two fierce and cruel dragons, a red and a white, who engaged in bitter conflict. The final victory went to the white dragon. At the sight, Merlin declaimed a prophecy which foretold the downfall of the British nation (the red dragon) overcome by the Saxons (the white dragon). However a conqueror was to arise,

> For out of Cornwall shall proceed a Bore
> Who shall the Kerk to pristine state restore,
> Bow shall all Britaine to his kingly beck
> And tread he shall on the white Dragon's neck.[1]

The legend of the toppling tower must be a primitive one referring back to the days of human sacrifice and adapted for a more humane audience.[2]

Then follows [3] the account of the machinations of Merlin in the bringing about of the union of Uter Pendragon and Igerna and the consequent birth of Arthur. This legend is told with greater elaboration of detail than in Geoffrey's *History*. Merlin

" must make proof of art mystical and unknown by which he would undertake by such unctions and medicaments as he would apply to metamorphose his highness into the true figure and resemblance of duke Gorlois (Igerna's husband), his friend Ulphin into Jordan of Tintegell, his familiar companion and counsellor ; and himself would make the third in the adventure, changing himself into Bricel, a servant that waited of him in his chamber ; and they three, thus disguised, would in the twilight of the evening

---

[1] *Op. cit.*, p. 54, Second Edition.
[2] Other instances not connected with Merlin in Llud and Llevis (*Mabinogion*), and in " Triad of Hengwort " (MSS. 54 and 536) (Skene, *Four Ancient Books of Wales*, ii. 265).
[3] *Op. cit.*, chap. 5.

whilst the duke in one place was busied in the defence of his castle against the assailants, command their entrance into the other fort in the name and person of the duke, where they should be undoubtedly received."

A prophecy of the prowess of Arthur is again given and explained in detail :

> The Cornish Bore shall fill with his devotion,
> The Christian World : the Islands of the Ocean,
> He shall subdue : the Flower de Lyces plant,
> In his own Garden, and prove Paramant
> The two-neckt Roman Eagle hee shall make
> To flag her plumes, and her faint feathers quake,
> Pagans shall strive in vain to bend or break him,
> Who shall be meat to all the mouths that speake him
> Yet shall his end be doubtful ! Him six Kings
> Shall orderly succeed, etc.[1]

As in the tale of the conceiving of Merlin, in which a mortal and a spirit created between them a strange prodigy, so the conjunction of history and legend has produced this strange book of curious and superstitious lore.

William Rowley also composed in 1662 a tragi-comedy called " The Birth of Merlin, or the Child hath found his Father."

An account of Merlin is found in the chronicles of the time, who for the most part repeat one another. Caxton's fifteenth-century chronicle contains a little poem on Merlin,[2] and there were in the early sixteenth century three editions of *A Lytel Tretys of the Byrth and Prophecies of Merlin*.[3] This wonder-worker also appeared in the poetical chronicles of England, such as Warner's *Albion's England*,[4] and the seventeenth-century *Polyolbion* by Michael Drayton.[5] Drayton relates the same story of Carmarthen and Merlin as the poet Spenser.

---

[1] *Op. cit.*, chap. 5, p. 64.
[2] Printed in 1498. This poem is a translation of a Latin poem in Higden's *Polychronicon*.
[3] Two were published by Wynken de Worde in 1510 and 1529 and one by John Hawkyns in 1533.
[4] Published in 1586.   [5] Published in 1612.

Some old alliterative Scottish prophecies,[1] which appeared in 1603, attributed to Merlin, Thomas the Rhymer and others, are of interest as having been used by Sir Walter Scott. They refer to Merlin's imprisonment.

> " Meruelous Merling is wasted away,
>   With a wicked woman, woe might shee be ;
>   For shee hath closed him in a Craige on Cornwel cost."

In the seventeenth century, in Dryden's dramatic opera [2] *King Arthur* or *The British Worthy*, Merlin appears as one of the personages. Dryden makes no effort to give him the traditional background he has in the Arthurian legend. He attends Arthur and with his magic philtre restores sight to Arthur's future bride Emmeline. He has his attendant sprite Philidel as the Saxon Enchanter, his enemy, has his Grimbald. Merlin has little individuality. He is merely a magician in a fairy-tale. Dryden's supernatural characters are always rather mechanical, like the puppets in a marionette show.

The figure of Merlin became so far removed from his background as to become a kind of mascot, by which to conjure. He was made use of by the astrologers in their predictions for the future. One of the chief of these was William Lilly [3] who published his *Merlinus Anglicus*, an almanack full of prophecies. One of these was " England's Propheticall Merline foretelling to all Nations of Europe."

In the nineteenth century, Merlin recovered his romantic prowess in Tennyson's " Merlin and Vivien " which illustrates the ever-recurring charm of the well-told fairy tale in literature. Wordsworth had, however, in 1830, attempted a tale of the magic of Merlin in the " Egyptian Maid," in which with great moral seriousness he upheld the ideal of purity. He does not show the same reverence as Tennyson for the traditions of Malory, but invents a story of his own and places it in an

---

[1] For list of these see Introduction to *Merlin*, ed. Wheatley (Early English Text Society), by W. E. Mead, p. lxxviii. To this account I am indebted for the information in this section dealing with the fifteenth to eighteenth centuries.

[2] Acted and published in 1691.   [3] 1602-1682.

Arthurian setting. The poet relates how Merlin, in one of his moods of wrath, caused a storm to arise and to wreck the Egyptian Maid :

> With thrilling word and potent sign
> Traced on the beach, his work the Sorcerer urges,
> The clouds in blacker clouds are lost,
> Like spiteful Fiends that vanish, crossed
> By Fiends of aspect more malign
> And the winds roused the Deep with fiercer scourges.

The Egyptian Maid is, however, finally rescued, almost moribund, and one and another of Arthur's knights pass before her as suitor for her hand—Sir Perceval, Sir Tristram, Sir Launcelot and Sir Galahad. Readers are led to understand that she was willing to be baptized, in order to wed a Christian knight. Only Sir Galahad was pure enough for her, and so this knight, of the most celibate reputation, is destined to be successful !

The poem is not a success and tradition seems unwarrantably altered. Wordsworth's genius was not for the narrative poem, but for the poem of a meditative and philosophic nature, when his deep emotions, " recollected in tranquillity," were expressed in simple and dignified language. The objects of Nature in her wild state, the dancing daffodils, the winding tranquil stream, the mountain peak, called forth this creative intensity of mood. But he was not capable of sketching in lightly, as Sir Walter Scott did, the outward and picturesque aspect of chivalry as a background for a story told in light and tuneful verse. Nor did he penetrate deeply enough into the heart of legend to find its symbolic and cosmic meaning. Legend, as legend, had no power to arouse the mysticism of his nature.[1] So this poem remains as a rather clumsy attempt to tell an unconvincing story in an artificial manner.

Tennyson goes back to Malory for inspiration. As he describes the appearing and disappearing of the magician,

---

[1] *Laodamia* may be cited as an exception to this general statement, but in this case the classical story, dealing with the issues of life and death, could bear the weight of the poet's philosophising on man's mortality.

his pen seems to be made of the same miraculous stuff as Arthur's sword, Excalibur.

His poem, " Merlin and Vivien," [1] in which the old sage Merlin is coaxed into telling Vivien of the magic spell, is an elaboration of Malory's account, which the latter took from the " Suite." The " Ordinary Merlin " gives another version. Tennyson gives a subtle study of the wily Vivien (Malory's Nimue), " The charm of woven paces and of waving hands," which loses Merlin to " use and name " is a spell which is also over his readers. Down to the lonely seashore Merlin is driven forth by one of those fits of melancholy to which seers are prone, for they pay the penalty of being able to read future destinies. At first the sage takes no notice of the enchantress Vivien, but gradually he becomes aware of her presence. By every wile she possesses, she tries to persuade him to tell her the magic spell. In vain she appeals to his sense of gratitude, of vanity, of fear and pity for her. He seems little moved. She tries every feminine trick. At last, aided in her purpose by a thunderstorm, she clings to him, half in real terror, half in conscious wile. At last, wearied by her persistency, he gives in to her. The end comes swiftly and Merlin remains a prisoner for ever.

Except for a rather long dissertation on the failing morality of the court, which seems rather out of place, though it serves to show up Vivien's spiteful nature, the allegorical and moral element is not overstressed. The story remains one of the finest romance stories in verse in English literature.

In a small poem " Merlin and the Gleam," [2] Tennyson makes Merlin a man who is always following the ideal, who finds the Gleam for awhile resting on Arthur's head, but discovers that it moves ahead, to elude him (Merlin) still. The poem is an example of how legend can give birth to a new and modern symbolism.

Swinburne treats the legend of Merlin in two ways. In " The Tale of Balen," Merlin performs the same function towards Arthur as in Malory. He accompanies and protects Arthur and is with him in battle. He is often overshadowed

---

[1] One of the *Idylls of the King*, published 1859.
[5] Published 1889.

by the spirit of prophecy as when he prophesies the coming of the Grail.

His wile holds fast the foe.

> With woven words of magic might
> Wherein the subtle shadow and light
> Changed hope and fear till fear took flight,
> He stayed King Lot's fierce lust of fight
>   Till all the wild Welsh war was driven
> As foam before the wind that wakes
> With the all-awakening sun, and breaks
> Strong ships that rue the mirth it makes
>   When grace to slay is given.[1]

He appears and disappears, often in disguise, warning and admonishing the headstrong Balen, who pays little heed to him. Merlin, like many prophets, has the power to foretell but not to avert disaster.

Swinburne also uses the legendary Merlin in another manner. In the poem of " Tristram of Lyonesse," in a long allusion, he makes use of the tale of Merlin and Nimue to give expression to his own pantheistic philosophy. He chooses, with his scholarly instinct for the finest version, the one given in the Ordinary Merlin where Merlin and Nimue are true lovers ; and where, to perpetuate their love and shut out the intruding world, they weave a magic circle to enclose themselves for ever. Thus Nimue uses the knowledge gained in the service of love.

It is fit that the ideal lovers, Tristram and Iseult, should discuss this story, for their theme of conversation is the magic draught which has made them indissolubly one. So are Merlin and Nimue one with each other in their magic circle and one with Nature.

(Merlin)

> Hears in spirit a song that none but he
> Hears from the mystic mouth of Nimue
> Shed like a consecration ; and his heart,
> Hearing, is made for love's sake as a part

---

[1] " Tale of Balen," p. 192, *Collected Poems*, Heinemann.

Of that far singing, and the life thereof
Part of that life that feeds the world with love :
Yea, heart in heart is molten, hers and his
Into the world's heart and the soul that is
Beyond or sense or vision ; and their breath
Stirs the soft springs of deathless life and death,
Death that bears life, and change that brings forth seed
Of life to death and death to life indeed,
As blood recircling through the unsounded veins
Of earth and heaven with all their joys and pains.[1]

Thus this legend has been lifted to the ideal or philosophical realm and the poet has used it to symbolise his theory of the Universe. This can be more successfully done in an allusion than in a complete story, for in the latter case the idealistic or allegorical treatment is apt to spoil the reality of the tale.

In his poetic drama " Merlin's Grave," [2] Gordon Bottomley makes use of the other tradition of the Caledonian Merlin.[3] In a note quoted from Andrew Lang, in the preface of this work, the following sentences occur :

" In the neighbourhood of Drummelzier near to where the Powsayl Burn, the 'Burn of the willows,' joins Tweed, you may see the grave of Merlin the Seer, the Wizard Merlin. Fleeing from the field of Arderydd (Arthuret near Carlisle) after the terrible defeat of the Pagans by the Christians in 573, Merlin found refuge among the hills of the Upper Tweed and there lived for many years, half-crazed, a homeless wanderer. In a poem still extant,[4] Merlin tells how he wandered long in the wild wood of Caledon,

Before I lost my wits, I used to be around its stem,
With a fair sportive maid, matchless in slender shape.

Not far from the churchyard of Drummelzier, to this day, they point out the grave where Merlin lies beneath a thorn-tree."

---

[1] " Tristram of Lyonesse " Part 6, *op. cit.*, p. 98.
[2] In *Scenes and Plays* by G. Bottomley.
[3] See above for discussion, p. 71.
[4] In W. F. Skene, *Four Ancient Books of Wales*, p. 370, *Black Book of Caermarthen*, " The Avallenau," attributed to Myrdhinn (Merlin).

In his play, Gordon Bottomley makes use of the two traditions, combining them skilfully, though his verse is somewhat unequal.

An old old man is seen pruning and tending a thorn-tree. This is Merlin himself. Two maidens are heard approaching in a boat. They have come to see Merlin's Cave. The old man approaches and asks the first maiden the name of the other maiden. When he learns that she is Highland, and lives in a tower upon an island, he realises that she is a reincarnation of the Lady of the Lake, Nimue. Once again the old drama is to be played again, as it is in every generation :

> " Age upon age,
> Have you been born,
> To turn at last to the Sage,
> Imprisoned under the thorn,
> And waiting, waiting for kindness,
> From a cruel spirit : for blindness
> To see love's glow in the old man's embers."

He goes on to ask where the white dog is, which she had when King Pellinor found her and brought her to Arthur's court. And, as before, he kneels to her and asks for love, for he is tired of reverence and fear and power. He continues :

> " In those isolations love had not found me
> Woman had let me be ;
> Yet I cannot grow old in my heart,
> Or keep from desiring loveliness,
> Had I not been too wise, the stress
> Of living had given me part
> In the human lot, a daughter
> Might cherish me now.
>
>   .   .   .   .   .
>
> You have come to give me at last
> The child in you : I sought her
> In the dark of the thorn and the past
> Hovering in delight to taste
> Love and daughter in one."

The woman asks the Wizard if she will partake of his power if she gives him what he asks. He answers that all he has is

hers.   But once again, the desire for power is too much of a
temptation.   She asks Merlin to tell her the spell.   He gives
her a spindle and tells her if she winds it round any place he
inhabits, he will become invisible until she unwinds it once
more.   He then asks for his reward, a kiss, but she persuades
him first to return to the thorn-tree.   Then, holding the
distaff in her hand, she dances slowly and solemnly round the
tree, until gradually by the movements of her body, the thread
is wound around him, and he is powerless.

She falls in exhaustion to the earth.   When she awakes,
as from a dream, she finds herself beside her companion.
The old man has vanished.   She has forgotten past events,
but the spindle is still in her hand.   She flings it into the
stream.   Thus is the key of Merlin's prison lost for ever,
and he remains a prisoner.

A chorus, sung by the curtain-bearer and folders, adds
to the suggestion of the stirring of old memories.   It is
reminiscent of the murmuring waters of the Tweed running
by, on whose banks the scene is enacted.   The English
Association, who, some years ago, gave a rendering of this
drama, brought out this effect by a kind of rhythmic incanta-
tion.   This is one of the passages recited :

> " Who can escape them, who can know,
> What things the ancients have laid on us ?
> A secret thing that one of us does,
> Can be remembered and done again
> By flesh that is not yet borne of our pain.
> This darkening earth, the hollow in hills,
> Invisible water that sings and fills
> The deeps of air with silences—
> Alert and watchful in unstirred trees—
> Remember too : and they tell the most,
> Without intercession of fetch or ghost
> To those in whom that memory brings
> The past and magic of all lost things."

Edwin Arlington Robinson, an American poet, gives in
his " Merlin " [1] (1917) a portrait which embodies his

[1] *Collected Poems*, 1896 and other editions, with Introduction by John
Drinkwater.

conception of the seer. He constructs a scene—out of the accepted tradition, but in keeping with it—and brings him in at a special period in the life of Arthur, the last period. Indeed the poem might have been called " The Return of Merlin," although the drama of his imprisonment and enchantment is given also in great detail.

The reader is first introduced to two old men, Sir Lamorak and Sir Bedevere, who talk in a shrewd and caustic manner of the situation at Arthur's court and of the betrayal of the King by Lancelot. The language reported is certainly not the conventional knightly speech :

> Sir Lamorak, shifting in his oaken chair,
> Growled like a dog and shook himself like one :
> " For the stone-chested, helmet-cracking knight
> That you are known to be from Lyonnesse
> To northward, Bedivere, you fol-de-rol
> When days are rancid, and you fiddle-faddle
> More like a woman than a man with hands
> Fit for the smiting of a crazy giant
> With armor an inch thick, as we all know
> You are, when you're not sermonizing at us.
> As for the King, I say the King, no doubt,
> Is angry, sorry, and all sorts of things,
> For Lancelot, and for his easy Queen,
> Whom he took knowing she'd thrown sparks already
> On that same piece of tinder, Lancelot,
> Who fetched her with him from Leodogran
> Because the King—God save poor human reason !—
> Would prove to Merlin, who knew everything
> Worth knowing in those days, that he was wrong." [1]

They speak of Merlin and his rumoured return. The narrative then, in the usual epic manner, turns backward and tells the story of Merlin's capture by the fascinating Vivian who dwells in Broceliande. The conversation between the two and the somewhat florid description of her charm is not told in the usual fashion of the romantic narrative, but rather in the manner of the modern novel. There is a certain psychological insight shown but often a loss of dignity.

[1] *Op. cit.*, p. 245, ed. 1922.

Such an effect is often created in Grand Opera when trivial
requests and conversations are sung. So here blank-verse
narrative seems to be the wrong medium for the coquettish
wiles of the gay and witty Vivian :

> Embroidering doom with many levities,
> Till now the fountain's crystal silver, fading,
> Became a splash and a mere chilliness,
> They mocked their fate with easy pleasantries
> That were too false and small to be forgotten,
> And with ingenious insincerities
> That had no repetition or revival.
> At last the lady Vivian arose,
> And with a crying of how late it was
> Took Merlin's hand and led him like a child
> Along a dusky way between tall cones
> Of tight green cedars : " Am I like one of these ?
> You said I was, though I deny it wholly."—
> " Very," said Merlin, to his bearded lips
> Uplifting her small fingers.   " O that hair ! "
> She moaned, as if in sorrow : " Must it be ?
> Must every prophet and important wizard
> Be clouded so that nothing but his nose
> And eyes, and intimations of his ears,
> Are there to make us know him when we see him ?
> Praise Heaven I'm not a prophet.   Are you glad ? " [1]

This loss of dignity is, however, regained in many passages
of description which show mastery of the blank-verse form.
The scene in which Merlin breaks out from the spell of
feminine enchantment to the world of events and to his
former lord, King Arthur, illustrates the poet's dramatic
insight. The prophet and seer belongs to a world which
the shallow, time-serving Vivian cannot enter. He is haunted
by visions which obscure the delights of his sensual paradise.

> He stared a long time at the cup of gold
> Before him but he drank no more.   There came
> Between him and the world a crumbling sky
> Of black and crimson, with a crimson cloud
> That held a far-off town of many towers,

---

[1] *Op. cit.*, p. 265.

> All swayed and shaken, till at last they fell,
> And there was nothing but a crimson cloud
> That crumbling into nothing, like the sky
> That vanished with it, carrying away
> The world, the woman and all memory of them.[1]

At other times he is besieged by memories of the past,

> A melancholy wave of revelation
> Broke over Merlin like a rising sea,
> Long viewed unwillingly and long denied.
> He saw what he had seen, but would not feel,
> Till now the bitterness of what he felt
> Was in his throat, and all the coldness of it
> Was on him and around him like a flood
> Of lonelier memories than he had said
> Were memories, although he knew them now
> For what they were—for what his eyes had seen,
> For what his ears had heard and what his heart
> Had felt, with him not knowing what it felt.
> But now he knew that his cold angel's name
> Was Change, and that a mightier will than his
> Or Vivian's had ordained that he be there.[2]

Thus Mr Robinson has given us in this narrative poem, with its dramatic situations, an interesting study of Merlin's character in its varied and not always harmonised elements. The effect of his verse, although on the whole harmonious, is intellectual rather than sensuous, and it is characteristic of him that in the " Merlin " as well as in his " Tristram "[3] he rules out the magical altogether. The traditional Merlin had obtained much of his glamour from this element.

[1] *Op. cit.*, p. 277.   [2] *Op. cit.*, p. 291.
[3] Published 1928, see below, Tristan section.

CHAPTER VII

LANCELOT

IF Gawain has been discredited by modern authors, it is not so with Lancelot. Like Gawain, he has his early origins in myth and folk-tale, though he has developed into something very different. In the earliest Lancelot romance of Ulrich von Zatzikhoven,[1] he is carried away by a water-fairy, hence his name Lancelot of the Lake. When he is fifteen years old, he is sent into the world and finally into Arthur's court, for his mother is sister to King Arthur.

In this loosely woven tale, many of his adventures are related, but the chief one which influenced future romances, is the one in which he assists King Arthur in the rescue of Guinevere from a king who abducts her. In a still earlier form, this must have been a story of the genus of the Rape of Proserpine by Pluto, a myth created by the Greeks to explain the change of the seasons from Summer to Winter and back to Summer once more. Ulrich gives no hint that Lancelot is the lover of Guinevere.

It was left for Chrétien de Troies to make Lancelot the lover of Guinevere, or, at least, to give literary form to the conception. The poet tells us himself that Marie of Champagne, the daughter of Eleanor of Aquitaine, commanded him to write this story and gave him " *san* " and " *matière* " —the plan and contents. He adapted the old story, which quite changed its character under the pen of the brilliant satirical court poet. As in the Grail story, Chrétien was no doubt handling material of whose antiquity he was ignorant. One of the earliest versions of the Guinevere rape, of which there are many, has been pointed out by scholars [2] in the *Vita Gildæ* ascribed to Caradoc of Lancarvon. Here the

---

[1] Dated before 1194, Lanzelet.
[2] One of the first of these was Gaston Paris in *Romania*, x. 465.

ravisher is Melvas,[1] King of the Summer country, and it is Arthur who goes to the rescue of Gwenhwyvar in Glastonbury. In Chrétien's "Lancelot" the Queen's abductor is Meleagant, son of Bagdemagus, whom Chrétien's continuator nominates the King of Goire. From this country which is reached by a sword-bridge no man ever returns. When Lancelot is inquiring concerning it, he is told that Guinevere is so enclosed that no mortal man can approach her. All this certainly seems to suggest an Other-world and mythical origin of a god or hero who has to pass over the sword-bridge or the bridge under the waves in order to free the captives there. Malory's abductor is Sir Meliagrance and the account is truncated and confused. It is the occasion, however, of the joyful passage on Love in May which has become a classic.[2] The season is significant and seems to point to a seasonal myth of the type of the Rape of Proserpine. Geoffrey of Monmouth, in his *History*, merely mentions the treachery of Mordred who has usurped the throne of Arthur, when at the late wars in France, and linked himself in unhallowed union with Queen Guinevere, Arthur's wife. Once again, the name Mordred has been equated with the fairy Queen Mider in the Gaelic story Mider and Etain.[3] In these conflicting accounts the only constant element is the unfaithfulness of Guinevere, which seems to be an early tradition,[4] although in Chrétien's story she is a fairly passive agent.

But Chrétien's interest was not in the origins of his story.

---

[1] Also Melwas, Chrétien de Troies in *Erec*, i. 1946, mentions King Meheloas of the Isle of Glass—Isle of Voire, signifying the Other-world. Celtic scholars treat these names as variants of the same noun.

[2] Malory, Book XVIII, chap. 25 ("Everyman" Edition).

[3] In the "Book of the Dun Cow." See Rhys, *Arthurian Legend*, pp. 25 ff. Etain is married to Airem in her second reincarnation. Her husband in her former reincarnation is Midir. He appears and offers to play a game of chess with Airem, on the condition that if he be victor, he will claim a kiss from Etain. He wins and the husband is forced to consent. But Midir, who has already obtained consent from Etain, transports her back again to the "Other-world," the Land of Fairy.

[4] Arthur Rhys (in *Arthurian Legend*, p. 40) says that in Wales to call a girl Guinevere is to accuse her of wantonness.

This poet, who had graduated with honours in the code of the school of courtly love, seized the opportunity to create in Lancelot a character who would be an example and model of that school with its artificial laws. Chrétien's Lancelot devotes himself to a supercilious and exacting lady who is above him in station, and married. At one time, when in the company of Gawain, he sees Guinevere passing, led captive by Meleagant, he is so overcome with emotion that he swoons and nearly falls out of the window. He holds himself ready to undergo any humiliation and indeed demeans himself to the uttermost by entering a " cart " used for the removal of refuse and sometimes of criminals. Unfortunately, he hesitates for one moment before entering it, and for this Guinevere cannot be persuaded to forgive him. Only when his life is despaired of does she relent. This incident bestows on him his title, Lancelot de la Charette. Thus, according to the chivalric code, Lancelot fulfils the rules of the perfect lover.

The latest researches of scholars have shown the main sources of Malory's Lancelot to have been the Prose Lancelot and Chrétien de Troies' " Lancelot de la Charette." [1] But Lancelot in Malory has become a much more lovable and human character than in Chrétien. He has stepped out of the artificial background woven by the French poet and become a living figure. Especially is this true in the last books of Malory. And in these Guinevere is brought to life also, having been up to then somewhat of a passive agent, as mediæval women often were.

How many noble qualities has this loyal, chivalrous gentleman ! He is braver than all, yet modest withal. Only in his last appeal to Arthur, when he is banished, does he permit himself to speak of his many deeds of chivalry. Never does he take advantage of another's weakness ; he often conceals his prowess in order to encourage a younger and less skilled knight. He is first to go to the rescue of any prisoner.

He is, save in the one respect, one of the most faithful followers of King Arthur and, along with Gawain, upholder of his realm in the early wars of France. His final banishment from the country of Logres is exceedingly bitter, yet, though

[1] See E. Vinaver, *Malory*, 1929. Sources : Appendix.

he has armed followers enough, he shows no sign of rebellion against his feudal lord.

And, in its essential qualities, if not in its circumstances, the love between Lancelot and Guinevere is a high and noble one, especially in its beginning. In the French prose romance, when Galehault introduces Lancelot to the Queen, it is related that, looking upon one another, they are drawn together instinctively by a bond of love which welds them forever. This love is of a free unrestrained nature which overleaps all bonds. When the Queen asks Lancelot why he has not returned the love of the Maid of Astolat, he replies, " Love must arise of the heart and not by no constraint." This passion, like that of Tristan and Iseult, is an unlawful and fateful one, yet no potion is assumed to explain it. It finally causes the destruction of the realm, and yet the very sorrow and tragedy it brings in its train, increase its depth and beauty, so that it stands for one of the great loves recounted in literature. It shines out beyond the other kinds of love pictured in Malory and in the romances of the Middle Ages, beyond the love which means merely a temporary attraction or possession or the conventional chivalric love described in Chrétien de Troies.

Thus Lancelot has become, for all time, the ideal lover as well as the ideal knight.

True, in the spiritual adventure of the Grail,[1] he fails. But Malory, by leaving out certain passages in his source and modifying others,[2] mitigates the severity with which he is treated in the *Queste*. And even here, he comes very near the threshold, seeing the Grail through the door and falling into a swoon, overcome by its excessive radiance. If he himself is not destined to be successful, the honour is given to his son Galahad, and Lancelot is found wanting, not because of lack of nobility, but because he is dedicated to another noble but more earthly type of love.

All these qualities, loyalty, generosity, idealism, capacity

---

[1] For further references see p. 132.

[2] See E. Vinaver, *Malory*, 1929. A close comparison between Malory and the *Queste* is given in Appendix 3. See also Appendix 2 for MSS.

to love and suffer for love, are those which attract throughout the ages, in Lancelot or any other modern hero.

The eighteenth century were more interested in the heroic King Arthur than in Lancelot, the *preux chevalier*. The poets of the Romantic Revival, such as Byron or Shelley, evidently found him too stereotyped a figure to bear the weight of their passionate revolt. It was not till the time of Tennyson and the Pre-Raphaelites that the sentiments of the age in what might be termed the Indian summer of the Romantic Revival welcomed this hero of chivalry.

The story of Lancelot had attracted Tennyson from youth, and in one of his earlier poems he has allowed his fancy to play round his knightly figure in a way he did not permit himself later, when he paid due reverence to the text of Malory. Though published twenty-six years before the " Defence of Guinevere " (1858),[1] the " Lady of Shalott " foreshadows the Pre-Raphaelites in the romantic treatment of its subject and in the exactness of its descriptions, from which a draughtsman could sketch a clear outline, or a black-and-white artist make a detailed drawing. Here is such a picture :

> Willows whiten, aspens quiver,
> Little breezes dusk and shiver
> Thro' the wave that runs for ever
> By the island in the river
>   Flowing down to Camelot.
> Four gray walls and four gray towers
> Overlook a space of flowers,
> And the silent isle imbowers
>   The Lady of Shalott.

The conventional trappings of chivalry are reminiscent of the illuminated miniatures in the manuscripts of Froissart's Chronicle.[2] This is the description of Lancelot's dress :

> His broad clear brow in sunlight glow'd ;
> On burnished hooves his war horse trod ;
> From underneath his helmet flow'd
> His coal-black curls as on he rode,
>   As he rode down to Camelot.

---

[1] The " Lady of Shalott " is published in the 1832 volume.
[2] MSS. Harley, 4379, 4380, reproduced by Studio, 1930.

The poem, however, has a certain untroubled clarity which brings to the mind the quality of Keats' " St Agnes Eve " rather than the troubled emotional atmosphere of Morris, which in such a poem as " The Defence of Guinevere " is caused partly by the repetition of the monotone.   There is more movement in Tennyson's poem.   There is an invigorating breeze blowing from the marshes where Tennyson lays his scene, an east wind which ruffles the drapery of the dead woman lying in the boat.   There is less of the enervating boudoir atmosphere which is often produced by Morris and Dante Gabriel Rossetti, in spite of their watchword " Back to Nature."   Nature, in Tennyson's poem, is described from an objective point of view by one interested to learn her laws as well as to feel her beauty.

The whole poem, with its chiming set of rhymes and double refrain, has a charm which the mature Tennyson did not often recapture, except perhaps in his lyrics, interspersed in his longer poems.   There is a soupçon of allegory, enough to arouse curiosity without distracting the mind.   The tragedy, reminiscent of the deeper one of the " Lancelot and Elaine " story, is lightly touched on and is like the echo of a distressed cry in a wood, with the same airy insubstantiality.

Lancelot has his part to play in a pathetic and moving drama which takes place, before the final struggle of passion and ambition which wrecks the ideals of Arthur's court. It is told in Malory's eighteenth book in all its simplicity and straightforwardness.   Tennyson has given a more detailed and elaborate version in " Lancelot and Elaine," the seventh of the *Idylls of the King*.   Both tell the story of the maiden of Astolat, who loved Lancelot " out of measure " with depth and passion and sincerity.   And since he could and would have none of her, she embraced Death instead.

It is all simply put in the letter she wrote, which Tennyson translated into verse :

" Most noble knight, Sir Launcelot, now hath death made us two at debate for your love.   I was your lover that men called the fair maiden of Astolat ; therefore unto all ladies I make my moan, yet pray for my soul and bring me at least, and offer ye my masspenny : this is my last request.   And a clene maiden I died. I take God to witness : pray for my soul, Sir Lancelot, as thou art peerless." [1]

This is Tennyson :—

> " Most noble lord, Sir Lancelot of the Lake,
> I, sometime call'd the maid of Astolat,
> Come, for you left me taking no farewell,
> I loved you, and my love had no return,
> And therefore my true love has been my death,
> And therefore to our Lady Guinevere,
> And to all other ladies, I make moan :
> Pray for my soul and yield me burial.
> Pray for my soul thou too, Sir Lancelot,
> As thou art a knight, peerless." [2]

This innocent sacrifice on Love's altar must have reminded Lancelot and the Queen of a time in early youth, when they themselves loved passionately but nobly. Since then, alas ! their love has become entangled in many deceits and contradictions. The contemplation of the dead maiden for the moment has subdued all ignoble jealousy, for it brings with it the sense of the transitoriness of mortal passion in contrast with Eternity. And so, for a few moments there is silence in the court, and a Cessation of all strife, as the barge sails slowly past with its dead maiden and her dumb servitor.

Tennyson, in his later work in the *Idylls*, emphasises the moral aspect of Lancelot's conduct throughout, the injury done to Arthur as a husband, the offence against the marriage-law. He did not make the struggle a conflict between a knight's loyalty to his liege lord, and his lady, which would more naturally have arisen in a feudal society.

In " Guinevere," Tennyson's second last *Idyll*, the Queen is a statelier and more regal figure than in Morris. The narrators of the Middle Ages had always a dignified retreat for their sinful and world-weary heroes and heroines in the convent. And Tennyson follows the tradition in causing Guinevere to take refuge at Almesbury. This poet multiplies words and images in describing her repentance. The sentences

---

[1] See Malory, " Everyman " Edition, p. 305.
[2] " Lancelot and Elaine," Tennyson, *Poetical Works*. Globe Edition, p. 416.

which Malory puts into her mouth are more effective in their brevity. This is what Guinevere says to her ladies concerning Lancelot :

"Through this man and me hath all this war been wrought, and the death of the most noblest knights in the world ; for through our love that we have loved together is my most noble lord slain."

And again :

"Sir Lancelot . . . as well as I have loved thee, mine heart will not serve me to see thee, for through thee and me is the flower of kings and knights destroyed." [1]

Tennyson manipulates skilfully the dramatic and sentimental possibilities of the scene, though the art is somewhat laboured. The repentance of the Queen is overdone, for in spite of her moral fault, the present-day reader does not like to see her "grovelling" before her self-righteous lord. Too much moralising is put into the King's mouth.

In the earlier part of the *Idyll*, the poet introduces a chattering little maid who, by repeating the gossip of the court, pierces with her idle words the heart of the listening Queen till she rises up in anger, thinking the little servant-girl has recognised her. But realising that it is her own conscience which has betrayed her, she renews her vow of repentance and her resolve never to see Lancelot again. Then she falls to musing on her first meeting with her knight. Tennyson has given us a memorable picture of this meeting which may be compared with his much earlier sketch. The earlier one is written in a light tripping measure, and the later in his mature and balanced blank-verse. His more juvenile poem runs thus :—

"Then, in the boyhood of the year,
Sir Launcelot and Queen Guinevere
Rode thro' the coverts of the deer,
With blissful treble ringing clear,
    She seem'd a part of joyous Spring.

---

[1] "Everyman" Edition of Malory's *Morte d'Arthur*, ii. 394.

> A gown of grass-green silk she wore
> Buckled with golden clasps before ;
> A light-green tuft of plumes she bore
>   Closed in a golden ring." [1]

This is the passage from the *Idyll* reproducing the scene from the past in Guinevere's mind, those " golden days " when she first saw her lover :

> When Lancelot came,
> Reputed the best knight and goodliest man,
> Ambassador, to lead her to his lord
> Arthur, and led her forth, and far ahead
> Of his and her retinue moving, they,
> Rapt in sweet talk or lively, all on love
> And sports and tilts and pleasure, (for the time
> Was maytime, and as yet no sin was dream'd)
> Rode under groves that look'd a paradise
> Of blossom, over sheets of hyacinth
> That seem'd the heavens upbreaking thro' the earth,
> And on from hill to hill, and every day
> Beheld at noon in some delicious dale
> The silk pavilions of King Arthur raised
> For brief repast or afternoon repose
> By courtiers gone before ; and on again,
> Till yet once more ere set of sun they saw
> The Dragon of the great Pendragonship,
> That crown'd the state pavilion of the King,
> Blaze by the rushing brook or silent well. [2]

This later blank-verse passage is more mature and dignified than the earlier lyric, but it has lost a charm of spontaneity and gaiety which the rhymed lines possess.

The Arthurian poems of William Morris, in which Lancelot and Guinevere are the chief figures, cannot be discussed without some preliminary remarks on the School to which he belongs and its aims.

The primary aim of the Pre-Raphaelites [3] in painting and

---

[1] " Sir Lancelot and Queen Guinevere " : a fragment, Globe Edition, 1929, p. 118.

[2] " Guinevere," Globe Edition of Tennyson's *Works*, 1929, p. 462.

[3] Good summary of the characteristics of the Pre-Raphaelites given in Lafourcade, *La Jeunesse de Swinburne*, 1928, ii. 70, 71.

poetry was to reject the classical convention and return to the simplicities of Nature. In literature, they turned for their subjects back to the Middle Ages and to the thirteenth and fourteenth century romances in England, such romances as " Sir Tristrem " and " Sir Degrevant " and such ballads as were found in Bishop Percy's *Reliques*. The form of the ballad and litany with refrain was copied and in some cases elaborated. In the Arthurian poems of Morris, however, the apparent simplicity was only on the surface. They have nothing of the *naïveté* of such ballads as " Chevy Chase " or " Sir Patrick Spens," or even the halting rhymed verse of " Sir Tristrem."

There were two chief influences to which Morris was subjected, which probably militated against simplicity in his Arthurian poems, " The Defence of Guinevere," " King Arthur's Tomb " and " Sir Galahad," published together in 1858. The first was the influence of Malory, who adapted romances which dealt with more or less settled chivalric and literary conventions. His compilation was written at a time when the first vigorous strength of the chivalric age had played itself out. Morris was a very close student of Malory, though he may at times differ from him in detail or use his own inventive faculty. For example, the first coming of Lancelot to Arthur's court in " King Arthur's Tomb " is imaginary. In the same poem it is related that Lancelot meets Guinevere at Glastonbury instead of Almesbury. Morris was also influenced by the later romances in the degradation of Gawain. He makes Gawain Lancelot's accuser, whereas in Malory, Gawain only becomes Lancelot's enemy when he discovers that Lancelot has slain his (Gawain's) two brothers. Lancelot maintains in defence that it has happened in the disorder of the fray. But in spite of these few changes, Morris, for the most part, took Malory's characters and incidents as he found them.

The second influence which prevented Morris obtaining the ballad simplicity in his Arthurian poems was what might be termed a " scenic " influence. The Pre-Rephaelites expressed their aims and ideals in painting as well as in literature, and Morris himself as a decorator had trained his eye to "scenic" effects. So his poems often appeal to the eye rather than to the ear. He could, when he liked, imitate in words quick movement as in the tournament scene in "The Defence of Guenevere," where the "clanging of arms about pavilions fair, mixed with the knights' laughs" is heard. But usually his Arthurian poems are a series of scenes which might be worked in tapestry or painted in panels in vivid colours. The painters of this school inspired the poets and the poets the painters. We have a painting by D. G. Rossetti, whose subject is inspired by "King Arthur's Tomb." The Oxford Union was decorated with frescoes [1] (which unfortunately faded very quickly) and some of these had Arthurian subjects. Morris himself attempted a decorated panel on "Tristan recognised by his dog."

The merits and demerits of a scenic painter can be traced in Morris's poetry. His poems may seem at first sight simple in form and wording, but they repay reading again and again for the carefully recorded effects of colour and light. Guinevere describes how in her hand

> "The shadow lies like wine within a cup
> Of marvellously colour'd gold."

The scene is easily imagined, wrought lovingly piece by piece by the careful craftsman, in the medium of stained glass.

Another influence which removes Morris's poems from the naïve simplicity of the mediæval rhymed chronicle, romance or ballad, is a certain "romantic" attitude, which is one of the characteristics of the Pre-Raphaelite temper. In Morris it was probably roused and encouraged partly by the revival of Church worship and liturgy, [2] which was called forth by the "Oxford Movement." Morris was influenced by it in his youth and when at Oxford, and spent many a happy day visiting churches and enjoying their ordered beauty. What would probably have been religious fervour in the Middle Ages, when the monasteries sheltered men of

---

[1] Executed about 1857, now restored by Professor Tristram. (See *Studio*, 111, 1936, "Pre-Raphaelites restored.")

[2] Newman's famous *Tract for The Times*, No. 90, was published in 1841.

learning and artists who employed their gifts for the Church, became in Morris and other Pre-Raphaelites a romantic and æsthetic fervour. In Morris's " Defence of Guenevere " this " romanticism " seems to have clouded his power of judging fairly. The argument is exceedingly weak. The reader is left uncertain of the Queen's guilt,

> " Nevertheless you, O Sir Gauwaine, lie,
>   Whatever may have happen'd these long years,
>   God knows I speak truth saying that you lie ! "

The Queen herself in an emotional appeal pleads that the choice in her life was made unwittingly, as if she had to choose in ignorance between two cloths, one standing for heaven and the other for hell. At her bedside was

> A great God's angel standing, with such dyes,
> Not known on earth, on his great wings, and hands,
> Held out two ways, light from the inner skies
>
> Showing him well, and making his commands
> Seem to be God's commands, moreover, too,
> Holding within his hands the cloths on wands :
>
> And one of these strange choosing cloths was blue,
> Wavy and long, and one cut short and red ;
> No man could tell the better of the two.
>
> After a shivering half-hour you said,
> " God help ! heaven's colour, the blue " ; and he said, " hell."

This is the clear picture she draws in order that she may awaken pity and forgiveness in the minds of her accusers. In " King Arthur's Tomb " she makes her own personal beauty an excuse for her conduct. She even reminds God, her Judge, of it, as weighing down the scales in her favour. There is the same passionate fervour in Dante Gabriel Rossetti's " The Blessed Damozel," though, of course, this does not necessarily apply to illegal love. Here the earthly passion, whose pulse beats strong through the poet's verse, becomes a rival to God's Love, even before His throne.

Perhaps in pointing out Morris's decorative qualities, critics have not laid enough emphasis on his realism and psychological insight. Although Browning has a greater range in his dramatic monologue, Morris also shows himself skilful in this subjective method, which in our time has been so often applied to the novel. If the treatment of character in Tennyson's " Guinevere " be compared with that of Morris in " King Arthur's Tomb " it will be seen how much more analytic and subtle Morris is in his depiction of the repentance of Guinevere, although Tennyson gives a more dignified presentation of the sorrowing Queen. In Morris's poem the subjective method is applied also to the landscape, as in Browning's " Child Roland to the Dark Tower Came " the mood of the spirit is reflected in the surroundings. For example, Morris tells us that the maid who brought the message from Lancelot to the tortured and repentant Guinevere did not know " what woe filled up all the room." And again the sudden change from love-longing to remorse is thus brought home to the reader,

> When suddenly the thing grew drear,
> In morning twilight, when the grey downs bare
> Grew into lumps of sin to Guinevere.

As often with Browning the psychological method and the intensity of feeling spoil the melody of the lines. Again, in order to convey to the mind the impression of fatigue, physical and emotional, the description of Lancelot's horse is effective,

> Still night, the lone
> Grey horse's head before him vex'd him much,
>
> In steady nodding over the grey road—
> Still night and night, and emptied heart
> Of any stories ; what a dismal load
> Time grew at last, yea, when the night did part,
>
> And let the sun flame over all, still there
> The horse's grey ears turned this way and that,
> And still he watch'd them twitching in the glare
> Of the morning sun, behind them still he sat,
>
> Quite wearied out with all the wretched night,
> Until about the dustiest of the day,
> On the last down's brow he drew his rein in sight
> Of the Glastonbury roofs that choke the way.

The effect of the whole is a series of clearly outlined groups against a modulated background of grey. And throughout the poem has a unity of effect which gives it artistic worth.

" Sir Galahad," a Christmas mystery, is another study in low tones. Sir Galahad, according to the poet's conception, is not shown in his most heroic mood, but in a very human one. If he is not tempted like Saint Anthony in the desert, by fleshly desire, he is tempted to envy the other knights who have fair ladies to love them and to sit mourning on their tombs when they die. When " Father Launcelot " rides out,

> Can he not think of Guinevere's arms round,
> Warm, lithe about his neck and shout
> Till all the place grows joyful with the sound ?

Even Palomydes, as he follows the questing beast, can have Iseult as his ideal, even though he never gains her love.

Galahad has to remind himself of the heavenly vision which has grown dim. However, an angel and four maidens appear who rouse him and challenge him :

> " O servant of the high God, Galahad !
> Rise and be arm'd, the Sangreal is gone forth
> Through the great forest, and you must be had
> Unto the sea that lieth on the north."

A speech of Sir Bors announces the Quest is a failure and the poem ends on a minor note.

The chief excellence of the poem is in the atmosphere which is produced by a careful attention to detail and the definite psychological effect of the monologue, in which we are not confused with more than one point of view. Along with Galahad we are sensible of the longest night before Christmas, the winter wind with its " moody tune " passing the chapel door and the cold which made him so drowsy, that less and less he saw " the melted snow that hung in beads " on his steel shoes. The accumulated detail, as in Keats' " St Agnes Eve," produces on the reader an almost physical effect of cold and weariness.

In these three poems the choice of scenes taken from the last books of Malory [1] have been chosen for their subjects,

[1] The third poem takes place at the end of the Quest.

dealing with sentiment rather than action. The poet is picturing a time at Arthur's court when the full glory of the summer day has passed and there remains the last gleams of sunset beauty. It was the appeal of this sad dying splendour which appealed to Morris at this early period of his life.[1]

Swinburne, also, at an early period, was influenced by the Pre-Raphaelites and attempted one or two poems on Arthurian subjects—" Queen Iseult " (1857),[2] " Lancelot," [3] and a few fragments. These are of interest as they show us how much these subjects were in vogue among the poets of the time as well as the painters. " Lancelot," for example, shows the marked influence of Morris in metre and treatment. Lancelot has a vision of the Grail :

> Ah ! dear Christ, this thing I see
> Is too wonderful for me,
> If I think indeed to be
> In Thy very grace,
> Clear flame shivers all about,
> But the bright ark alters not,
> Borne upright where angels doubt ;
> The blessed maiden looketh out
> White, with bared face and throat
> Leaned into the dark.
> On her hair's faint light and shade
> A large aureole is laid,
> All about the tresses weighed.

However, this vision wavers and changes into the figure of the Queen. Lancelot speaks :

> " Lo between me and the light
> Grows a shadow on my sight,
> A soft shade to left and right,
> Branchèd as a tree.
> Green the leaves that stir between,
> And the buds are lithe and green,
> And against it seem to lean
> One in stature as the Queen
> That I prayed to see."

---

[1] He was twenty-four years of age when he wrote this poem.
[2] Fuller treatment on pp. 207-210.
[3] Published in *Works*, ed. Sir E. Gosse, vol. i.

Swinburne, however, was not long to remain such a slavish disciple of the Pre-Raphaelites. His genius, like a vessel built for a deeper ocean, soon swept on to breast stronger and fiercer waves than ever swept the tide-locked inland sea of this school of poets.

Lancelot and Guinevere, a play by Richard Hovey (published in 1891), does not rise to great heights in substance or style. Lancelot and Guinevere are treated as in a second-rate modern novel ; the latter even at one time beseeches Lancelot to take her away and marry her. The playwright causes Arthur, who has newly wed Guinevere, to be called away on the affairs of the kingdom, and thus he does not substantiate his marriage. This, and the fact that Lancelot has seen a wondrous vision of Guinevere, in her early mountain home, is meant to form an excuse for the conduct of the lovers. Morgause, Arthur's revengeful sister and the wife of King Lot of Orkney, has Peredure, Guinevere's brother, in her toils, and thus is enabled to play the spy. She accuses Lancelot and Guinevere in open assembly, on the return of Arthur, and the terms she uses are not influenced by any feeling for a romantic situation ! Arthur, however, refuses absolutely to believe any evil concerning his trusted knight and Guinevere.

The prose scenes are full of echoes of Hamlet and the Grave-diggers, Dogberry, and Mrs Malaprop.

There is a certain amount of ingenuity shown in the construction of the plot, but the effect left on the mind of this play is not of high tragedy. The passionate love between Lancelot and Guinevere seems to fall to the level of an intrigue. The drama illustrates the method in which traditional matter should not be modernised if it is to retain its nobility and dignity.

John Davidson, in *The Last Ballad* (published 1899), gives a very different rendering of the Lancelot story from that of Morris. He makes no attempt to reconstruct the conventional mediæval atmosphere. He chooses one set of incidents in Lancelot's life and changes the details in order to give an interpretation which suits his own moral conception. Though the poem is named a ballad, it has not the impersonality of the true ballad nor even of his own more perfect example, *A Cinque Port*. Neither is it a pure lyric, though there is a personal and passionate cry ringing through it, the passion of one who has lost his early beliefs, for whom,

> Down no silver beam the Holy Grail
> Glided from Heaven, a crimson cup that throbbed
> As throbs the heart divine ; no aching sounds
> Of scarce-heard music stole into the aisle,
> Like disembodied pulses beating love.[1]

And yet this poet must find outlet for his unsatisfied idealism. In this narrative poem, he finds expression for it in idealising the love of Lancelot for Guinevere. There is also discerned through the verses the Puritan conflict between flesh and spirit, a hatred of the drive of physical necessity :

> " King Arthur's trust,"
> He [Lancelot] cried ; " ignoble, fateful, blind :
> Her love and my love, noxious lust." [2]

This was a product of the poet's own circumstances [3] and temperament rather than a probable heritage of the hero of chivalry, Lancelot.

Though the personal judgment lends vigour and sincerity to the work, the hard metal is not quite fused in the creative heat. Lines, here and there, are irradiated by flashes of genius, though the poem as an artistic whole is unequal. Yet this modern conception of Lancelot is original and of significance. In spite of some crudities in the workmanship the ballad cannot be termed commonplace.

The incidents are placed at a later part of Lancelot's life. The main narrative tells how Lancelot had been driven by his remorse and despair out of the court and into the wilds. There he succoured the weak and withstood tyrants. But, wherever he journeyed, the vision of Queen Guinevere

---

[1] "A Ballad in Blank Verse of the Making of a Poet," *Poems* by John Davidson, in the Modern Library, 1924, p. 26.

[2] *The Last Ballad*, verse 20.

[3] See the Introduction by R. M. Wenley, *op. cit.*, which gives an interesting account of this poet's life.

accompanied him. He longed for a sight of her, but though he approached King Arthur's court beside the Usk, his conscience would not allow him to stay and behold her face. Finally he drifted into Lyonesse and wandered into the forest, living on roots and herbs like a wild beast. All evil things came out to mock him, while innocent things fled before him :

> The viper loitered in his way :
> The minx looked up with bloodshot leer ;
> Ill-meaning fauns and lamiae
> With icy laughter flitted near.[1]

But at Eastertide, when all Nature began to flower, deliverance came to the haunted man, with the appearance of a " spirit clad in flame " riding on a milk-white steed. It was Galahad, and as he held his father fast and shed " tenderer tears than women shed," Lancelot's madness passed and the natural human joy saved his reason. Galahad brought his father to a castle and cared for him in body and mind for a while. But once again the mystic quest claimed the son and he went forth to seek the Grail.

Lancelot would fain have followed him, but the vision of Guinevere's face came between him and his spiritual objective. Nevertheless, it purified his deeds and served him as the Grail served Galahad, as an ennobling influence :

> . . . for evermore on high
> When darkness set the spaces free,
> And brimming stars hung from the sky
> Low down, and spilt their jewellery,
>
> Behind the nightly squandered fire,
> Through a dim lattice only seen
> By love, a look of rapt desire
> Fell from a vision of the Queen.

Thus Guinevere becomes to Lancelot a symbol of the ideal.

John Masefield, in his collection of poems *Midsummer Night*,[2] concerns himself with the dramatic possibilities of the

[1] *The Last Ballad and Other Poems*, by John Davidson, 1899, p. 8.
[2] Also in *Collected Poems*, 1932.

final episodes, rather than with the moral or psychological aspect. His narration of the single-handed fight of Lancelot in the tower, against his enemies, is interesting to compare and contrast with the account of the same scene by Morris. The contest is described by Guenevere in reminiscent mood :

> " There was one less than three,

> " In my quiet room that night, and we were gay ;
> Till sudden I rose up, weak, pale and sick,
> Because a bawling broke our dream up, yea,

> " I looked at Launcelot's face and could not speak,
> For he looked helpless too, for a little while ;
> Then I remember how I tried to shriek,

> " And could not, but fell down ; from tile to tile
> The stones they threw up rattled o'er my head,
> And made me dizzier ; till within a while

> " My maids were all about me, and my head
> On Launcelot's breast was being soothed away
> From its white chattering, until Launcelot said—

> " ' By God, I will not tell you more to-day,
> Judge any way you will—what matter it ? '
> You know quite well the story of that fray,

> " How Launcelot still'd their bawling, the mad fit,
> That caught up Gauwaine—all, all, verily,
> But just that which would save me ; these things flit." [1]

The manner is characteristically Pre-Raphaelite with its intensity of feeling and its subjective point of view.

The treatment of Masefield is an arresting contrast ; the lines are short and the action swift, the similes are apt but not digressive. Masefield has modernised the story by simplifying it. The struggle is far removed from the conventional fights of Malory by knights, top-heavy with armour. Here is a tale which is for all ages, the poem proclaims. Here is presented a man, alone, unarmed and fighting with his

[1] *Defence of Guenevere*, ed. R. Steele, 1904, pp. 13 and 14, " The Defence of Guenevere."

back to the wall for a woman's honour. The poet leaves the circumstantial morality to take care of itself. Sufficient is it to show that Lancelot's foes performed their act of justice (if it were one) in a revengeful spirit and dishonourable manner. They stole to the tower and tiptoed up the winding stairway. They beat at the doors and flung coarse taunts at Lancelot and Guinevere. In a short speech Lancelot proclaimed the beauty and steadfastness of his love, which shone like a clear light in a dingy room.

Then he turned from words to deeds and went out to challenge his enemies. Only one at a time could stand on the narrow platform. So when Colgrevaunce leapt at Lancelot the latter gave him a blow with his fist and laid him dead on the turret floor. Then Lancelot, swift as lightning, put on his foe's armour, and taking the dead man's sword, stepped out once again to the boarding. One by one, as they came on, he grappled with them, and one by one they were hurled back, falling sheer into the depths below. With that intuitive psychology, which is one of Masefield's great gifts, the poet reveals to us the last thoughts of these men thus hurled to destruction.

Mador of the Wye was one of those engaged in this life-or-death struggle. Lancelot bade him remember their ancient quarrel about the right of pasture. They rushed on each other " as a wild boar rushes, in some oak glade of Dean."

One by one they were slaughtered by Lancelot, all but Modred, who fled at last in terror.

As dramatic as the fight was the silence that followed, which made Lancelot prophetic :

> A silence followed in the tower
>   Save for the Knight's deep breath,
> Horror had followed on the power
>   Of dealing death.
>
> By the dim flicker of the taper
>   Sir Lancelot discerned
> How in her face as white as paper
>   The Queen's eyes burned.[1]

---

[1] From John Masefield, *Midsummer Night*, " Fight on the Wall."

Lancelot realised that a fateful hour had struck and that all the hours of joy which he and the Queen had had together were over. He foresaw the kingdom breaking asunder and the death and destruction of all.

> " Here is the prelude of the story
> That leads us to the grave.
> So be it : we have had a glory
> Not many have.

> " Though what to-morrow may discover
> Be harsh to what has been,
> No matter, I am still your lover,
> And you, my Queen." [1]

Laurence Binyon, in his play *Arthur*,[2] gives a straightforward dramatic recital of events from the incident of the Maid of Astolat's fatal love right on to the defeat and passing of Arthur. He takes from Malory the story of Lancelot and Elaine, Lancelot's abduction of the Queen, the siege of Joyous Gard, the intervention of the Pope, the return of Queen Guinevere to Arthur, the banishment of Lancelot, the treachery of Modred and the last destructive battle.

The drama is well sustained and the style clear and pregnant. But it shares the misfortune of many plays made out of novels, being rather a series of scenes than a progressive and dramatic unity.

Originality in this case can only be won by a different view-point, a deep insight into character and a high standard of dramatic poetry. These qualities are lacking. It proves rather a modern reading of Malory in dramatic form, dignified but somewhat unreal.

[1] *Op. cit.*, p. 106.   [2] 1923.

CHAPTER VIII

THE WELSH TRADITION

I

In the late eighteenth and early nineteenth century, the interest shown by scholars and poets in Wales, its myths and legendary stories, was part of the general movement towards study of a romantic past. Thomas Gray's *Bard* in 1757, for example, shows knowledge of, and passionate sympathy with, Welsh history and literature.

Thomas Love Peacock, who must have known Welsh and had access to such sources of Welsh literature as the " Triads," [1] attempted an historical novel which gives a very different picture of Arthur and his bards and followers from that of the French romances and Malory. *The Misfortunes of Elphin*, published in 1829, is a spirited tale. Peacock is not altogether unsuccessful in portraying sixth-century Wales, for he himself, living in that country, is imbued with the love of it, and has a pleasant gift of describing its scenery. The learned and informative portions of his work are introduced appositely, though not woven into the body of his creation. They often show up, like a cotton lining behind a garment wrought of shimmering silk. Such, for example, is the description of Christmas festivities at the court of King Arthur, at Caer Lleon, which gives him the opportunity for a learned disquisition. In the same sober style is the description of the amusements at Caer Lleon :

---

[1] A heterogeneous collection of Welsh literature, *The Myvrian Archaiology of Wales*, including the "Triads," had been published with a translation in 1801-1807, edited by Owen Jones, E. Williams and W. Owen Pughe. The more reliable book, the *Four Ancient Books of Wales*, was not published till 1868 and the *Mabinogion*, 1838. As Peacock married a Welsh lady, he probably knew or learnt Welsh.

" The chase, in the neighbouring forest ; tilting in the amphitheatre ; trials of skill in archery, in throwing the lance and riding at the quintain, and similar amusements of the morning, created good appetites for the evening feasts ; in which Prince Cei, who is well known as Sir Kay, the seneschal, superintended the viands, as King Bedwyr did the liquor, having each a thousand men at command, for their provision, arrangement and distribution ; and music worthy of the banquet was provided and superintended by the king's chief harper, Geraint, of whom a contemporary poet observes, that, when he died, the gates of heaven were thrown wide open, to welcome the ingress of so divine a musician." [1]

The social milieu of the chief—here King Arthur— surrounded with his followers, including the group of bards, is described vividly and with touches of broad humour. Song and wine and good fellowship prevail. Seithenyn ap Seithyn [2] and his flowing potations and cry of " Wine from Gold ! " is a rollicking figure, worthy to be set in the company of Falstaff. He makes us leave our sober moralities and join in the revels. These are the circumstances of one of these scenes.

Seithenyn in a very low voice, " cocking his eye, and putting his finger on his lips," is telling Taliesin, one of the most famous of bards, that King Melvas has got in his castle " the finest woman in Britain." This is of course Gwenyvar (Guinevere) who has been wrested away from King Arthur.

" That I doubt," said Taliesin.

" She is the greatest, at any rate," said Seithenyn, " and ought to be the finest."

" How the greatest ? " said Taliesin.

" Seithenyn looked round, to observe if there were any listener near, and fixed a very suspicious gaze on a rotund figure of a fallen hero, who lay coiled up, like a maggot in a filbert, and snoring with an energy that, to the muddy

---

[1] *The Misfortunes of Elphin*, chap. 12, last paragraph.

[2] He is not mentioned in the " Taliesin " belonging to the *Mabinogion* tales, but in a poem in the *Black Book of Caermarthen*, No. XXXVIII. The first stanza is addressed to Seithenyn, calling upon him to see that Gwyddnen's plain has been flooded by the sea.

apprehensions of Seithenyn, seemed to be counterfeit. He determined by a gentle experiment to ascertain if his suspicions were well founded ; and proceeded, with what he thought great caution, to apply the point of his foot to the most bulging portion of the fat sleeper's circumference. But he greatly miscalculated his intended impetus, for he impinged his foot with a force that overbalanced himself, and hurled him headlong over his man, who instantly sprang on his legs, shouting, ' To arms ! ' Numbers started up at the cry ; the hall rang with the din of arms, and with the vociferation of questions, which there were many to ask, and none to answer. Some stared about for the enemy ; some rushed to the gates ; others to the walls. Two or three, reeling in the tumult and the darkness, were jostled over the parapet, and went rolling down the precipitous slope of the castle hill, crashing through the bushes, and bellowing for some one to stop them, till their clamours were cut short by a plunge into the Towy, where the conjoint weight of their armour and their liquor carried them to the bottom. The rage which would have fallen on the enemy, if there had been one, was turned against the author of the false alarm ; but, as none could point him out, the tumult subsided by degrees, through a descending scale of imprecations, into the last murmured malediction of him whom the intensity of his generous anger kept longest awake. By this time, the rotund hero had again coiled himself up into his ring ; and Seithenyn was stretched in a right line, as a tangent to the circle, in a state of utter incapacity to elucidate the mystery of King Melvas' possession of the finest woman in Britain." [1]

This description shows the true Welsh love of exaggeration combined with a scholar's precision of detail. The hyperbole is, however, consciously employed for the sake of heightening the humorous effect, not for the love of the marvellous, as it is in such a tale as " Kilhwch and Olwen."

The real hero of Peacock's story is Taliesin, and in his person he unites two stories which have little to do with each other, the one of Elphin and his misfortunes, which is taken and amplified considerably from the unfinished

[1] From *The Misfortunes of Elphin*, chap. xi.

" Taliesin " in the *Mabinogion*, and the other, the abduction
of Gwenyvar (Guinevere) by Melvas (Melwas), King of the
Summer Country. The latter story is incorporated in the
life of Gildas (*Vita Gildæ*), though in this form the mediation
is through St Gildas, not through Taliesin, as our romancer
makes it. The primitive mythological tale must have been
similar to that of the Greek " Rape of Proserpine," which is an
attempt to explain the change of seasons from summer to winter.

Elphin, according to Peacock's version, is taken prisoner
by his enemy, Maelgon Gwyneth (Maelgwn Gwynedd in the
" Taliesin ") along with his beautiful daughter, Melanghel (not
mentioned in the " Taliesin "). Taliesin, who is a foundling,
and has been rescued from the sea and brought up by Elphin,
is in love with Melanghel. He therefore has a doubly strong
motive to go to the rescue of both, and sets out for the court
of King Arthur to obtain help for the undertaking. Taliesin
knows, however, that Arthur will not listen to him, till his
own wife, Gwenyvar (Guinevere), is rescued. She has been
stolen away when she was hunting in the woods by Melvas [1]
of the Summer Country. So Taliesin sets out to attempt her
rescue, as a preliminary to his own quest. He persuades
the Abbot of Avallon (Glastonbury) and the famed toper
Seithenyn to accompany him to the court of King Melvas.
Thus King Melvas is to be confounded with a threefold argument, presented by the wily abbot with all the force of his
skilful persuasion, by the bard with all the powers of his art,
and by the pleasure-loving drunkard with his " wine from gold."

To those arguments, wittily put forth, the king finally
gives way. The sly abbot suggests that if the king will not
surrender the lady, King Arthur will come and take her by
force, therefore it would be more politic to give her up now,
and gain the greater glory. Also, if so disposed, the king
might claim from King Arthur " the fairest princess of his
court to wife, and ample dower withal." Seithenyn remarks,
" Another ray from the golden goblet will set it (the argument)
in a most luminous view." " And Taliesin summons all the
energies of his genius to turn the passions of Melvas into the
channels of anti-Saxonism."

[1] Another form of this word is " Melwas."

The final result is that Gwenyvar, under an honourable guidance, is returned to King Arthur warranted by the word of a king, backed by that of his butler, " As pure as on the day King Melvas had carried her off."

" None here will doubt that," said Gwenvach, the wife of Modred. Gwenyvar was not pleased with the compliment, and, almost before she had saluted King Arthur, she turned suddenly round, and slapped Gwenvach on the face, with a force that brought more crimson into one cheek than blushing had ever done into both. This slap is recorded in the Bardic Triads as one of the three fatal slaps of the Island of Britain. A terrible effect is ascribed to this small cause ; for it is said to have been the basis of that enmity between Arthur and Modred, which terminated in the battle of Camlan, wherein all the flower of Britain perished on both sides ; a catastrophe more calamitous than any ever before or since happened in Christendom, not even excepting that of the battle of Roncesvalles : for, in the battle of Camlan, the Britons exhausted their own strength, and could no longer resist the progress of the Saxon supremacy. This, however, was a later result, and comes not within the scope of the present veridicous (*sic*) narrative." [1]

Now that Gwenyvar is happily restored in good condition, Taliesin can return to his own affairs. Arthur, before an assembly of his followers, pronounces judgment on Elphin's enemy Maelgon Gwyneth. Taliesin has every occasion for joy and for bardic lyrics of triumph. He is to wed the fair maiden of his choice, the daughter of Elphin. As a punishment for his treachery, Maelgon is to pay all marriage expenses. Thus all ends well as true romance should.

Peacock, as the above extracts show, has a finished prose style which has balance and rhythm. He places emphasis in the right place, and uses just the correct incisive force which makes his prose such a fit instrument for satire. His sentences may be said to resemble a serpent fastening on its prey, whose venom is not the least deadly because of the symmetrical and glittering beauty of its coiling form.

Perhaps the definiteness of the quality of Peacock's satire

[1] From *The Misfortunes of Elphin*, chap. xvi.

has obscured somewhat the more positive qualities of his prose and verse, which spring from enthusiasm and admiration, not from criticism in its more negative aspect. For even in his verse it is his satiric poem " The War-Song of Dinas Vawr " which has gained the praise of critics.[1] Although, with the exception of this War - Song, his verses lack the precision and penetrating force of his prose, yet there is a certain lyrical quality which makes them linger pleasantly in the memory, like the echo of one of the mountain streams of which he writes. He may not enter the realms of the highest poetry in content or form, yet there is a spontaneous freshness which makes the poetic effect of his poem, taken as a unity, greater than that of the separate stanza or line. The introduction into his tale of the bards and bardic circle, with their competitive festal gatherings, gives the author the opportunity of putting into the mouths of Taliesin and others, Welsh songs and poems which are often his own translations and adaptations. These manifest on the part of Peacock a personal love of Nature and Welsh scenery.

Especially interesting to the Arthurian student is a free rendering of " Avallenau Myrddhin "—Merlin's Apple-Trees —from the poem in the *Black Book of Caermarthen*. The six verses given below illustrate its descriptive charm, not untouched with melancholy.[2]

Fair the gift to Merlin given,
Apple-trees seven score and seven ;
Equal all in age and size ;
On a green hill-slope that lies
Basking in the southern sun,
Where bright waters murmuring run.

Just beneath, the pure stream flows ;
High above, the forest grows ;
Not again on earth is found
Such a slope of orchard-ground :

[1] Especially Professor Saintsbury in Introduction to Macmillan's edition of *The Misfortunes of Elphin*.

[2] Given with more literal translation in W. F. Skene, *Four Ancient Books of Wales*, 1868, p. 373. References to Merlin's Apple-Trees is also found in *Vita Merlini* (line 90 ff.).

Song of birds, and hum of bees,
Ever haunt the apple-trees.

Lovely green their leaves in spring ;
Lovely bright their blossoming :
Sweet the shelter and the shade
By their summer foliage made ;
Sweet the fruit their ripe boughs hold,
Fruit delicious, tinged with gold.

Gloyad, nymph with tresses bright,
Teeth of pearl, and eyes of light,
Guard these gifts of Ceidio's son,
Gwendol, the lamented one,
Him, whose keen-edged sword no more
Flashes 'mid the battle's roar.

War has raged on vale and hill ;
That fair grove was peaceful still.
There, have chiefs and princes sought
Solitude and tranquil thought :
There, have kings, from courts and throngs,
Turned to Merlin's wild-wood songs.

But the singer hears the sound of the hostile axe and fears his apple-trees are doomed.

" Well I know, when years have flown,
Briars shall grow where ye have grown :
Them in turn shall power uproot ;
Then again shall flowers and fruit
Flourish in the sunny breeze,
On my new-born apple-trees." [1]

Thus, Peacock in this tale, *The Misfortunes of Elphin*, by his skilful reconstruction and humorous treatment of incidents, makes a noteworthy contribution to the Welsh side of the Arthurian legend.

[1] From *The Misfortunes of Merlin*, chap. xv. In the *Imrama*, Irish travel tales, apples are a characteristic of the Other-world.

II

The publication in 1838 of Lady Charlotte Guest's *Mabinogion*, with an English translation, marked an epoch in the literary history of the Arthurian legend. For here, like a spring of water, gushing up clear and unsullied, was disclosed a new source of inspiration. Malory's *Morte Darthur* had, up to this date, been the chief compilation of stories, but Malory had come to the end of a long literary tradition, and at times the characters seem to have the qualities of marionettes, pushed and pulled by the numerous strings of a traditional convention.

But here was a book of a different range of qualities. In it, one could breathe the true fairy-tale atmosphere. Once inside this enchanted realm, the reader is made free of a world which is a genuine world of art, in that it is a kingdom which possesses its own laws. Like the world of the child, it is a self-contained whole. No cold disturbing air from the prosaic world of fact blows upon it. Marvel is piled upon marvel, like cloud upon cloud at the time of sunset, till the whole irradiated fabric dazzles our astonished eyes.

These characteristics are especially true of the earlier tales. The various stories may be divided for convenience into four sections. There is first the early and non-Arthurian tales proper to the *mabinogi* or apprentice bards [1]; secondly, the two narratives of " Kilhwch and Olwen " [2] and the " Dream of Rhonabwy," early and both definitely Arthurian ; the third section comprises the later stories, " The Lady of the Fountain," " Peredur, the Son of Evrawc," and " Geraint, the Son of Erbin." These latter are strongly influenced by French romance—especially Chrétien de Troies. [3]

[1] See M. Loth, *Les Mabinogion*, 1913, p. 13, Introduction.

[2] This is Lady Charlotte Guest's spelling.   M. Loth spells it " Kulwch and Olwen."

[3] A fierce discussion has raged round the point of the origin of these stories ; the insular or Welsh faction, headed by Gaston Paris, believes that they belong to Wales, and were carried by professional story-tellers to the Continent ; the Armorican faction, headed by Zimmer and Förster, that the phrase " matière de Bretagne " applies neither to Great Britain nor to Wales, but to Little Britain or Brittany in France and thus Brittany

The fourth section comprises the romance " Taliesin," which is from late manuscripts, but probably compiled in the thirteenth or fourteenth century.[1]

M. Loth, from the study of its linguistic characteristics, places " Kilhwch and Olwen " in the late eleventh or early twelfth century. It is particularly interesting to the student of origins, because it shows no knowledge of Geoffrey of Monmouth nor influence of the French romances. It has more the qualities of the folk-tale, the story of a quest and its usual accompaniments of marvel. Also, the fact that in this quest, the animals, including the ouzel, the stag and the lion, are called in to help, is significant. There is also the refrain so dear to children and the primitive audience : " It will be easy for me to compass this, although thou mayest think that it will not be easy." As in so many cases where a story has gone through various stages of oral transmission, the original incident may have been related of another hero and affixed to Arthur later. As Dr Chambers points out,[2] there are certain displacements in the story which favours this theory ; for example, all the original tasks mentioned at the beginning of the narrative are not carried out.

The quest itself, the hunting of the boar " Twrch Trwyth," is mentioned in Nennius. Here, in " Kilhwch," it is given in great detail. The story runs as follows :—

In order to gain the hand of Olwen, the daughter of Yspaddaden Penkawr, Kilhwch was faced with a succession of very difficult tasks. One of the most terrible was to seize from the fierce boar " Twrch Trwyth " the comb and scissors which were between his ears. The boar was once a king and had been transformed by magic into animal form. His seven sons also were changed into seven pigs.

King Arthur promised to come to the rescue of Kilhwch, and summoned all his warriors, those in France, Normandy,

was their original home. The facts of history prove that the relations of France and England at this time were very close. Thus the exact share of each country's folk-lore is difficult to apportion exactly.

[1] See Loth, *Les Mabinogion*, 1913, vol. i. 359, note. Lady Charlotte Guest translates it in her edition of the *Mabinogion* with notes.

[2] See E. K. Chambers, *Arthur of Britain*, p. 71.

Armorica and in the Summer Country and went into Ireland. The Irish joined Arthur, for they had suffered from the boar's frightful ravages. They pursued him into Wales. There was a furious combat, and one by one the small pigs were slain. Finally, Twrch Trwyth made his way to Cornwall, but before he reached that country, Arthur and his followers had plunged him into the Severn and obtained the razor and scissors. A still further and fiercer hunt ensued for the comb and finally the boar was driven into the sea and " it was never known whither he went." " And thus did Kilhwch obtain Olwen, the daughter of Yspaddaden Penkawr."

The origin of the story evidently lies in myth. Nutt believes that the tale is allied to the Irish romantic sagas. The giant Yspaddaden [1] with his lowered eyelids shows certain resemblances to the Irish " Balor," a god who also had his eyes habitually cast down. This was perhaps as well for anyone who happened to be near him, for he had the power of slaying his enemy by one piercing glance ! Again, the whole incident may be looked upon as having been originally an " agricultural myth " and Arthur may have been a " culture hero " who comes from the Other-world to win the gifts of civilisation for men (here the comb and the scissors). [2]

There is also probably a double reference, historical as well as mythological. Mr Rhys demonstrates that the route the boar pursued can be traced on a map of Britain. Mr Moore [3] tries to show that this is a Welsh version of an historical episode, a Danish slave-catching expedition from Ireland to the West Coast of Britain in 835, a raid mentioned in the *Anglo-Saxon Chronicle*. Ragnar Ladbrok, the head of the expedition, according to this theory, is the same person as the " Turges " of the Irish annals, who alludes to himself as the " old pig " and his sons as the " young pigs." Whether this interpretation

---

[1] See Loth, *Les Mabinogion*, i. 296, note.

[2] A suggestion from Dr E. K. Chambers who points out that hair-clipping was an initiation ceremony for knighthood among the Celts (*Arthur of Britain*, p. 215).

[3] *Athenæum*, 1st February 1913, " The Historical Basis of Tristan and Iseult."

be correct or not, the definite topography seems to point to a definite happening.

The " Dream of Rhonabwy," in which the dreamer is a twelfth-century chieftain, shows signs of a knowledge of Geoffrey's *History* through the Welsh translations, especially in relation to the battle of Camlan. For example, in accordance with Geoffrey, " Medrawd " is mentioned as the nephew of Arthur. In spite of this evidence of being post-Galfridian, the story retains qualities which place it among the earlier tales of the *Mabinogion*. There is the same atmosphere of marvel : magic carpets, rings and stones play their part. In its pages, Arthur and his warriors move through the bright clear atmosphere like gay birds of plumage. In Rhonabwy's dream, the dreamer sees Arthur on his way to the battle of Camlan. The " Emperor," as he is called, stops on his way to the battle to play a game of chess with Owain. In the progress of the game a brightly-attired youth enters to ask Owain if he will call off his (Owain's) Ravens, who are harassing Arthur's men. Arthur also joins in the request, but all Owain says is " Play this game, Lord." They go on playing. Five separate young men enter with the same request and the sixth and last tells Arthur that the Ravens have slain his household and the sons of the chief men of the island. Arthur once again beseeches Owain to call them off, and taking the golden chessmen off the board, crushes them to dust. Then, at last, Owain orders Gwres, the son of Rheged, to lower his banner. All is peace once more.

Once again there seems to be a double reference, a mythological and an historical. The raven in Celtic mythology and other mythologies, was the typical bird of prey following the warrior to feast upon his victims. In Norse mythology, Odin, the god of war, was depicted with two ravens, one on each shoulder, who whispered to him all they had heard and seen, thus standing also for counsel and wisdom. The *Anglo-Saxon Chronicle* (878) records the capture from the Norse of a banner called the Raven.[1] By transference, in the " Dream of Rhonabwy " the Ravens may refer to a band

---

[1] From the *Revue Celtique*, i. 53, " The Ancient Irish Goddess of War."

of men.   They are certainly described as avenging spirits of
war, whether human or symbolic.

" So the youth returned back to the place where the strife
bore hardest upon the Ravens, and he lifted up the banner ;
and as he did so they all rose up in the air, wrathful and
fierce and high of spirit, clapping their wings in the wind,
and shaking off the weariness that was upon them.   And
recovering their energy and courage, furiously and with
exultation did they, with one sweep, descend upon the heads
of the men, who had erewhile caused them anger and pain
and damage, and they seized some by the heads, and others
by the eyes, and some by the ears, and others by the arms,
and carried them up into the air ;   and in the air there was
a mighty tumult with the flapping of the wings of the
triumphant Ravens, and with their croaking ;   and there was
another mighty tumult with the groaning of the men, that
were being torn and wounded, and some of whom were
slain." [1]

In the *Four Ancient Books of Wales*, published in 1868 by
W. F. Skene, there are interesting references to, and poems
on, Arthur.   The Four Books are, the *Red Book of Hergest*
(which included the *Mabinogion* [2]), the *Book of Taliessin*,
the *Book of Aneurin* and the *Black Book of Caermarthen*.[3]   One
of the earliest poems which may be pre-Galfridian is by
Taliessin, " Preiddeu Annwfn " (The Harryings of Hades),[4]
which describes Arthur's descent into the Other-world in his
ship *Prydwen* to find there a magic cauldron.

In *The Black Book of Caermarthen* there are three poems
which may be dated approximately not later than the first
half of the twelfth century.   One mentions the grave of
Bedwyr and Arthur, but nothing concerning the return of
the latter.   One is called " Gereint filius Erbin," who is

---

[1] Lady C. Guest's translation from the *Mabinogion*.
[2] Published separately.
[3] More scholarly translations of Arthurian poems are found in Rhys,
Arthurian Legend, and preface of Malory, " Everyman " Edition, vol. 1.
[4] So translated by Professor J. Rhys, see Malory, " Everyman " Edition,
Preface, vol. i.   Lady Charlotte Guest names it " Preidden Annwn "
and translates it the " Spoils of Hell."

regarded in the poem as a follower of Arthur. He may be equated with Gerontius in the eighth century.[1]

The third and perhaps most interesting poem for our purpose is a dialogue between Arthur and a porter, Glewlwyd Gavaelvawr, who appears also in " Kilhwch and Olwen," and "The Lady of the Fountain." The poem mentions also Manawyddan, son of Lyr, who is evidently the Irish sea-god Manannan Mac Lir appearing in Irish saga. In these verses, Arthur, Bedwyr and Kei are mighty heroes slaying monsters. Kei (Kay) is connected with Palug's Cat and Arthur with a hag.

Thus the picture of Arthur and his followers in the *Mabinogion*, the *Four Books* and the " Triads," has a certain consistency. He and his associates have the traits of the early mythological heroes, celebrated also in Irish legend. It is altogether a different picture from that of Arthur in the pseudo-histories.

The *genre* of Malory's work as an inheritor of the courtly romanticists is absolutely different, much more sophisticated and conventional. There are one or two characters and incidents, however, which the Welsh romances and Malory have in common. According to Welsh legendary tradition,[2] Rhitta the Giant King of Wales, in order to punish the insane arrogance of the two kings of Britain, marched against them, vanquished them and cut off their beards. They were then turned into oxen for their crimes. Some of their arrogance, however, seems to have entered into the soul of their conqueror, for, having made it a practice for some time to disbeard all the kings he conquered, he made himself a mantle out of the beards, which extended from head to heel. It will be remembered, in Malory, he had the audacity to send for Arthur's beard and was promptly reprimanded and the request refused.[3] This " Rhitta Gawr " or " King Ryons," as Malory calls him, is not actually mentioned in " Kilhwch and Olwen," but the two transformed kings are, namely,

---

[1] See E. K. Chambers, *Arthur of Britain*, p. 66.

[2] See *Mabinogion*, ed. Lady Charlotte Guest, " Everyman " Edition, p. 325 ; also Loth, *Les Mabinogion*, 1913, i. 303 note.

[3] Book I, chap. 26, Malory, " Everyman " Edition.

Nynniaw and Peibaw whom God turned into oxen on account of their sins.

Another celebrated personage sung by Welsh bards and Norman *trouvères* is Caradawc (Caradoc or Craddocke). In Welsh story he is a warrior who had won his fame at the battle of Cattraeth where he fell mortally wounded. Lady Charlotte Guest identifies him with the Caradoc " Brise-Bras," a hero of the Round Table.[1] His " brawny arm " through an error of translation became the " wasted arm," and the story of an enchanter who caused a serpent to fasten itself upon him with injurious results, was invented to explain his appellation. His wife, Tegau Eurvron, is in bardic literature renowned for her chastity and possessed three treasures—a knife, a goblet of gold, and most famous of all, a mantle. Only the irreproachable in wifely virtue could wear this mantle, otherwise it shrank. A coarse but forcible English *fabliau*, " The Boy and the Mantle," [2] gives an account of chastity tests and their dire results, and in this the " mantle " also appears. The French representative tale, " Le Mantel mal taillé," [3] has the same subject, somewhat elaborated. The story of the " Horn " test which varies a good deal from the *fabliau* is given in Malory.[4] It is sent to Arthur, on account of the rumours of the infidelity of Guinevere, but is intercepted and brought to the court of King Marke, whose Queen also failed to " drinke it cleane." Spenser must have had some such incident as the mantle story in mind when he wrote of Florimel's girdle :

> That girdle gave the virtue of chaste love
> And wivehood true to all that it did beare ;
> But whosoever contrarie doth prove,
> Might not the same about her middle weare,
> But it would loose or else asunder teare.[5]

The poet also adapts in a characteristic way for his own

---

[1] See *Mabinogion*, " Everyman " edition, p. 346.
[2] Percy's *Reliques of English Poetry*, vol. ii.
[3] It is not determined which was the earlier.
[4] Book VIII, chap. 34, " Globe " Edition.
[5] Book IV, Canto 5, Stanza 3.

romantic purpose the story of the beards in the *Faerie Queene*.[1]
Sir Calidore rescues a Squire, bound hand and foot, who tells
him that on a rocky hill there stands a castle belonging to
the Lady Briana. She has initiated a cruel custom of
demanding of the passers-by, as toll, the locks of the ladies'
hair and the beards of the knights. Her lover, Crudor, has
refused to yield to Lady Briana's love unless she provide
him with a mantle lined with these locks and beards.
Sir Calidore, however, the knight of Courtesy, naturally
objects to this discourteous custom, and having overcome
the Seneschal of the Castle and the knight Crudor in
battle, sends the knight back to the lady to accede to her
demand and to marry her without condition or dowry.
The knight has also to promise courtesy to all errant
knights and ladies in future, who must needs pass by the
Castle.

If some references to these Welsh traditions are found in
Malory and Spenser, a collection of Welsh stories was not
made common property till Lady Charlotte Guest wrote her
translation of the *Mabinogion*. This came into the hands of
Tennyson and he was attracted to one of the less primitive
tales and worked it into his plan of the *Idylls*. While less
interesting to the student of myth, the Welsh " Geraint, the
Son of Erbin " provides a more coherent story.

The two parts of the story were published as "The Marriage
of Geraint" and its sequel "Geraint and Enid" in the first series
of the *Idylls of the King* in 1859. The same narrative with
variations is told by Chrétien de Troies in " Erec and Enid."
The relation of the two tales is a matter of dispute among
scholars. In some respects, both show a high degree of
civilisation. For example, in the *Mabinogion*, glass is
mentioned, and in Chrétien, information is given that white
sheets were provided on the beds. In contrast to this, there
are examples of the coarser manners of an age when women
were merely men's chattels and possessions. If a woman's
knight or husband were killed she could become any man's
possession who cared to protect her. Tennyson emphasises
this fact, which he found in his source.

[1] Book VI, Canto 1, Stanza 11 ff.

When Enid sat wailing beside her lord, whom she thought
was dead,

> (And) many past, but none regarded her,
> For in that realm of lawless turbulence,
> A woman weeping for her murder'd mate
> Was cared as much for as a summer shower.
> One took him for a victim of Earl Doorm,
> Nor dared to visit a perilous pity on him ;
> Another hurrying past, a man-at-arms,
> Rode on a mission to the bandit Earl ;
> Half whistling and half singing a coarse song ;
> He drove the dust against her veilless eyes.[1]

Then Earl Doorm came along and took them both to his
hall.   He would have made her his own, if her husband
had not suddenly risen from his death - like swoon and
defended her.

There are considerable differences between Chrétien de
Troies and the *Mabinogion* both in plot and atmosphere.
The chief one is that in Chrétien it was Erec's (Geraint's)
honour as a warrior that was at stake, in the *Mabinogion* and
consequently in Tennyson, his honour as a husband.   Chrétien
relates that when Erec was half asleep he heard Enid bemoan-
ing that men questioned Erec's bravery, since he had become
her doting husband.   Therefore, rousing himself up, he set
out in wrath to find adventures which would demonstrate
his prowess.   He commanded her to follow him in silence.
In the *Mabinogion* version, he misunderstood what she said
and thought she was grieving concerning her unfaithfulness
to him.   Tennyson's story is pivoted round this idea :

> " O noble breast and all-puissant arms,
> Am I the cause, I the poor cause that men
> Reproach you, saying all your force is gone ?

> .   .   .   .

> Am I so bold, and could I so stand by,
> And see my dear lord wounded in the strife,
> Or maybe pierced to death before mine eyes,

---

[1] Tennyson, "Globe" Edition, 1899, p. 362, " Geraint and Enid."

And yet not dare to tell him what I think,
And how men slur him, saying all his force
Is melted into mere effeminacy ?
O me ! I fear that I am no true wife." [1]

Geraint awoke and, hearing only the last words, took it for a confession of unfaithfulness.

There is no evidence that Tennyson knew Chrétien, for he was not, like Swinburne, a student of Old French. But nevertheless it repays the modern reader of Tennyson to read Chrétien and compare him with Tennyson. For both were faced by the same problem ; they had to adapt an older source to their own age. If Chrétien had some earlier source, written or oral, which he did not altogether understand (as happened in the *Perceval*), he yet found enough material in it to adapt it successfully to the brilliant society of his own time, rich and leisured, with much of the feudal element in it. To this society this story, which relates incidents concerning fighting, tournaments, hawking and love would appeal. In contrast to the *Lancelot*, written at the request of Marie of Champagne (Eleanor of Aquitaine's daughter), it is a story of true and constant wedded love.

Tennyson had a more difficult task. He did not, however, attempt to modernise the story but relied on his skill as a story-teller to make the mediæval tale of interest to his readers. Its subject attracted Tennyson as upholding the ideal of faithful obedience and loyalty in marriage. To the Victorian, the qualities of meekness and constancy in woman were primary virtues. Nowadays, however, so little is the " Patient Griselda " type liked, that this story is often condemned altogether, without regard to its outstanding artistic merits.

An examination of Tennyson's narrative shows that it possesses coherence, skilful character-drawing and poetical charm.

Modern readers of the novel usually agree that prose is a better medium for a coherent tale than verse. But, as this poem shows, a poetical tale can be clear and straightforward. Once the dramatic device used in these two stories is

---

[1] " The Marriage of Geraint," " Globe " Edition, p. 342.

grasped the tales go straight ahead. This dramatic device is that of the epic, and of some modern novels. The story-teller plunges *in medias res*. In this case, we are brought to the core of the story at once, to the situation where the married Enid addresses her sleeping husband and the consequent misunderstanding. Then the past events of the marriage between Geraint and Enid are told as a memory of Enid's. Apart from this device, the narrative is straight-forward and coherent, and irrelevancies, found in the source, are omitted. One of these is the story of Earl Owain and the magic games, one of those Welsh legends in which marvel follows marvel.

As regards character-drawing, even those who dislike Enid's type must allow that she is drawn with sympathy. The changing moods of Geraint are described with subtlety and the gradual softening of his anger. The *Mabinogion* merely informs us of the fact of his wrath, nor does it dwell later on the reconciliation between husband and wife, which is really the climax of the story. Chrétien, a psychologist by nature, emphasises this point also.

Geraint made full amends for his suspicion of his wife and churlish conduct. He has just awakened from his swoon in Earl Doorm's hall :

" Enid, I have used you worse than that dead man ; [Earl Doorm]
Done you more wrong : we both have undergone
That trouble which has left me thrice your own :
Henceforward I will die rather than doubt." [1]

It may be easier on the whole for the prose writer to obtain swift movement and coherence in a story. But the writer of a poetical tale aims at a more difficult kind of unity. This quality may, I think, be sensed in this narrative. By means of simile and harmonious description, the emotional tensity is heightened. Yet these similes and descriptions are not ends in themselves or mere " purple patches." While giving a certain variety of design, they yet emphasise the main design as a well-constructed pattern does. Thus, in this poem, the references in the similes are connected with the

[1] Tennyson, " Geraint and Enid," *op. cit.*, p. 365.

main theme as in the one quoted below, where the place-reference is apt.

The poet is telling the reader that Geraint's wrath at what he considered Enid's treachery, fought with his pity, when he saw her trying to drive three riderless horses before her, according to his own command. It caused him pain,

> And suffering thus he made
> Minutes an age : but in scarce longer time
> Than at Caerleon the full-tided Usk,
> Before he turn to fall seaward again
> Pauses, did Enid, keeping watch behold [1]
>
> .   .   .   .   .
>
> Three other horsemen waiting.

Tennyson also elaborates the touches of sentiment he found in his source almost to the verge of the sentimental. A characteristic example of this is the stress he lays on the part Enid's poor faded dress plays in the story. It was this dress on which Enid's eye lit, when Geraint told her roughly to put on her poorest dress and ride forth with him. It recalled to her the days of her betrothal, when her lover told her to don her oldest dress so that Guinevere might have the pleasure of fitly arraying the bride-to-be.

Later on in the tale, this dress is referred to again. When Enid sat in Earl Doorm's hall beside the seemingly lifeless body of her husband, she refused to dress in the rich garment the Earl brought her :

> A splendid silk of foreign loom
> Where like a shoaling sea the lovely blue
> Played into green, and thicker down the front
> With jewels than the sward with drops of dew
> When all night long a cloud clings to the hill
> And with the dawn ascending lets the day
> Strike where it clings : so thickly shone the gems.[2]

The poor faded robe, not this magnificent one, was dearer to Enid as a symbol of the bereaved and sorrowing state.

[1] Tennyson, " Geraint and Enid," *op. cit.*, p. 356.
[2] *Op. cit.*, p. 365.

The tale of Geraint and Enid is a typical mediæval story with nothing specifically Welsh about it, except perhaps the descriptions of wild nature. So that although the *Mabinogion*, translated by Lady Charlotte Guest, will always hold its own, because of its literary value, the Welsh stream of tradition has not, in modern literature, directly changed the current of the French tradition, interpreted by Malory. This fact is illustrated also by the attitude which Tennyson presented to the Welsh " Peredur " which he ignored altogether. Though of great value to scholars, as one of the earlier forms of the Grail stories,[1] it was, in its somewhat undeveloped and contradictory form, of no use to the poet in his *Idylls*. If he had lived later and studied the origins of the Grail-story, he might have chosen the more complete and rational dramatic story of Wolfram von Aeschenbach's *Parzival*.

[1] See J. L. Weston, *The Legend of Sir Perceval*, 2 vols, 1906-9, *passim*.

CHAPTER IX

THE HOLY GRAIL : EARLIER VERSIONS

THE origins and early texts of the Holy Grail have been the subject of study, conjecture, and controversy, of many eminent scholars, English, German and French, of late years.[1] A knowledge of these texts and their relationship and of the main discussions concerning these, is of course of value to those studying modern Arthurian poets. But for the present argument, it is sufficient to emphasise the general nature of these origins, and to confine our particular study of texts to two, which are later and which have determined in the main the traditions which modern poets have accepted.

At this stage, it will be sufficient merely to mention them. One of these is the anonymous twelfth-century *Queste* [2] (the actual manuscript of which is lost) which Malory transcribed and abbreviated in his thirteenth to seventeenth books of the *Morte Darthur*. It is an exceedingly fruitful exercise to read these together and note the differences and the reasons for change or abbreviation. It makes the reader realise as nothing else does, how, especially in these books, Malory is chiefly an abbreviator and transcriber. His real originality is in the magic of his style.

The second text, which Dr Weston has given us in a most vigorous translation, in stanzas, is that of Wolfram von Aeschenbach's *Parzival* [3] (thirteenth century). It is one of the finest poems of the Middle Ages. Though lengthy and very detailed (it contains the adventures of Gawain as well

---

[1] See J. D. Bruce, *Evolution of Arthurian Romance from the Beginnings down to Year 1300*, (1923), bibliography at end of volume.

[2] For study, see E. Vinaver, *Malory*, 1929, list of manuscripts, Appendix 2. For comparison, Appendix 3. See also Pauphilet (A.), *La Queste del Saint Graal*, 1921.

[3] Translated by J. L. Weston, 1894.

as Parzival), it is, on the whole, a unified, purposeful tale, and moves on steadily to its end and climax. It has considerable literary merit. Wagner followed, in the main, the events in this poem for his drama, the *Parsifal*,[1] and thus its story has become familiar throughout Europe, associated with the heart-stirring Grail music. Wolfram von Aeschenbach himself proclaims that he took the story from a certain " Kiot." Some have doubted this declaration and scholars suspect this source does not exist. But as this statement of Wolfram's has not exactly been disproved, others have taken it as it stands, as Dr Weston does in the notes of her translation of the *Parzival*.

In regard to the general origins of the Grail, scholars mainly agree that the foundation of the story lies in the far-off region of pagan myth. Dr Weston considers that " close parallels exist between the characters and incidents of the Grail story and a certain well-marked group of popular beliefs and observances, now very generally recognised as fragments of a once widespread Nature-cult." [2]

This Nature-cult, she tells us, was connected with sex-rites and fertility and the coming of Spring (as in the " Adonis " rites in Greece). Thus the feast of the Grail was, according to this theory, a celebration of the awakening powers of Nature and the cup and lance, male and female phallic symbols. The special servants of the Grail were those " initiated " into the hidden powers of life and they had to go through certain rites. This theory also attempts to explain the central incident of the suffering Grail-king, who was wounded in the thighs and who could only be healed by the asking of a certain question. The disability was connected with the reproductive faculties and in this misfortune the " wailing land " shares. The question, of course, is one of those magic formulæ like the " Open Sesame " with which we have been familiar from our childhood. When the hero rode up the second time to recite the formula, *i.e.* ask the required question, the land rejoiced. It had been freed from the curse.

[1] See below, Chap. XII.
[2] See *From Ritual to Romance*, 1920, p. 132.

The whole legend became in course of time rationalised into a hero-story, Christianised and moralised.

In the earlier texts the primitive element is not altogether absent. We trace it here and there, jutting out like the peaks of high rocks in the ocean, which the tide has not altogether submerged. In Chrétien de Troies, for example, his mention of the " wailing of the land " and the " wailing of the women " (also mentioned in the "Adonis" legend) seems to demand an explanation not given in the actual events of the tale. Chrétien did not finish his poem so we do not know how he would have treated the Grail, but from indications in his poem, probably he regarded it only as a wonder-working talisman, worthy of reverence. The process of rationalisation is far advanced in this poet. Chrétien explains Perceval's first failure to achieve the sick king's healing as a punishment for his having caused his mother's death through heedless folly.

In its later form in the continuators of Chrétien, and especially in the Robert de Borron texts (or those ascribed to the latter), the Grail legend has come into contact with the Joseph of Arimathea legend and the process of Christianising has been taking place. The cup in which Joseph of Arimathea catches the drops of Christ's blood has been identified with the cup of the Last Supper. Joseph of Arimathea had taken it with him over to England to Christianise that land and it had performed many miracles, such as feeding him and his followers in prison. Then it disappeared, only to reappear to certain favoured ones.

In the *Queste* and in Malory, this food-producing vessel and life-giving feast is identified with the Mass and Eucharist. All manner of meat and drink is still provided, when it first appears to King Arthur's knights sitting at meat. But one of the chief qualities it possesses is the producing of a kind of spiritual ecstasy. " Then I shall tell you," said Galahad, " the other day when we saw a part of the adventures of the Sangreal I was in such a joy of heart, that I trow never man was that was earthly." It can only be seen by the pure in heart, which implies strict celibacy. The sight of the Grail for its own sake thus becomes the goal of the seekers rather than the healing of the sick king. True, Galahad does touch the maimed king with the blood of the sacred spear and heal him, but this is not made the central incident. To care so much for one's own spiritual satisfaction seems to the modern mind a selfish aim, even though disguised under the symbol of holy things.

In Wolfram of Aeschenbach the conception of the Grail is far otherwise. The central incident is the healing of the sick king and the whole theme of the poem the perfecting of the hero Parzival for this end. It is important to notice, however, that the Grail is not connected with Our Lord's Passion, though it is with Christianity. It is a magic stone which produces food and restores youth. Borne in procession by the Grail-maidens, it evidently has some moral implication, as those maidens must be chaste and pure of life. The power of the stone is renewed every Good Friday by a dove bearing a wafer, so it shows Christian influence. No unbaptized heathen such as the chivalrous Feirefis can view it. Its surroundings are magical rather than mystical in the more spiritual sense, " Unawares must they chance upon it for I wot in no otherwise." The conception of the Grail is also influenced by the Crusades and there exists a military knighthood at Monsalvasch,[1] who guard it, which descends from father to son. The Grail keeper can marry but not his attendants, unless they go to foreign lands.

Though Wagner has shown in his opera, *Parsifal*, the dramatic possibilities of the story of Perceval and the Holy Grail, this version was not followed in English literature. There was, however, an early Welsh rendering of the story, of extreme importance in the history of origins [2] in "Peredur" in the *Mabinogion*. It had some incidents in common with Wolfram von Aeschenbach—the description of Peredur's early life and upbringing, his appearance in the hall of the wounded king, who inhabited with his courtiers the " wailing land." There is also a strange admonition to the hero *not* to ask any questions, which seem to point originally to some form of taboo. It is evidently some tale of revenge ; there is mention

---

[1] This form of the word is taken from Dr Weston's translation, vi. 170 (*Parzival*).

[2] See J. L. Weston, *The Legend of Sir Perceval*, 2 vols, 1906-9.

of the bloody spear, the gory head in a charger carried by two maidens but of no Holy Grail as such ; nor has this story any religious atmosphere.   Peredur has also many adventures of the usual chivalrous kind, such as rescuing distressed maidens.

The other source, the *Queste*, which Malory used and abbreviated and which commended itself to Tennyson and other English poets, is of a very different nature.   It is of great interest to the student of religious life in the Middle Ages and has a moral, spiritual and some literary value.   But it has not the living interest of Wolfram.

Pauphilet, in his able study on the *Queste*,[1] points out that it is a *tableau* of Christian life probably written and adapted by a Cistercian monk.   It is of the most ascetic character and makes reference to means of spiritual grace adopted in the monastery, such as fasting, confession and Mass with its attendant doctrines.   For example, in Mass the presence of the " real body " is assumed, that is, the doctrine of Transubstantiation as held by the Catholic Church at that time.   In Book XVII, chapter 20, of Malory, it is written how Galahad and his fellows were fed of the Holy Sangreal and how Our Lord appeared to them.   "And then the bishop made semblant as though he would have gone to the sacring of the mass.   And then he took an Ubblye (a wafer) which was made in likeness of bread.   And at the lifting up there came a figure in likeness of a child, and the visage was as red and as bright as any fire, and smote himself into the bread, so that they all saw it that the bread was formed of a fleshly man." [2]

The order of the moral virtues is altogether different from that assumed in the chivalric code adopted elsewhere by Malory.   The chief virtues are humility and sexual purity in its most severe form.   One of the sins most severely censored is *la luxure* in which marriage as well as irregular love is condemned.   Next comes pride, especially the pride which is aroused by successful combats.   Lancelot is therefore one of the chief transgressors, though, to the modern reader, he is the most interesting character in the *Queste*, which is not

[1] Albert Pauphilet, *Études sur la Queste del Saint Graal*, 1921.
[2] From *Morte Darthur*, " Everyman " Edition, ii, 265.

strong in character-drawing. He has to repent of his irregular love of Queen Guinevere, if he is to have any hope of seeing the Holy Grail. Again, he is reproved for putting his trust in his sword rather than in God. Malory, translating closely from the *Queste*,[1] gives it thus : " The dwarf smote him and said ' Oh man of evil faith and poor belief, wherefore trowest thou more on thy harness, than in thy Maker.' " There are combats in this world but they are waged against spiritual enemies with spiritual armour. Galahad's chief weapon is trust in God.

In order to provide a hero to fit into these lofty but intangible ideals, a man had to be found of mysterious origin, without family ties. He is named Galahad, and like Parzival is the one promised aforetime. It is prophesied that he will sit in the perilous seat, enter the magic ship, fit together the broken sword and behold the Grail. Having beheld the Grail, he seems too lofty and pure for this mortal and sinful life and is translated to the Heavenly Kingdom. Perceval (the form in the *Queste* of the name) [2] is also one of the questers and has retained his ingenuity and air of candour and, most important of all in this monastic treatise, has retained his virginity. In the earlier forms of the *Queste*, as Dr Weston has pointed out in her series of studies,[3] Gawain was the original hero. In these earlier romances he is depicted as courteous, chivalrous and a loyal companion, ready for all adventures. But, alas ! he has many loves, probably because as a favourite English hero, many stories of love and adventure, which did not originally belong to him, became attached to his name. At any rate, he did not suit the monkish writer of the *Queste*. To him, as to Thomas à Kempis, earthly graces were very different from heavenly ones. So Gawain becomes in this treatise the example of a worldling, light and frivolous, and is condemned by its severe standards. In the *Queste* the incidents related are far removed from the possibilities of real life. They form a contrast to Wolfram's story, which,

[1] For comparison with MS. similar to that which Malory used, see Vinaver (E.), *Malory*, 1929, Appendix 3.
[2] Other forms : Percivale (Malory), Parzival (Wolfram von Aeschenbach), Parsifal (Wagner).
[3] For list see Appendix C, p. 266.

in spite of its mediæval chivalrous setting, has yet an air of reality about it, not far removed from that of Froissart's *Chronicle* of his own times.[1] But the incidents in the *Queste* are more intangible and impossible than the most romantic incidents of Malory in his other books. They tell us of phantom ships, neophytes who subsist for long periods on the grace of God alone, and of the champions of impossible feats. The writer loves the elaborate allegories and long moralisings in which the Middle Ages indulged.

One of the most elaborate, interesting and obscure allegories is that of the miraculous ship, described thus by the modern poet William Morris :

> There shall you find the wondrous ship wherein
> The spindles of King Solomon are laid,
> And the sword that no man draweth without sin,
> But if he be most pure.[2]

In the course of their adventures, Galahad, Perceval and Sir Bors enter a strange and empty ship, borne over the waters miraculously and silently. In it they find a bed with magnificent silk coverings, and at its foot a sword hanging, whom no one but the chosen Galahad can dislodge from its sheath.

The story is a curious mixture of Celtic magic, Bible lore and moralising allegory. This sword with the strange girdle " espee as estranges renges " is a sword whose first girdle was of hemp which contrasted strongly with the magnificence of its scabbard of serpent's skin and its scaly handle, made from the scales of beasts that possessed magic properties, so that he who handled it should never feel weary. It has been prophesied that a new girdle would be made by a king's daughter and she must be a maiden. This virgin is, of course, Perceval's sister, who makes a girdle of her own hair bound with gold and set with precious stones.

The tale of the building of the ship is connected with Solomon and his wife and goes still further back to the

---

[1] There is no date given of first edition of Froissart's *Chronicle*. The second edition is 1505, and Berner's English translation, 1525.

[2] " Sir Galahad " in *Defence of Guenevere*, King's Poets, 1904, p. 48.

beginning of things in the Garden of Eden. The three wooden spindles, from which the sword hangs, are made of three different kinds of wood, white, green and red, from the Tree in the Garden of Eden. The Tree was white at the time of our parents' innocence, it became green when Abel was conceived and red when Cain was murdered.

The story, with its numerous allusions to mediæval legends and beliefs, is difficult to understand without commentary,[1] and Malory, in abbreviating it, makes it even more so (Book XVII). But Malory's style, like the sauce of a good cook, makes this strange mixture palatable, and the passage describing the ship and the fair bed (chapter 3) has a charm for the ear if not for the rational sense.

From this short summary of the contents it can be seen that the aims, ideals and subject-matter of the *Queste* are very different to those in Malory's other books, where it is the idealised love of woman, usually another man's wife, which is the chief motive of action, especially of fighting and adventures. Lancelot, the noblest and most chivalrous of them all, fits in uneasily to the new régime. All his former glories and attainments are counted to him as sins. He has to repent them utterly. In the original *Queste*, Lancelot remarks that the new (spiritual) life pleased him a hundred times better than the old. But Malory, purposely or otherwise, omits this saying in his rendering ![2]

Thus, though Malory's adaptation of the *Queste* is of value in itself, it does not add to the unity of purpose of the *Morte Darthur* as a whole. So when Malory returns to his last books, leading to the destruction of the Round Table and the death of Arthur, through the treachery of Modred, we read that the court made glad when Sir Lancelot " began to resort unto Queen Guenever again, and forgat the promise and the perfection that he made in the quest." [3]

---

[1] Dr Weston in her interesting pamphlet, *Apple Mystery in Arthurian Legend* (reprinted from the Bulletin of John Ryland's Library), 1925, explains some of these symbols, centring round the apple.

[2] Vinaver states and shows that " by omission Malory defends Lancelot's character." See his *Malory*, p. 80.

[3] Malory, " Everyman " Edition, ii. 271.

CHAPTER X

THE HOLY GRAIL : MODERN VERSIONS

A MODERN poet, having the version of Malory's "Holy Grail" before him, is faced with two difficulties. There is the inherent difficulty of the story itself, which has gone through so many changes in form and meaning, and there is the difficulty of its relation to the other stories of the *Morte Darthur*.

Tennyson, perhaps, was not so conscious of the trans-mutations the story of the Holy Grail had gone through as he would have been if he had fallen heir to the findings of more modern Arthurian scholarship. From one point of view it simplified matters for him, but it caused him to miss altogether what is now considered the finer and more human version of Wolfram von Aeschenbach. The poet laureate, following Malory's version in his "Holy Grail," [1] depicts the Grail in its most unsubstantial form, a cup which appears and disappears. In Malory, it provides all manner of meats and drinks, but Tennyson does not stress its material aspect. Often, however, in his poem, it is but a shining light, the sight of which causes a strange spiritual ecstasy but does not send the favoured recipient forth to conquer evil. We are certainly told that Galahad, when he sat in the perilous seat, " lost himself to find himself," but apart from this risk, he does not seem to do much for others. His sister, who gives her blood and dies to save another, seems to partake more of the spirit of sacrifice and holiness.

Apart from the difficulty inherent in the subject-matter, there seems to have been a conflict in Tennyson's own mind, which can be traced in the poem and spoils its unity. On the one hand, the story and spiritual ideals of the Holy Grail greatly attracted him. He had to some degree the mystical temperament and was subject to those " fallings away of sense " and " vanishings " which Wordsworth as a fellow-

[1] One of the *Idylls of the King*, published 1870.

poet and mystic shared with him. In Tennyson's *Life*, by his son, we are told that the story of the Holy Grail expressed the poet's own spiritual ideals. In a conversation to his son he is reported to have said, " ' The Holy Grail ' is one of the most imaginative of my poems. I have expressed there my strong feeling as to the Reality of the Unseen. The end, when the king speaks of his work and of his visions, is intended to be the summing-up of all in the highest note by the highest of human men." "These three lines in Arthur's speech are the central lines of the *Idylls*," the poet continued :

> " In moments when he feels he cannot die,
> And knows himself no vision to himself
> Nor the High God a vision." [1]

On the other hand, perhaps because the temper of the Victorian age was, in the main, practical and limited, or perhaps because there was an inherent tendency to this failing in the poet's own temperament, Tennyson realised in full the danger of emptying experience in order to purify it, and of other-worldliness. So the poet of the Grail laid stress in his poem on the fact he found in Malory, that the Quest of the Holy Grail led the knights to forsake Arthur. Arthur, to Tennyson, even more than to Malory, was a man of high moral perfection and had set out to perform a noble work in the world. He and his knights were to rescue the land from savagery and heathendom. At one time, Tennyson seems to take his stand beside this perfect kingly figure and to agree with him that the appearance of the Grail was " a sign to maim the order which I [Arthur] made." Those who pursue it follow false ideals and false fires. They are haunted with the sense of illusion and everything falls to dust in their hands. Tennyson can give his readers this feeling of illusion, for he uses every device of his poetic skill to produce it :

> " But even while I drank the brook, and ate
> The goodly apples, all these things at once
> Fell into dust, and I was left alone
> And thirsting, in a land of sand and thorns." [2]

---

[1] *Tennyson. Memoir by his Son*, 1899, p. 492.
[2] " The Holy Grail," from the *Idylls of the King*, Tennyson's Poems, " Globe " Edition, 1889, p. 425.

These two conflicting judgments are met with in the poem.
For the Holy Grail is connected with Christ's Passion, and, as
such, was to Tennyson the symbol of a high spiritual ideal.
Lancelot is punished for his sin against Arthur in not being
permitted to see the Holy Grail, though he views it from afar.
But if it is a false fire and illusion, where is the deprivation ?
Another implication which Tennyson makes that the Grail
vision is only for such a pure and unworldly nature as Galahad,
but not for the other knights, is surely a very limited idea
of the spiritual kingdom :

> " Ah Galahad, Galahad," said the king, " for such
> As thou art is the vision, not for these." [1]

No, in Tennyson's scheme of the *Idylls*, the Quest of the
Holy Grail, placed where it is, at the time when Arthur's
kingdom and wars against the savage are beginning to fail,
owing to treachery and dissensions among the knights themselves, is a Quest, the following of which breaks up still more
the unity of the Round Table. Approached from such a
negative attitude, the true beauty and spirituality of the
Quest cannot be brought out. Where it is, and where we
feel the poet is in sympathy with it, it has attraction in spite
of the logical judgment that the Quest is a false one. Thus
the poem as a whole, in relation to the plan of the *Idylls*, is
not altogether a success. Of course it must always be
remembered that the inherent contradiction is in Malory
and the source he used. Tennyson, however, has striven to
make the *Idylls* more consistent, whereas Malory was quite
content to follow in the main the manuscript he was using,
though abbreviating and modifying it considerably.[2]

There are in Tennyson, of course, passages of descriptive
beauty. There is, for example, the passage describing the
appearance of the Grail, which corresponds to the classic

---

[1] Same as above, p. 423. This is not necessarily Tennyson's own
belief.

[2] For a study of this see A. Pauphilet, *Études sur la Queste del Saint
Graal*, 1921. Also E. Vinaver, *op. cit.*

one in Malory of the same event. This is Tennyson's account :

> Then on a summer night, it came to pass,
> While the great banquet lay along the hall,
> That Galahad would sit down in Merlin's chair.
>
> And all at once, as there we sat, we heard
> A cracking and a riving of the roofs,
> And rending, and a blast, and overhead
> Thunder, and in the thunder was a cry.
> And in the blast there smote along the hall
> A beam of light seven times more clear than day :
> And down the long beam stole the Holy Grail
> All over cover'd with a luminous cloud,
> And none might see who bare it, and it past.
> But every knight beheld his fellow's face
> As in a glory, and all the knights arose,
> And staring each at other like dumb men
> Stood, till I [Percivale] found a voice and sware a vow.[1]

The following quotation is from Malory, which, it will be observed, Tennyson has here followed very closely. It is characteristic that the poet omits the mention of the feeding properties of the Grail :

" And so after upon that to supper, and every knight sat in his own place as they were toforehand. Then anon they heard cracking and crying of thunder, that them thought the place should all to drive. In the midst of this blast entered a sunbeam more clearer by seven times that ever they saw day, and all they were alighted of the grace of the Holy Ghost. Then began every knight to behold other, and either saw other, by their seeming, fairer than ever they saw afore. Not for then there was no knight might speak one word a great while, and so they looked every man on other, as they had been dumb. Then there entered into the hall the Holy Greal covered with white samite, but there was none might see it, nor who bare it. And there was all the hall fulfilled with good odours, and every knight had such meats and drinks as he best loved in this world. And when

---

[1] Tennyson, " Globe " Edition, 1899, p. 421.

the Holy Greal had been borne through the hall, then the Holy Vessel departed suddenly, that they wist not where it became." [1]

In Tennyson's poem, sympathy is awakened for Lancelot, as the poet describes how he strove to tear his unlawful love for Queen Guinevere out of his heart, in order to gain the spiritual prize. He tells us how his madness came upon him and "whipt him into waste fields far away" and how he fled along a bleak shore. He entered a boat and was driven along the strand until the boat grated on the shingle. Before him he saw the enchanted towers of Carbonek. Here he breasted two lions and passed into the empty sounding hall. All he saw was the rounded moon shining through the oriel window and all he heard, a voice clear as a lark, singing in a tower. He climbed up a thousand painful steps and heard a choir singing

> "Glory, joy and honour to our Lord,
> And for the Holy vessel of the Grail." [2]

Overcome by his madness, he tried to burst in, but all in vain. He caught but a glimpse of the Holy Thing veiled and covered, ere he swooned away. The Quest and its accomplishment was not for him.

Tennyson makes Gawain altogether light and frivolous and incapable of spiritual vision :

> "I will be deafer than the blue-eyed cat,
> And thrice as blind as any noonday owl
> To holy virgins in their ecstasies." [3]

This is a later conception of Gawain. In Malory, Gawain is one of the first to make a vow to "labour in the Quest of the Sangreal," and though he loses patience when he does not achieve it, he is not a mocker. Dr Weston maintains that he was the original hero of the Quest and attained it.

R. S. Hawker and Thomas Westwood,[4] contemporaries

---

[1] From " Everyman " Edition of Malory, ii. 171.

[2] Tennyson, " Globe " Edition, p. 432.

[3] Tennyson's *Poetical Works*, " Globe " Edition, 1899, p. 432.

[4] Though Westwood is classed as an imitator of Tennyson, his *Quest of the Sancgreall* was published in 1868, whereas Tennyson's was not published in the *Idylls* till 1869, though planned some years before.

of Tennyson, show that the subject of the Grail was occupying poets' minds at this time.

Robert Stephen Hawker, born near Plymouth (1803) and afterwards vicar of Morwenstowe in Cornwall, shows himself in his verse to be a true lover of romantic legend. His poem, " The Quest of the Sangraal," partakes of the nature of the rugged sea-bound cliffs of his Cornish parish. For although the stanzas of varying length are written in the usual metre of blank-verse (iambic pentameter), yet the rough and vigorous effect produced on the ear and mind differs from the smooth melodious cadences of Tennyson. Such verses [1] as the following ring out like a war trumpet with challenging effect and the verse pattern is varied skilfully :

> Now feast and festival in Arthur's hall :
> Hark, stern Dundagel softens into song !
> They meet for solemn severance, knight and king,
> Where gate and bulwark darken o'er the sea,
> Strong men for meat, and warriors at the wine,
> They wreak the wrath of hunger on the beeves,
> They rend rich morsels from the savoury deer,
> And quench the flagon like Brun-guillie dew !
> Hear ! how the minstrels prophesy in sound,
> Shout the King's Waes-hael, Drink-hael the Queen !
>
> Then said Sir Kay, he of the arrowy tongue,
> " Joseph and Pharaoh ! how they build their bones
> Happier the boar were quick than dead to-day."

Hawker, as country vicar of Welcombe and Morwenstowe, entered into the life of the fishing village, doing heroic rescue work. As he went about his duties, he showed a lively interest in legends and tales, many of which are published in his works. In connection with the Arthurian legend, Tintagel in Cornwall has literary associations with the story of Arthur's being cast up a naked babe on the shore, and with King Mark in the Tristan legend. It was, however, the story of the Grail which attracted Hawker after his wife's death, and into his poem he weaves Cornish names and

---

[1] In *Poetical Works*, 1879, with Introductory Sketch of Life.

descriptions of Nature penned amidst the sublimities of tor and rocky precipices. His short poetical summary of the Grail's early connections with Joseph of Arimathea shows knowledge of the mediæval "Histories." He speaks of Perceval, "a chosen knight, the ninth from Joseph in the line of blood."

In his treatment Hawker shows originality. A skilful symbolic use is made of the fact he introduces, that the knights are sent in their Quest, north, south, east, west. Merlin casts lots, in the form of silver arrows, to determine in what direction each knight is to go. To Sir Lancelot falls the far north, the abode of fiends and demons, cloud and storm ; to Sir Perceval the gentle perfumed south ; to Tristan, appropriately the west, the land of the sea and setting sun ; to Sir Galahad is apportioned the Orient, the east, " for his chosen hand unbars the gate of day."

In Merlin's and Arthur's prophetic vision of the accomplishment of the Quest, the Grail does not appear, as in Malory, to the knights as they sit round the Council table, but in a majestic vision in the sky. A youthful rider in the semblance of Sir Galahad appears holding a vase on high, " one molten gem like massive ruby or the chrysolite," the light gushes from it in flakes falling on the hills from " grey Morwenna's stone to Michael's tor."

> Then saw they that the mighty Quest was won :
> The Sangraal swooned along the golden air ;
> The sea breathed balsam, like Gennesaret :
> The streams were touched with supernatural light :
> And fonts of Saxon rock, stood, full of God,
> Altars arose, each like a kingly throne,
> Where the royal chalice, with its lineal blood,
> The glory of the Presence, ruled and reigned.

This poem of Hawker's on the Grail-Quest is unfortunately unfinished, and was to have included four chants in all, only one of which was completed and the opening lines of the second.

Though he does not possess Milton's power of sustained sublimity and sonorous and measured phraseology, he shows evidences of grandeur of conception and architectonic skill which might have been fulfilled in the completed poem. Like Milton he used for poetic purposes the notion of wide spaces, the contrast of light and darkness and a definite conception of a cosmic system which he takes the trouble to define in his own footnote. There is occasionally a kind of Apocalyptic splendour in his images but his power of expression is not equal to his conceptions. Although often defective in rhythm and music, abrupt in transition from one image to another and unpolished in phraseology, Hawker does not irritate by being imitative in conception or trite in phrase. The general impression left on the mind by this unfinished poem is that of arresting but unequal power.

Thomas Westwood published *The Quest of the Sancgreall* in 1868. He shows the influence of Tennyson both in theme and style. He is very much of a copyist, and like many copyists, he emphasises the weakness of his model rather than his strength. In this poem of five parts, after the appearance of the Grail, the knights set out on the usual vague quests, armed with magic talismans, riding through haunted lands and fighting with ghostly combatants. Lancelot and his son Sir Galahad are both carnally tempted by fair sinuous maidens. Neither of the temptations is interesting or convincing. The war-hardened and emotionally experienced Lancelot would never have fallen a prey to such a crude form of sensuality. Galahad is so guarded by the heavenly powers in his rôle of chosen knight, that he does not even get a chance to sin, but is rescued by holy visions !

The poet invents two incidents, but they follow the already well-trodden path and the miraculous is constantly appearing to the detriment of the interest of the adventures. When it is a foregone conclusion who is going to win, much of the interest of a combat is lost.

The last section contains some good, if imitative, descriptive passages, and gives the circumstances and setting of the Grail in more detail than Tennyson. It identifies it altogether with the Eucharist. When the knights are sitting in assembly at Carbonek its appearance is thus described :

Two ministering angels bear

> Wax tapers, and a spotless linen cloth,
> That, reverent, o'er the holy cup they laid.
> The bishop from his place beside the board,
> Made semblance, as to consecrate the mass,
> With lifted hands, and moving lips that prayed ;
> And holding up a wafer, from the midst
> There came a shape, in image of a child,
> Red-visaged, bright as fire, that smote itself
> Into the bread, whereat the knights were 'ware
> The bread was fashioned of a fleshly man.

The vision of the Grail causes Galahad, as Malory also relates, to long to leave the world. So he and the questing knights are borne away in a ship wafted by no earthly wind. He becomes king in Sarras and the Grail heals many sick and renews faith. But finally Galahad and the Grail are translated to heaven :

> Then suddenly he fell asleep in Christ,
> And a great multitude of angels bore
> His soul to heaven. And out of heaven there came
> The semblance of a Hand, that reaching down,
> Caught up the Grail, and no man saw it more.

This last passage and others are very reminiscent in phraseology of Tennyson, copying his more languorous style and not his stronger rhythms or the deeper movements of his stanzas.

The fact is mentioned by Westwood that the Grail fed and healed the multitude. Otherwise, the Quest in Malory and his followers seems often to be a mere selfish one, and the Grail, when found, a private possession, even though a spiritual one.

James Russell Lowell (1819-1891), the American poet, writes a short poem to protest against this interpretation. His poem, " The Vision of Sir Launfal," is a narrative poem which ranks as pleasant verse with a high moral, rather than poetry in the stricter sense of the word.

The lesson conveyed is the same as in Van Dyke's beautiful prose story, *The Third Wise Man*, and also as that in Wolfram's

Parzival, by whom the American poet was probably influenced. The young knight, " Sir Launfal " (the name has been adapted from Marie of France's " Sir Lanval "), falls asleep and dreams. In his dream he sees himself setting out to find the Grail, but in his proud attitude to the leper at his gates, he shows how little fitted he is for that high quest. After much experience of the world and its sorrows and poverty, he again meets the leper. This time, as he himself is destitute, he gives him all he possesses, water from the stream in a wooden bowl and a mouldy crust of bread. But on this occasion he gives it with true sympathy—" the heart within him was ashes and dust." Thereupon the beggar becomes transfigured into the image of Christ, and in a voice " calmer than silence " he says :

> " Lo, it is I, be not afraid !
> In many climes, without avail,
> Thou hast spent thy life for the Holy Grail ;
> Behold it is here,—this cup which thou
> Didst fill at the streamlet for Me but now ;
> This crust is My body broken for thee,
> This water His blood that died on the tree ;
> The Holy Supper is kept, indeed,
> In whatso we share with another's need ;
> Not what we give, but what we share,
> For the gift without the giver is bare ;
> Who gives himself with his alms feeds three,
> Himself, his hungering neighbour and Me." [1]

The knight awakes and now realises that the Holy Grail can be found in his own castle. He therefore spends his life in succouring the poor and needy at his own gates.

The researches which scholars, such as Dr Weston, have lately made on the origins of the Holy Grail [2] correspond with many of the findings of modern psychology. Influenced by this factor, there have been two recent literary experiments, one in verse and the other in prose. One of these is T. S. Eliot's " Waste Land," and the other is T. Powys' *Glastonbury Legend*.[3]

---

[1] Lowell, *Works*, " The Vision of Sir Launfal."
[2] Especially in *From Ritual to Romance*, 1920.   [3] Published 1933.

The subject of this recent poem " The Waste Land " [1] is perhaps characteristic of a certain school of post-War poets. It is not the healing of the Grail king and the victory of the Grail seeker which interests this poet ; it is the part of the legend which describes the Grail hero, riding through a sterile land with a curse upon it, full of wailing women, mourning for its fruitlessness. As the author, T. S. Eliot, tells us in his own notes, the main allusions are taken from Dr Weston's *From Ritual to Romance*, which has inspired the poem.

The incident is treated as symbolic of the present period of disillusionment after the War—a period which seems to suffer from fatigue-neurosis. It may be compared to the world-weariness Macbeth felt, after he had committed his murder, and had worn out his emotions. Thus he had come to the end of desire :

> " To-morrow and to-morrow, and to-morrow,
> Creeps in this petty pace from day to day,
> To the last syllable of recorded time :
> And all our yesterdays have lighted fools
> The way to dusty death. Out, out, brief candle.
> Life's but a walking shadow, a poor player
> That struts and frets his hour upon the stage
> And then is heard no more : it is a tale
> Told by an idiot, full of sound and fury,
> Signifying nothing." [2]

Mr T. S. Eliot, in a very different manner, attempts to represent the weary and disillusioned world-consciousness of this post-war period. He uses a subjective method. He gives us a cross-section of his own mind, in this mood of disillusionment, and tries to represent the separate layers of consciousness and what is below consciousness, by disconnected phrases. It is the method of free association, not of logical thought. Unfortunately the difficulty of the poem is increased by the fact that the associations are for the most part merely personal ones and require the author's own explanations,

---

[1] From T. S. Eliot, *Poems*, 1909-1925, " The Waste Land," new edition, 1932.

[2] Shakespeare's *Macbeth*, Act v, Scene 5.

given at the end of his volume, to elucidate them. Take, for example, the allusion to the " hooded figure who walks always beside you." [1] The natural inference in the connection would be that the unknown figure is the Christ. But this deduction is corrected by the note and the poet remarks in this connection that he refers to a party of explorers, of which he has read, who, " at the extremity of their strength had the constant delusion that there was *one more member* than could actually be counted." The change is made by using a personal association instead of one which has a common basis. If this method is carried to extreme, the poets of this modern school will find themselves writing for themselves alone.

What Mr Eliot is trying to do can be done much more effectively in another more fluid medium, namely in music. In Wagner, for example, the musician induces a certain mood and yet can blend with it other emotions at another level of consciousness. Thus in Lohengrin, fear begins to enter into and finally ousts the " Love-motive." The associations are formed in the first place by certain phrases of music being associated with certain compelling emotions called up by dramatic incidents in the opera. In this case, therefore, there is a logical link in the chief actions of the drama. In Mr Eliot's work there is no such link.

The best way to approach the poem before us, I think, is to get hold of the recurring themes, round which the associations are centred, and then to give full play to the associative power of the phrases and words, helping ourselves as far as possible by the author's own guiding clues in his own commentary.

The main subject is, then, the desert land. To it, Spring brings no refreshing rain, nor do even thunder-storms bring any moisture :

> Here is no water but only rock,
> Rock and no water and the sandy road,
> The road winding above among the mountains
> Which are mountains of rock without water.[2]

---

[1] T. S. Eliot, *op. cit.*, p. 105.   [2] *Ibid.*, p. 103.

Again, with reminiscences of Ezekiel (ii, verse 1) :

> What are the roots that clutch, what branches grow
> Out of the stony rubbish ?   Son of man,
> You cannot say, or guess, for you know only
> A heap of broken images, where the sun beats,
> And the dead tree gives no shelter, the cricket no relief
> And the dry stone no sound of water.[1]

And in the mental sphere life is without ideals and romance. Thus the springs of life and imagination dry up and there are only (as the same poet expresses it in " Gerontius ") " thoughts of a dry brain in a dry season."   When the hope of finding the Grail or of freeing the land and the king from his curse disappears, life becomes monotonous and banal. Mr Eliot expresses this by giving disjointed sentences from the most trifling and even sordid conversations of city dwellers :

> " What shall we do to-morrow ?
> What shall we ever do ?
>   The hot water at ten.
> And if it rains, a closed car at four.
> And we shall play a game of chess,
> Pressing lidless eyes and waiting for a knock upon the door." [2]

The last lines represent the horror that monotony breeds and that waits to seize upon the unhappy modern who has exhausted all his sensations.

Another way of expressing the banality of modern existence and also of satirising romance, is to place a romantic line and a prosaic one together, to produce an effect of extreme bathos :

> The river's tent is broken : the last fingers of leaf
> Clutch and sink into the wet bank.   The wind
> Crosses the brown land, unheard.   The nymphs are departed.
> Sweet Thames, run softly, till I end my song.
> The river bears no empty bottles, sandwich papers,
> Silk handkerchiefs, cardboard boxes, cigarette ends
> Or other testimony of summer nights.   The nymphs are
>   departed

---

[1] In T. S. Eliot, *op. cit.*, p. 84.   [2] *Ibid.*, p. 94.

And their friends, the loitering heirs of city directors ;
Departed, have left no addresses.
By the waters of Leman I sat down and wept . . .
Sweet Thames, run softly till I end my song.[1]

and so on.

It will be remembered in Wolfram von Aeschenbach's story, that when Parzival failed to ask the question which was to release the curse of the Grail king, he was courteously conducted to his chamber for the night. In the morning he found that all the inhabitants of the castle had disappeared and only his horse, tethered, was left in the empty courtyard. As he rode across the bridge, he seemed to pass from the country of the dead and so probably it was, for many of these bridges in early Celtic story were bridges to another world.[2]

So the modern hero in this poem, to whom the Waste Land seems a dwelling-place rather than a temporary adventure, only meets dead people, as he crosses London Bridge :

Unreal City,
Under the brown fog of a winter dawn,
A crowd flowed over London Bridge, so many,
I had not thought death had undone so many,
Sighs, short and infrequent, were exhaled.
And each man fixed his eyes before his feet.
Flowed up the hill and down King William Street,
To where Saint Mary Woolnoth kept the hours
With a dead sound on the final stroke of nine.[3]

Then the verses end in what sounds like a frenzy of delirium.

This poem is interesting as showing that the Grail legend, as a subject, has attraction for this very modern school. Taken as satire rather than as lyric the attempt may have some literary value. But it is an experiment in a medium which is tentative and not familiar to the reader, or not used in a customary manner, so that at the first reading at least, it

[1] In T. S. Eliot, *op. cit.*, p. 94.
[2] Freud's theory is that the bridge, in the subconscious mind, represents the gate of birth ; see *New Introductory Lectures*, 1933, p. 37.
[3] In T. S. Eliot, *op. cit.*, p. 86.

fails of direct aesthetic effect. It thus appears to be a psychological problem rather than a poem.

Another work in prose on the subject of the Grail has also been influenced by recent psychology and academic research on origins.

J. C. Powys, in his *Glastonbury Legend*, writes a prose tale round Glastonbury, attempting to pierce deeper into the Grail myth, and analyse the mystic influences the author evidently believes are still emanating from that place, which is so full of traditions of Joseph of Arimathea and the Grail.

The *milieu* of this very long and complicated story is placed in Glastonbury. This place has many associations with the Arthurian story, most of them purely legendary, although claims have been made that these had a foundation in historic facts.

One of the chief and earliest authorities on the Benedictine Abbey of St Mary and its church comes from William of Malmesbury. In his first version of the *Gesta Regum* in 1125 he considers the original church was built in the eighth century by Ina of Wessex. In a later treatise, *De Antiquitate Glastoniensis Ecclesiæ*, dedicated to Henry of Blois, he traces the foundation further back and accepts as genuine a donation of land, " Ineswitrin," by the king of Dumnonia (Devon) in 601, associating the church with St Gildas, St Patrick and St Bridget.

There is nothing in this historical narrative concerning Arthur. Scholars [1] consider that the matter describing the burial place of Arthur and Guinevere, is later interpolated matter and may be contemporary with two other chroniclers, Ralph of Coggeshall and Giraldus Cambrensis. The passage of the pseudo-William of Malmesbury runs thus :—

" I pass over Arthur, the famous king of the Britons, entombed with his wife in the graveyard of the monks between two pyramids and over many other British princes. This Arthur, in the year of the incarnation, 542, was mortally

---

[1] See W. W. Newell, *The Antiquity of Glastonbury*, Public Modern Language Association, America, 1903, p. 478. On this subject see also J. Armitage Robinson, *Two Glastonbury Legends*, 1926 ; F. Lot, " Glastonbury and Avalon " (*Romania* xxvii. 528, 1903).

wounded by Mordred near the river Camba in Cornwall, and thence was borne to the island of Avallon for the healing of his wounds, and died there in the summer about Pentecost being nearly a hundred years old, or thereabouts." [1] The identification of " Iniswitrin " with Avalon is also considered a later interpretation.

Giraldus Cambrensis in his *De Principis Instructione*, of which the first book was probably composed between 1193-99, tells of the actual finding of the coffin with the inscription " Hic jacet sepultus inclitus rex Arthurus cum Wenneveria uxore sua secunda in insula Avallonia." The mention of Guinevere as a second wife is curious. Ralph Coggeshall in the *Chronicon Anglicanum* (1187-1224) mentions the same discovery but with less detail. He adds that Glastonbury was surrounded by marshes and was called the Island of Avallon, which meant the Isle of Apples. Merlin in Welsh poems is connected with apples [2] and the wounded King Arthur in the *Vita Merlini* is borne to the Fortunate Isle, which is also the Isle of Apples, to be healed by Morgan and her eight sisters. In the Irish *Imrama* and travel tales, the apple is a characteristic fruit of the other world.

As regards the story of the finding of Arthur's tomb (placed about 1190), which is an example of deliberate fabrication of legend, Dr Chambers [3] suggests that the motive for pressing the claim of possessing the tomb of Arthur was due to the desire to attract pilgrims to Glastonbury for money which was then urgently required. It is at least a tribute to the fame of Arthur.

For the student of legend the most interesting stories which were fathered from this bastard script centre around Joseph of Arimathea. [4] In the genuine document of the *De Antiquitate* Joseph is not mentioned. William of Malmesbury gives to the church an apostolic origin and suggests that the apostle in question may have been Philip. In the pseudo-preface of the *De Antiquitate*, Joseph of Arimathea is connected with Philip the apostle, the head of the band of twelve missionaries

---

[1] For translation, see E. K. Chambers, *Arthur of Britain*, p. 117.
[2] For paraphrase of such a poem see above, pp. 113-114.
[3] *Arthur of Britain*, p. 119.
[4] This information is taken from J. Armitage Robinson, *op. cit.*

who set out to evangelise Britain in the west, arriving in
63 A.D. It is not clear whether this is meant to imply that
Joseph accompanied them.

A marginal note to the final edition of the *De Antiquitate*
tells us that Joseph was accompanied by his son Josephe
and many others and that he (Joseph) died in the island.
The Grail legend is mentioned as the source of this information.

The *De Antiquitate*, with its interpolations and glosses, was
evidently consulted by John of Glastonbury when, at the
end of the fourteenth century, he gathered together in his
Chronicle [1] the various legends, oral and written. He had
beside him also the simplest form of St Joseph's early story
from the Gospel of Nicodemus (*Gesta Pilati*). He refers to
it as a " treatise concerning Joseph of Arimathea, drawn
from a certain book, which the Emperor Theodosius found at
Jerusalem in Pilate's Judgement Hall." John of Glastonbury
also probably made use of the charter of St Patrick (1120)
which connects Joseph with Philip, the same link as in the
pseudo-preface of the *De Antiquitate*. This same John also
mentions the " book which is called the Holy Grail." From
this he obtained the narrative of Joseph's voyage to Britain
on the miraculous shirt of his son Josephe, his imprisonment
by the king of North Wales and the release of King Mordrains.
Then is added the story of the gift of the island of Yniswitrin,
bringing us back again to the pseudo-introduction of the
De Antiquitate. The incidents of the building of the chapel
and Joseph's death and burial in Glastonbury localise the
doings of the saint. Finally, the writer concludes, the place
was to become deserted and waste until the Blessed Virgin
should cause her oratory to be brought to the memory of
the faithful. A noteworthy fact is that in this story of Joseph
no mention is made of the Grail itself. The incident, drawn
from the *Vindicta Salvatoris*, during which he was miraculously
sustained by the Grail, is rejected. This seems to uphold
the theory that the Grail cult never received ecclesiastical
sanction, though it developed along lines parallel with the
Christian Eucharist and Mass, especially in its later evolution.
The Glastonbury variation substitutes for the incident of

---

[1] *Chronica, etc.*, published by Hearne in 1726.

the imprisonment the primitive legend found in the Gospel of Nicodemus, which brings Joseph conveniently to Glastonbury in 63 A.D. That tradition is also favoured in which St Joseph is related to have brought with him two silver cruets filled with the blood and sweat of the Lord. These cruets, the tale runs, were buried with him. They appear on the coat of arms in the south window of the chancel of the parish church of St John's. These cruets are represented in other places in Glastonbury,[1] including the east window of Langport Church, where there is a figure of Joseph of Arimathea carrying these vessels on a white cloth in his right hand. Both these representations do not probably go back earlier than the fifteenth century and may belong to the sixteenth.

Other measures were taken in these centuries to impress through the eye the pilgrims who visited Glastonbury. Archbishop Ussher [2] quotes from the " Magna Tabula " of Glastonbury, which was a kind of folding frame with six interior wooden leaves. The writing on these has been evidently copied from John of Glastonbury's book, with the exception of the closing section which is new and headed " of the Chapel of Saints Michael and Joseph and all saints who rest in the cemetery." Also a column north of the Lady Chapel bore an inscription which related, among other matters, the coming of Joseph of Arimathea. The base of this column, about seven feet in diameter, uncovered in 1921, was erected to indicate the exact site of the earliest church.[3]

Other legends circulated round the name of Joseph of Arimathea. In 1502 a poem was written under the title " The Lyfe of Joseph of Arimathea." [4] Here are mentioned the cruets in the heraldic shield and the building of the Lady Chapel.[5] Miraculous cures wrought by the saint are

---

[1] For list, see Armitage Robinson, *op. cit.*, p. 65, Appendix.

[2] In *Britannicarum Ecclesiarum Antiquitates* (1639).

[3] Not really known.

[4] Printed by Pynson in 1520 and reprinted by Skeat in the Early Eng. Text. Soc., 44 (1871), pp. 37-52.

[5] Part of the primitive legend of Joseph, taken from the *Transitus Mariae*, relates his attendance on the Virgin and his presence at her Assumption. See Armitage Robinson, p. 33 ; also Tishendorf, *Apocalyptes Apocryphae*, pp. 113 ff.

recorded at length. Here also is the first mention of the "Holy Thorn."

> Thre hawthornes also, that groweth in Werall,
> Do burge and bere green leaves at Christmas
> As freshe as other in May.

There is a later version of this " Holy Thorn " legend which is said to have sprung from Joseph's staff when he rested with his company on Wery-all-Hill in Glastonbury. Another example of a flowering staff will be remembered in Tannhäuser. In both these, this burgeoning is symbolic of spiritual rebirth.

This short survey of the traditions and history of Glastonbury is sufficient to show that in his *Glastonbury Legend* J. C. Powys has good material for his novel. Unfortunately, the combination of the realistic and the romantic is not a satisfactory one. There is in the descriptions a vague mysticism, in which there blend together pagan influences of the sun, emanations from strange unearthly fish and supernatural visions of the Grail. The whole story centres in a pageant play of the Grail, engineered by the mayor of Glastonbury. The sensations of each character and their conscious and subconscious reactions to these supernatural influences are analysed at great length and the general effect is what may be termed a mystic sensuality. But in a novel, a clever Freudian analysis of motive does not necessarily mean skilful character-drawing. Also, in the art of literature, suggestion of the supernatural is more potent than detailed description or lengthy analysis. This is why Coleridge's *Ancient Mariner* affects the imagination so powerfully that, once read, it can never be forgotten.

> " The many men so beautiful !
> And they all dead did lie ;
> And a thousand thousand slimy things
> Lived on ; and so did I.

> " I looked upon the rotting sea,
> And drew my eyes away,
> I looked upon the rotting deck,
> And there the dead men lay.

" I looked to heaven, and tried to pray,
But, or ever a prayer had gusht,
A wicked whisper came and made
My heart as dry as dust."

Here the images are clear in the foreground and yet the background stretches away into the unknown and the kingdom of the supernatural. But the descriptions of Powys, on the contrary, though they show imaginative power, deal in " huge cloudy symbols " which confuse the mind. The senses are also overpowered by the torrent of words, raising one obscure image after another.

Yet, if his book had aimed at being a romance rather than a realistic novel, his powers might have had more scope. It is almost impossible to give any idea of his method and style by a short quotation. The experience of Sam Dekker when he beholds the Grail may be chosen as typical.

" All these places lay behind him [1] as he sat in that barge on the Brue, for his face was turned directly towards the three eminences of the Isle of Glastonbury, Wirral Hill, Chalice Hill, and the Tor. Thus rested Sam Dekker ; and then—without a second's warning—the earth and the water and the darkness *cracked*. . . . Whence it came, whether it came of its own volition and whether it was that same transformation of matter which had been affecting him so of late, carried one degree further, Sam never knew ; but he knew what was happening to him and he knew it without the least doubt or question.

" What he saw was at first accompanied by a crashing pain. That was the word Sam himself thought of to express it—the word *crashing*. But as the vision clarified before him and grew distinct, this pain died away. But it was dazzling, hurting, blinding, at first, and it was associated in his mind with the sense of a sharp, long-shaped thing piercing his guts. His sensation was indeed strangely definite. The pain was so overwhelming that it was as if the whole of Sam's consciousness became the hidden darkness of his inmost organism ; and when this darkness was split, and the whole atmosphere split, and the earth and the air split, what he felt to be a gigantic spear was struck into his bowels and struck *from below*.

" He had ceased to be a man sitting on a coal sack at the stern

---

[1] List mentioned in preceding paragraph of novel.

of a barge. He had become a bleeding mass of darkness. His consciousness was a dark surface of water ; and up through this water, tearing it, rending it, dividing it, turning it into blood, shivered this crashing stroke, this stroke that was delivered from abysses of the earth, far deeper than the bottom of the Brue.

" Whatever this ' spear ' was that struck him, to his whole animal nature quivering under it, it was as much the shock of something totally unknown, something new to human experience, outrageous in its strangeness, that tore so at his vitals, as the crashing pain that it brought with it.

" But when the vision appeared, and it came sailing into the midst of this bleeding darkness that was Sam's consciousness, healing everything, changing everything, each detail of what he saw he saw with a clearness that branded it forever upon his brain. He saw a globular chalice that had two circular handles. The substance it was made of was clearer than crystal ; and within it there was dark water streaked with blood, and within the water was a shining fish.

" Sam's first thought was ' This is the Grail ! This is the Grail ! It has come back to Glastonbury ! ' His second thought was ' I must tell Father and Nell about this.' His third thought was more realistic ; and it was so congruous with his deepest being that the mere fact that he had had it—when he remembered the whole thing—put the seal of authenticity upon his vision. He thought in his heart : ' What is that fish ? It is a Tench. Surely it is a Tench ! ' . . . Is it a Tench ? Is there a fish of healing, one chance against all chances, at the bottom of the world-tank ? Is it a Tench ? . . . Is cruelty always triumphant, or is there a hope beyond hope, a Something somewhere hid perhaps in the twisted heart of the cruel First Cause itself and able to break in from outside ? and smash to atoms this torturing chain of Cause and Effect ?

" The crystal goblet with the two curved handles was quite close to him now. He could see the darkness in the throat of the shining fish, balanced motionless in its centre, but because of its position he could not see the Creature's eyes.

" *Is it a Tench* ? And then all at once it began to fade away. . . . He felt sure afterwards that it was not his leaping to his feet or his raising his voice as he did, that made it vanish and he stood there in crushed humility like a man who says to himself : ' It cannot be I who have seen this ! it is a mistake ; it was surely meant for another ! ' " [1]

---

[1] J. Cowper Powys, *A Glastonbury Romance*, 1933.

The comparison of Powys' treatment of the supernatural, and that of Malory describing the appearing of the Grail, is a study in the use of symbols. Powys, in the passage just quoted above, brings in most of the mythical symbols connected with the Grail—the sword, the cup (here called a goblet), the fish—and even tries to combine the two latter in one image. But, though he protests that his hero Sam Dekker has never read any Grail legends, the reader feels that the author, at any rate, is well versed in them ! But it seems academic knowledge, acquired by reading treatises on the Grail rather than entering profoundly into the meaning and significance of the symbols.

This modern author has, in truth, a very difficult task, compared to that which the author of the *Queste* had. Pauphilet [1] identifies the Grail cult with the Cistercians. It is certainly true that the religious, mystical and ascetic traditions of these monks, especially in their conception of the Mass and their doctrine of Transubstantiation, had many points in common with the Grail cult, at least in its later developments. Thus in his treatment of the supernatural and in the symbolism used, the author of the *Queste* was dealing with the familiar, though something that transcended the ordinary. And the most telling spiritual symbols are often the most familiar ones, for the mind in this case has not to grapple with strange or unknown material. Thus it is in a passive state, open to suggestive influences, which are more potent emotionally than the arguments of the intellect. It is the province of the artist, especially when he is dealing with the supernatural as a subject, to create this suggestive state of mind, and having created it, to introduce subtly those images or symbols with the greatest associative value for his special purpose. Unfortunately, the modern artist, having, in this case, no such religious tradition behind him as the mediæval artist had, has often to create his own symbols. If they are too complex or erudite, as those of T. S. Eliot or Powys are apt to be, the reader is left either to confusion of mind or to a series of footnotes. [2]

[1] Pauphilet (A.), *Études sur la Queste del Saint Graal*, p. 132.
[2] As in T. S. Eliot's *Waste Land*.

In reviewing these modern poems and prose works, it has to be confessed that there is in the nineteenth and twentieth centuries no great Grail poem of an epic or philosophic nature. One reason for this omission may be the fact that Malory chose for his adaptation such a monastic and ascetic version. If he had chosen a rendering with the broad humanism of the *Parzival* of Wolfram von Aeschenbach, poets might have found the subject suitable for a long poem with a complex structure. There is splendid material for a drama, bringing in the evolution of Parzival's character, or for an epic, treating Parzival as a great representative of the race.

CHAPTER XI

BALIN AND BALAN

THE conception of the Grail with its deep symbolism appears to belong especially to the Middle Ages. Though it may have sprung originally from a Nature and esoteric cult not approved of by the Christian Church, yet it borrowed, in the course of its development, familiar symbols belonging to the Eucharist and Mass. It thus appealed in its literary form of the *Queste* to those trained to regard common things such as food and drink in a sacramental light, so that to them there was nothing abrupt in the transition from a food-producing talisman to the symbol of Christ's sacrifice, who gave His body for bread to the people.

The Grail-concept in the Middle Ages was a plant which had sent deep roots into the soil and was nourished from a whole system of religious beliefs and culture. When it is transplanted into the thinner and less nourishing soil of the more sceptical modern age, it produces a much less rich bloom. It becomes the symbol of the ideal, divorced from the religious system which engendered it. As such, it appeals to a wider public, but loses in concrete representation. Attenuated thus, it may suitably provide the subject for a lyric, such as John Masefield's fine poem on " Sir Bors." Here the Quest of the Grail has become almost a personal aspiration and is individually ascetic, not communally so.

The story of Balin and Balan may be taken at this point, although Balin is not primarily one of the Grail heroes. Indeed his connection with the Grail only brings misfortune upon him. Malory relates that King Pellam turned on Balin and smote him in revenge for the slaying of the invisible knight Garlon. Balin, fleeing for his life and swordless, entered unawares into the chamber of the Holy Grail and grasped the marvellous and holy spear lying on a golden

table.   With this spear he smote King Pellam through the
thighs a " dolorous stroke," which brought many years suffering
to the king and the curse of unfruitfulness to three lands.
This explanation, of course, is only one of those given for the
cause of the land's barrenness.   The story is connected with
the *Parzival* [1] form of the Grail story.

The tale of Balin and Balan has been treated by two English
poets, Tennyson and Swinburne, and a comparison between
these proves interesting.

Swinburne made a happy choice when he took the tale
of Balin and Balan [2] and set it to a ringing ballad metre in
The Tale of Balen.

It must have been a congenial task, because Balin is a
knight of Northumbria (Northumberland) where the poet
himself often rode in his youth on a galloping steed beside
the north-easterly sea with its cold, keen winds.   So in Balen's
last hour the poet makes him see visions of his boyhood such
as the poet had himself spent.

In Malory, Balin is put in prison by Arthur for " slaying
of a knight, the which was cousin unto King Arthur."   But
Swinburne invents a patriotic motive.   He tells us the cause
of the slaying is an insult offered to Balen's " wild North "
and the poet's native country.

Swinburne, in the actual events of Balen's career, follows
Malory very closely.   But the artistic effect is somewhat different.   In Malory, the tale is pathetic.   Balin is unfortunate ;
he is always doing right and noble things in a wrong way.
When he proves himself the foreordained knight, who can
relieve the distressed lady of her heavy sword and of her
consequent curse, he refuses, in spite of her warnings, to
return her the sword which is to lead to his undoing.   He is to
slay with it the man he loves best and die himself, at the
same time.   When, again, he slays a knight and takes a just
revenge, a lady comes and kills herself, falling on the top of
her lover's dead body.   Thus Balin is made unwittingly the
slayer of two people.   It is pathetic and, to modern minds,
somewhat humorous.   Even Balin sees the irony of it, for

[1] See Grail, Chap. IX.
[2] Swinburne names Balin " Balen."

he exclaims when he hears a horn blow, as it had been the
death of a beast, "That blast," says Balin, "is blown for me,
for I am the prize, yet am I not dead."

But in Swinburne, the story is more than pathetic; it
rises to the height of tragic doom and illustrates the theory
of blind fate. Interwoven with the sense of doom is that
of a strange beauty invoked by the poet through his descriptions
of Nature, of Spring, Summer, Autumn, Winter. These
seasons, which appear successively, are used as symbols of
Balen's story at different periods. There is first the Spring,
a Spring in Northumbria, when the " whin is frankincense
and flame " ; in it, the hero sets out in all the hope of youth,
which pays no heed to warnings. Then comes the hot
Summer, when the fierce lust of battle rages. In some fine
battle-stanzas, the poet describes the clash of arms between
the hosts of Lot and Arthur.

> Then thundered all the awakening field,
> With crash of hosts that clashed and reeled,
> Banner to banner, shield to shield,
> And spear to splintering spear-shaft steeled
>   As heart against high heart of man,
> As hope against high hope of knight
> To pluck the crest and crown of fight
> From war's clenched hand by storm's wild light,
>   For blessing given or ban.[1]

Then the poem turns to Autumn, when the vigorous breeze
that shakes lustily the decaying autumn leaf, is a harbinger
of winter and death. So Merlin

> gave his (Arthur's) soul to see [2]
> Fate, rising as a shoreward sea,
> And all the sorrow that should be
>   · Ere hope or fear thought long.[3]

Last of all comes Winter, but as Winter makes northern

---

[1] Swinburne, *Collected Poems*, Heinemann, iv., 193.
[2] The context does not seem very clear ; but the following verses
seem to indicate King Arthur, not Balen.
[3] *Op. cit.*, p. 196.

men rejoice, so, in spite of the dark wind of fate which blows round his head, Balen faces God's doom to live or die with equal joy and sorrow.

> Sorrowing for ill wrought unaware,
> Rejoicing in desire to dare
> All ill that innocence might bear
>   With changeless heart and eye.[1]

The details of the last fight, where he fights with his brother, both being disguised, follow Malory closely. Balan rises on knees and hands and crawls " by childlike, dim degrees " to his brother's side.   He looses his helm to discover his marred countenance.   Thus Balen speaks :

> " O Balan, oh my brother ! me
> Thou hast slain, and I, my brother thee !
> And now far hence, on shore and sea
> Shall all the wide world speak of us." [2]

Not only over Balen hangs the tragic issue of all his brave deeds, but in his doom we can read also a foreshadowing of the destruction of Arthur and his Round Table. Arthur's incestuous begetting of Modred (though done in ignorance) shines like a baleful light over the raging battle between Lot's forces and Arthur's.

> For, Arthur's, as they caught the light
> That sought and durst not seek his sight,
> Darkened, and all his spirit's might
> Withered within him even as night
>   Withers, when sunrise thrills the sea.
> But Mordred's lightened as with fire
> That smote his mother and his sire
> With darkling doom and deep desire
>   That bade its darkness be.[3]

The " weight of the fear that brings forth fate " hangs on all their hearts.

All through the tale, which belongs to the earlier story

[1] *Op. cit.*, p. 214.   [2] *Op. cit.*, p. 228.   [3] *Op. cit.*, p. 195.

of the Round Table, there are reminders of future events, such as the evil which was to fall on the land, because of Balin's " dolorous stroke."

These foreshadowings of doom are found in Malory, prophesied by Merlin. Swinburne emphasises them, not by moralising over them as Tennyson does, but by using similes and images from Nature, thus making his readers partake of that high beauty and awe which is the atmosphere in which true tragic feeling is engendered. Thus, without seeming to change his source much, the poet has made his poem original in the best sense, recreating it first in his own heart and mind so that the heroic ballad glows with light and fire.

Using the same source as Swinburne, Tennyson has created quite a different character in Balin.[1] Swinburne has made Balin a frank, straightforward warrior impelled by clear and simple motives. He never doubts himself, but goes open-eyed and guiltless to meet his contrary fate. But Tennyson names Balin " Balin the Savage," and makes his conflict not so much with relentless Fate as with himself.

He is torn with dark and savage moods in which he commits deeds whose consequences work him future woe. He bears the emblem of Guinevere, the crown on his shield (this is an invention of Tennyson's), but he is not civilised enough for Arthur's court. He has the outlook of the pagan. He does not seize the spear, as in Malory, in a moment of urgent necessity, but in a mood of rebellion against holy things. The final scene in Tennyson is pathetic rather than tragic. The misfortune is brought on by the wild mood of Balin. It is not, as in Malory and Swinburne, the climax of a series of deeds, justifiable in themselves, which a malign fate has brought to an evil issue.

Tennyson, in the events of Balin's story, follows Malory less closely than Swinburne. His study of character is less definite, and in his poem the figure of Balin is not so clearly outlined against its background as in Swinburne. One reason for this is that it is a tale among others in a special scheme, whereas Swinburne's is a complete unity in itself. Tennyson

[1] *Idylls of the King,* " Balin and Balan."

uses Balin's tale for a moral purpose.   Balin, he tries to show, would have had his savagery and want of religion modified and would have learnt chivalry and reverence, if there had been a purer ideal at court.   But already the poisoning miasma caused by the guilty relations of Lancelot and Guinevere has begun to spread.

CHAPTER XII

WAGNER : PARSIFAL ; LOHENGRIN ; TRISTAN

IT is difficult to overestimate the importance of Wagner in the history of Arthurian legend. This great musical artist and dramatist gave to certain of the great legends of the world their rightful place. It is true his chief mode of expression was the Art of Music, not of Literature, yet because of the universality of that medium he revived interest in the legends he chose. His versions are now the best known throughout Europe. Those with subjects taken from Arthurian legend are, in chronological order of publication, *Lohengrin* (1848), *Tristan* (1859) and *Parsifal* (1882). The *Parsifal* and *Lohengrin*, connected with the legend of the Holy Grail, and the *Tristan*, repay close study as to sources, story and interpretation.

THE "PARSIFAL" OF WAGNER, ITS SOURCES AND INTERPRETATION

The main essence of Wagner's story is taken from Wolfram von Aeschenbach's *Parzival*,[1] which also contains adventures of Gawain. This is a very long narrative poem, well worth studying along with Wagner's Opera. The changes Wagner made are those which any dramatist might make in using the material provided by a long narrative. In drama, the action must centre on one or two salient points, and the successive series of actions rise to a climax, sometimes falling again (though not in this drama).

In comparing the story of Parzival (the form of name is, in Wagner, " Parsifal ") in Wolfram and in Wagner it will be convenient to divide it into three series of episodes. First of all, there are the incidents dealing with Parzival's youth

---

[1] There are several editions, including Lachmann (E.), ed. Werke, 1833. The translation used here is from J. L. Weston, 2 vols., 1894.

and upbringing, with its resulting *naïveté*, up to the first experience of the Grail and the sick king. This series represents Parzival, the ingenuous, the " Perfect Fool."

Wolfram relates at great length how Parzival was brought up by the widowed Herzeleides far from the haunts of men and ignorant of war and chivalry. As her warrior-husband had died in battle, she, his mother, wished to keep him from all possibility of danger. But Fate and his knightly heredity were too strong for her. One day Parzival met three Arthurian knights riding through the clearing of the wood in glittering armour. With interest, the fair boy examined the armour of one of the knights and his shining sword. His ambition was fired and he resolved to be a knight at Arthur's court.

He hastened back to his mother and begged for a horse and armour to ride forth on adventure. His mother, in order to make the adventure bitter for him, so that he might return to her for comfort, gave him a fool's dress. She also gave him advice which was to influence his future career. He was ever to be fair and courteous and not to despise the teaching of a grey-haired old man if he met him. She also told him he should try and win from a maiden her ring and take a kiss from her lips. Thus the strength of his manhood would increase.

Thereupon, innocent and untried, Parzival rode forth to these adventures, resolving to follow his mother's advice literally. Fortune soon provided him with a fair lady, Jeschuté, sleeping in a tent, from whom he stole a ring and a kiss, thus arousing the wrath of her lord, who refused to believe in his innocence or rather his ignorance. He came in due time to the court of King Arthur, where he found the grey-haired sage of whom his mother had prophesied. The latter taught him knightly prowess and wisdom, but gave him advice which Parzival was to follow to his own undoing. He told him to beware of asking too many questions.

Thence follows a recital of many adventures, including the killing of the knight Ither for the sake of his armour, a rash deed of which Parzival was later to repent. In the course of his wanderings, he fell in love with and won as his wife, Kondwiremur, to whom he was faithful in thought and deed all through his adventures in far-off lands, until he was restored to her in joy and honour.

Parzival, after many journeyings, met the Fisher King, fishing by a lake and was invited by him to the Grail Castle. Here there were no tournaments, for all was in sadness owing to the illness of King Anfortas. The king himself lay on a couch in the palace beside great fires and clad in robes of sable. Parzival entered and then strange doings took place. A squire entered bearing a bleeding lance. Then followed a procession of maidens all clad in costly silk robes. (Wolfram gloried in detailed descriptions of their magnificence.) Last of all came the chief Grail maiden, the queen, bearing aloft on a cushion " the crown of all earthly wishes, fair fulness that ne'er shall fail." [1]

The procession came and went and the company were feasted. Parzival saw all, wondering, but alas ! silent. The question which was to remove the evil spell and relieve the king of suffering remained unasked. The promised deliverer was in the company, but the day of salvation was not yet at hand.

How has Wagner dealt with this series of incidents describing Parzival's youth ? He has telescoped the idea of Parsifal's ignorance, savagery and want of thought in the incident of his ruthless shooting of the swan. This is a happily-chosen incident in that its germ is found in Wolfram, in the picture of the young Parsifal with his home-manufactured bow and arrow going forth to shoot the wild deer. He did not realise, as young boys often fail to do, the pain and terror he was inflicting.

The swan also was a sacred bird to the keepers of the Grail, and it will be remembered that the legend of the Swan is the nucleus of *Lohengrin*, a version of which is given at the end of Wolfram's *Parzival*. Wagner makes Kundry relate a few incidents of Parsifal's early life, his meeting with the Arthurian knights in the forest, and his forsaking of his mother. She also informed him that as a result of his thoughtlessness his mother had died of grief. Thus Parsifal was introduced to

---

[1] *Parzival*, translated from the German of Wolfram von Aeschenbach, by J. L. Weston, 1894.

his first sorrow.   It is quite logical therefore that this raw, wondering youth should be present at the mysteries of the Grail and see the suffering king and hear the prophecy concerning himself and yet remain in dumb amazement.

The second series of incidents in Wolfram deals with " Parzival the Learner," as he might be named, at the time of probation.   The innocent fool has to be taught his folly and see the results of his savage, ignorant deeds ere he can attain to the wisdom and sympathy which is to result in his asking the question which is to undo the curse laid upon Anfortas.

Parzival learned through a meeting with his cousin Ségune the great opportunity he had lost at the Grail Castle. He had also to learn the result of one of his ignorant deeds, the robbing of Jeschuté, whom now he found in rags, and forsaken by her lord who believed her unfaithful.   However, Parzival fought him and thus seemed to convince him of the innocence of his wife !   Our hero confessed his folly :

> A fool-man was I,
> Nor yet had I waxed to wisdom.[1]

Parzival was not yet finished with reproaches, for, at the court of Arthur, the hideous Kondrie arrived.   Her nostrils were slit, she had the ears of a bear, but her bridle and her garments were costly.   She carried a scourge to punish Parzival for his sin in not asking the question, which she said was due to lack of sympathy.

So the knight, with his heart full of shame and remorse, rode forth on a long series of adventures, seeking the Grail Castle.   He knew now wherein his failure lay and that if he got another chance he must ask the question.   He was to be further enlightened as to the history and meaning of the Grail and taught the grace of humility from the hermit Trevrezent at the holy season of Good Friday and Easter. The hermit gave him and his horse all the hospitality he, in his simple way of living, could afford.   Parzival confessed to him his sins and asked pardon.   Trevrezent related to Parzival the whole story of the Grail, how the king was wounded in

----

[1] Dr Weston's translation.

the thighs because he had sinned in serving earthly love rather than heavenly. He described to him the Grail procession, the maidens, the bleeding spear and the Grail itself, with its mystic writing promising a deliverer. In parting, Trevrezent gave Parzival absolution and bade him go on and be steadfast and true of heart.

We are now told in Book XV of Parzival's meeting with the heathen king, Feirefis Angevin, half black, half white, who turned out to be his step-brother. Then at a feast of the Round Table of King Arthur, Kondrie, the Grail messenger, appeared with news of Parzival's election to the Grail kingdom. His weary purgatorial pilgrimage was now ended. He had been purified and softened by sorrow and humbled from vain and worldly pride.

Wagner had to change the second series of events, which showed Parsifal as a learner of the experiences of life. The slow development of character which, for the modern mind, is one of the most interesting characteristics of Wolfram's *Parzival*, cannot be shown so successfully in a drama as in an epic or novel. Wagner represents the testing of Parsifal by causing him to undergo (Act II) one fierce temptation. This took place in Klingsor's garden, and with its magician's cave, scenic marvels and temptress, in the person of Kundry, savours not a little of the melodramatic. The foundation of the ingenious story is found in Wolfram in the story of Klingsor, who had given way to unlawful love and been punished in one of the most deeply humiliating physical ways. Wagner amplifies the story thus. In revenge, he relates that Klingsor had sent Kundry to tempt Anfortas and the king had been wounded through the thigh. He had also lost the sacred spear to the enemy, the spear which had pierced the side of the Lord and which was a holy relic, kept by the Grail keepers. Parsifal, as the promised saviour, had to undergo carnal temptation in the person of Kundry, made youthful and lovely. Just as he was about to submit to her wishes, he experienced within himself the dreadful burning of Anfortas' wound. This symbolizes the mystery of vicarious suffering. Parsifal had begun to share, with Christ, in the redemption of the world. He was thus liberated from his own personal temptation. The wrathful magician, Klingsor, now appeared and hurled the sacred spear at Parsifal. Parsifal seized it, and uninjured, made with it in triumph the sign of the Cross. With this spear he was later to heal the king's wound.

The last scene (which is the last Act in Wagner) depicts the arrival of the mature Parzival, the promised Saviour. Wagner takes most of his details from Wolfram, except that in the mediæval poet it is the eagerly-awaited question, " What aileth thee here, mine uncle ? " which has the magical effect. Wagner substitutes an action in the healing of the king, the touching of the sufferer by Parsifal's spear.

Also Wolfram, as is the way of an epic or novel, gathers up the unfinished ends of his story by telling us how Parzival became at Monsalväsch the King of the Grail, with his wife Kondwiremur at his side.

Wagner, as a dramatist, stops at the climax. In his Opera it is narrated that Gurnemanz, the hermit, saw an unknown knight in armour approaching and reproached him for being armed on Good Friday. On looking closer, he discovered it was the " Fool " who had a long time ago shot the sacred swan. On asking whence Parsifal came, the youth replied, " By ways of search and suffering I came." He informed the hermit that this time he had come to heal the king and that he had recovered the sacred spear. Gurnemanz was overcome with joy. He told Parsifal that all was going to ruin, because Anfortas had deprived himself, the knights and the old king Titurel, of the service of the Grail, hoping that much-longed-for death might come to him (Anfortas). Titurel had died in consequence. Parsifal hastened into the Castle hall just in time to see the covered Grail brought in, and also the coffin of the old king Titurel. Anfortas paid no heed to the urgent and impassioned request of the knights to serve the Grail. He implored them to kill him first, to bury their swords in his wounds, and end his agony.

At this moment Parsifal stepped forth and extended the spear, saying that that which made the wound would alone heal it. He recited the words:

> " Be whole, forgiven and unstained !
> For now thy charge from thee I take.—
>   Thy suffering be hallowed.
> By which the highest strength of fellow pain
>   and sheerest wisdom's might
>   were taught the backward fool.
>   The holy spear
>   I bring you home again." [1]

So at last the great act of healing was performed on the king and, delivered from pain, his face lighted up with spiritual ecstasy. The Grail, glowing with sacred light, was now uncovered, and Parsifal swung it as a censer before the assembled knights. Kundry sank lifeless to the ground. At Parsifal's feet in reverence fell Anfortas and Gurnemanz. Parsifal, the Saviour, had accomplished his work.

This stirring drama is, of course, accompanied by the orchestra, which represents in its minor chords and gradual transitions the yearning of pain as well as the final triumph over pain. By welding music and drama, Wagner has created a great symbolic work of art. In following those who associated the story with Christ's Passion and redeeming grace, Wagner has made it more deeply Christian than Wolfram has done. It is ascetic in some measure, as Parsifal's chief victory over temptation was a conquering of the senses. But it has not yet the severe monastic, ascetic and inhuman detachment from humanity of the *Queste*.

The Christianity is of a more redemptive and universal kind. The mourning land now mourns on Good Friday and rejoices on Easter Day. Thus, as an old pagan festival became Christmas, so the pagan mourning of the earth has also been translated into holy grief, and its rejoicing into Christian gladness.

Perhaps the greatest originality of the *Parsifal* as far as the conception of the plot and characters go is in the depiction of Kundry. In Wolfram, Kondrie [2] is typical of one of the characters of mediæval legend, a " loathly damsel " with her slit nostrils and ears of a sow. She may have come into

---

[1] *Parsifal*, translated by A. Forman, p. 70 (Act III).
[2] Name is spelt thus in Wolfram von Aeschenbach.

Wolfram's pages from an older tradition of the " beauty and beast " type of story, where a prince is compelled to marry an ugly maiden (transformed by witchery). When he does so, she becomes beautiful again. Such a story was connected with the early Gawain. Kondrie, however, in Wolfram, rides on a magnificent horse, with costly trappings, and is a messenger of the Grail, bearing its emblem on her breast, that of doves.

Wagner has ingeniously combined with this a legend which is the *Wandering Jew* in another form. Kundry had, at the time of Christ, mocked and spit at the Saviour as He passed, carrying His cross. So she is condemned to wander remorseful through the ages, sold to evil, until she redeems herself by service. She has come under the power of the magician Klingsor, and yet her real longing is to perform humble service to the Grail keepers. She is pictured in the first Act of the *Parsifal* an old woman arriving with a balsam fetched in peril from afar for the sick king's healing, and yet in a later Act she is forced by the power Klingsor has over her to become a temptress to the young and untried Parsifal. She transforms herself into a beautiful young damsel and tries to win Parsifal over by her loveliness and sympathy, speaking to him of his dead mother. In resisting this temptation he not only is enabled to cure Anfortas, but he also saves Kundry. At the very end, when she falls dead at his feet, she is liberated from her curse. The constant struggle between good and evil in Kundry and the final triumph of the good makes her a more interesting character than the mere fairy-tale original.

LOHENGRIN

In the twelfth and thirteenth centuries there existed several stories of the Swan-Knight. There seem to have been two main forms of the story, one in which the hero was called Helias, the other in which his name was Lohengrin.

In the more complicated form known in France the hero's name was Helias. His five brothers and one sister were turned into swans. Five of these, four brothers and one sister, were restored to their human form by means of the chains which they had possessed as children, which were put again round their necks. One swan, however, was left, a brother to Helias. In the second form of the tale the swan was brother to the heroine, not the hero.

One day Helias saw in the river a swan drawing a boat. Recognising him as his enchanted brother, he entered the small ship. In four days he arrived in the land of Bouillon, where the duchess of the country was looking for a champion. Helias waged successful battle for the duchess and married her daughter. After some years, through the advice of an envious lady, the young duchess asked her husband questions concerning his origin, which he had forbidden her to ask. So the knight was compelled to leave her and go sorrowfully back to his land and family.

The remaining brother recovered his shape and the family lived happily united. But Helias still mourned for his wife and child. However, he was comforted by a prophecy that from his offspring should come the brave knight, Godfrey of Bouillon, leader of the first Crusade.

The stories which follow this form did not make the Swan-Knight son of the Grail king. Wolfram von Aeschenbach in his *Parzival* was one of the earliest known to us who did this. In his version the hero is called Loherangrin. Curiously enough, it is the failure to ask the question which caused suffering, in the *Parzival*. In *Lohengrin* it is the asking of the question which is the grave fault. In the former case the question may have originally been some necessary spell, like the " Open Sesame " of the *Arabian Nights* ; in the latter, some form of taboo or forbidden words.

Wagner took, in the main, his story from Wolfram, who places his events in Flanders. The opera-writer quickens the action by making Lohengrin fight Telramund, the accuser of Elsa (the heroine), on his immediate arrival. Also Elsa asks the forbidden question on the night of her marriage, not after some years, as in Wolfram. In Wolfram's story there are no swan-brothers nor swan-sister ; the enchanted swan is brother to the heroine. The duchess herself, not the daughter, becomes the Swan-Knight's betrothed.

Wagner, according to the critics, was also influenced by

another romance written probably between 1276 and 1290, *Der Schwanritter*, by Konrad von Wurzburg. The names of the hero and heroine differ from any of the romances of which we have spoken, nor is the story connected with the Grail. But the Emperor, as in Wagner's Opera, is holding a levee on the bank of the river when a white swan appears dragging a boat in which is a knight asleep. The knight is destined to be the champion of the two ladies in distress, who are appealing to the Emperor. When the boat lands, the knight awakens and addresses the same words to the swan as in Wagner.

" Fly now on thy way, dear Swan, and when I need thee again I will call thee."

Wagner's Opera is so well known that a brief summary of the plot will prove sufficient.

Elsa, accused by the Count Frederick of Telramund, before all the people, of murdering her brother in order that she may become ruler of Brabant, appeals for aid to a knight she has seen in her dreams.

Heralded by strains of heavenly music, a knight appears in a boat, drawn by a swan. This warrior has come to be Elsa's champion on condition that Elsa will never inquire concerning his abode, rank or name. He fights with and overcomes Count Frederick.

Elsa has given her promise not to inquire concerning the knight's name. Later, however, she allows herself to be influenced by her enemy, Ortrud, an ally of Telramund, who claimed the throne for him. So on the eve of her marriage, Elsa, giving way to the fear of losing her newly-made husband, begs him to unfold the mystery. " Speak, who art thou? Whence hast thou come? What is thy rank?" The fatal and forbidden words have been pronounced and Elsa herself has courted her doom.

In the last Act, in front of the assembled people, Lohengrin reveals his holy origin and dwelling. He possesses the mysterious power of the Grail as long as his name remains unrevealed. Now, however, he must return. As he pronounces the words once again the swan appears to take him back to his sacred dwelling-place. One act of restoration, however, is performed by means of the power of the Grail. Elsa's brother, whose transformation into a swan has been caused through the evil magic of Ortrud, is here and now transformed, restored to his sister, and a dove substituted to draw the boat.

Analysing the tale in its various forms, it can be seen that the nucleus of the story is a transformation legend of the " beauty and the beast " type. Intertwined with this is probably a narration of incestuous love, of very early times. This would explain the caution of secrecy, as the knowledge of the bridegroom's name would increase his bride's guilt. In a society with a higher developed sense of morality, this subject would offend taste, so in the evolution of the legend the incestuous relationship would tend to disappear. As it stands, the events seem to relate the story of a heavenly visitant. It is reminiscent of a modern opera, the *Immortal Hour*, founded on the Celtic myth of Midir and Etain. It is interesting to remember that these two of heavenly origin also take the form of swans as they disappear to the fairy mountains of Slievenamon.

The idea that the swan is a sacred animal, belongs to an early tradition. This is the totemic belief of a magic and religious bond between a certain animal and a certain group of people. To harm the animal is to harm the group also. Sometimes the god may have taken the form of the animal and been worshipped as such. Jupiter, it will be remembered, is reputed to have visited Leda and done his wooing in the shape of a swan.

Thus the Lohengrin story, as treated by Wagner, is one of the best examples of a legend being rationalised and idealised. The story, while keeping some of its original characteristics, has been raised to another level and endowed with a moral and spiritual meaning. This is suggested by the heightening of the emotional tension in the various musical " motives " and also in the dramatic action.

Wagner resorts to his usual system of recurring motives with gradual transitions. The Prelude of *Lohengrin* is not, as in former operas, a digest of the various recurring motives to be used, but rather sets the emotional key, the " Stimmung " in which the Opera is to be heard. Here it is the helpless maiden's cry of distress addressed to the Grail knight. Therefore the first motive is that of the Grail itself, delicately rendered by the highest tone of the violins and the flute. Musicians point out that the first two chords of the second bar are used both in this drama and in the *Parsifal* as the Swan motive.

In the second Act another motive, that of evil, fear and doubt, is subtly conveyed. The outward dramatic impersonation is given by Ortrud, the wife of Telramund, a former suitor of Elsa's. Wagner's evil characters tend to be melodramatic, probably because they are types and have not the light and shade which makes a human character interesting. Ortrud, for example, embodies the bad qualities of envy, discord and cunning, without any compensating good. She visits Elsa in her own apartment and wins her way into Elsa's confidence, sowing seeds of doubt and fear in the heroine's mind. These are destined to bear fruit in her breaking of her promise and in asking the fatal question.

The last Act brings the climax. The Act opens with a martial prelude, leading up to the famous wedding-march. But soon there breaks into the notes of triumph the motive of Ortrud's evil magic and warning. Elsa, driven on by a frenzy of fear, asks the fatal and forbidden question. Into the music which is played, as the knight pronounces his own name " Lohengrin " and that of his father, " Parzival," come the Grail-motives once again. In the recitative Lohengrin tells of the abode on the sanctuary of Monsalväsch [1] and of the Brotherhood of the Grail, which he is rejoining. The louder martial strains of the Grail knights die away into the heart-breaking tones of farewell.

The story is one of human failure and triumph of evil, yet the impression left on the mind and emotions is not that of hopelessness. The final scene is one of bodily parting, yet between the lovers there remains still an indissoluble spiritual bond. With this thought Lohengrin tries to comfort the grief-stricken Elsa.

---

[1] This form of the word is taken from Dr Weston's translation of the *Parzival*, p. 170. Wagner uses the form " Montsalvat."

According to Wagner's own interpretation, Lohengrin looked for a woman who should trust in him, who should not ask him how he was called or whence he came, but love him as he was and because he was whate'er she deemed him.   He sought the woman who would not call for explanations or defence but who would love him with an unconditioned love. His longing was not for worship nor adoration, but for the only thing sufficient to redeem him from his loneliness, to still his deep desire for love, for being understood through love.

The dramatic opera of *Lohengrin* may not suggest to all hearers this interpretation, and the logical meaning of a work of art must never be forced, because it is created to suggest rather than to teach.   Yet it must be admitted by all that the story is one of tragic failure of trust between lovers, one of whom ranks higher in spiritual order than the other.   The corresponding music heightens the effect of anticipation, realisation, ecstatic love, doubt and agony of parting which the story in its human aspect displays.   And those who wish to, can discover within the drama the struggle between materialism and idealism, between the demands of the senses which demand objective proof, and the spiritual, which has laws of its own.   Thus the tale, simpler in the elements than the *Parzival*, is a good example of a fairy-story given human interest and idealised till it is made, through its dramatic appeal and its music, of greater significance for all.

TRISTAN

Wagner's genius in presenting the *Tristan* legend through music, dramatic action and recitative, has influenced the conception of this legend very profoundly.   The appeal is made through different artistic media, and thus the combined product is difficult to analyse.   A critical knowledge of music as well as of dramatic art would be required for a complete criticism, for the effect produced on the audience is a blending of both.   Or, at times, there may even be a conflict, and this means faulty art.   The music, for example, may hold up the action to a degree that spoils the dramatic scene, though the music is in itself of great artistic worth.

Again, the recitative cannot be judged by itself alone for literary merit or want of it, for it is designed to lend itself to musical treatment. In the *Tristan* it is a mixture of the alliterative " Stabreim " (Staff-rhyme) and end-rhyme. Each syllable usually has a note to itself, to enhance distinctness of enunciation. Wagner considered this of great importance. To take an example :

" So starben wir,	" So should we die
um ungetrennt,	that ne'er again
ewig einig,	Our souls might suffer
ohne End'	parting's pain—
ohn' Erwachen,	that unawakened,
ohne Bangen,	unforbidden,
namenlos	for reach of name
in Lieb umfangen,	too deeply hidden,
ganz uns selbst gegeben	our beings we might blend
der Liebe nur zu leben."	in love without an end." [1]

From a general point of view, however, considering the main purpose of this thesis, there are two main matters to be considered; first, the handling of the plot and any important changes in the traditional incident, and second, the special interpretation according to Wagner's philosophy.

The writer of this Opera had the skill to choose for his *Tristan* drama [2] three of the salient and most tragic incidents in this story, the last being the death of Tristan and (as it is generally interpreted) of Isolde.[3] These three dramatic events are taken as the most moving and representative happenings which take place in man's life—intensified on a grand and heroic scale. True, Tristan belongs to no one nation ; he is not, like Aeneas, a national hero, but is representative of all mankind, wherever overwhelming passion and outward events are at cross-purposes.

There is, in Wagner's adaptation of the Tristan story (mainly from Gottfried von Strassburg's version),[4] the greatest economy of actions and personages, so that we may, as it

[1] Forman's translation of the *Tristan*, p. 44.
[2] Produced at Munich in 1865.   [3] Form of name in Wagner.
[4] See also Chap. XIII.   Tristan: Sources.

were, have the main incidents in our mind and yet not be distracted with too much detail. And these main incidents have for us an emotional content—here expressed in a series of musical " leitmotifs " which deal with great and universal themes : "The Look" (a blending of attraction and repulsion), the " Magic Potion " (the triumphing ecstasy of awakening love, mingling with a sense of foreboding), and so on.

A study of Wagner's methods of treating the story, together with his own comments thereon, scattered throughout his published letters, reveals to us that he has a definite if not an original philosophy. As regards the *Tristan* itself, he writes : " In comparing Tristan and Siegfried, both Tristan and Siegfried are in bondage to an illusion, which makes this deed of theirs unfree, woo for another their own eternally predestined bride and in the false relation hence arising, find their doom." [1] Again, Tristan, as a hero of the material world, in the glory of his manhood and pride, is, according to Wagner's extremely Buddhistic conception, a victim of illusion. Wagner expresses this by one of his musical transitions. In the *Tristan* the hero-motive of the first Act becomes by a simple change the motive of Day (and hence Illusion) in the second Act.

Wagner takes liberties with Gottfried's story, but careful inspection shows us that there is always some dramatic reason behind it. There is a most startling change in the first Act which adds, however, to the dramatic strength of the story. Isolde offers to Tristan what she considers is a potion of death and resolves to drink half of it herself. But Brängane, [2] choosing what she considers is the lesser of two evils, substitutes the love-potion for the death-potion. Thus, when Isolde hands Tristan the love-potion, she is ready to embrace death and, as she thinks, deal it out to the man who is indifferent to her. Isolde's emotion is at first a curious blending of hate and attraction, expressed in all its complexity in the " Look " motive. She had first been drawn to Tristan by pity, when he was a sick man in disguise as " Trantris," and this stayed her hand, when she discovered he was the murderer of her lover Morold (not her uncle, as in Gottfried). She

---

[1] Epilogue to *Niebelung's Ring*.　　[2] The German form in Wagner.

hated him before she has tasted the love-drink, because he is carrying her away from country and home, with her parent's consent rather than her own. His indifference to her also tantalises her. But her hate has within it the germ of budding love. The magic of the potion causes this love to come to its fruition. Tristan's passion awakes simultaneously. The orchestra interprets these sudden, overwhelming emotions by harmonies in which the majestic strains of life and death, ecstasy and foreboding are commingled.

Though borne up on this wave of joy and suffering, Tristan and Isolde have immediately to face realities. The facts of circumstance which surround their lives have not changed. The ship has meanwhile been making for the shore. It is now safe in harbour. Marke [1] and his courtiers, with a fanfare of trumpets, are here to welcome the king's bride. Marke is come to receive her with all honour and to thank Tristan for the loyal fulfilment of his pledge. Tristan can only attain the accomplishment of his desire by breaking his faith to his liege-lord and uncle :

> O sweetness bitter fruited
> O bliss in faith-break rooted.[2]

The second Act is founded on one chief incident—that of King Marke's discovery, through Melot, of Tristan's faithlessness. Wagner has here once more kept to the finest tradition which does not deprive Marke of all noble traits. His sorrow at Tristan's betrayal is dignified. He feels that if Tristan be false, there is no truth in the world :

> Where looks he now for trueness
> Whom Tristan has betrayed.[3]

Tristan has no excuse except that of Fate, but here his idea of Fate is wrapped up in metaphysical language. Marke is not enlightened as to the magic drink which is the representative of Blind Fate, and which excuses Tristan's conduct.

[1] So spelt in Wagner. [2] Translation by A. Forman, 1891, p. 18.
[3] *Op. cit.*, p. 49.

This is the most criticised Act of the *Tristan*. To some it consists of a long-drawn-out love duet. Wagner has, on the one hand, been accused of sensuality—in other words, of " doping " his audience by his music. On the other hand, as the recitative certainly bears witness, Wagner may be challenged as giving us an abstract metaphysical dialogue. The lovers seem much more concerned in the blending of their souls in another life than of a more earthly union in this one :

> So should we die
> That ne'er again
> Our souls might suffer
> Parting's pain—
> That unawakened,
> Unforbidden,
> For reach of name
> Too deeply hidden,
> Our beings we might blend
> In love without an end.[1]

The longing for death and the long-drawn-out simile of Day and Night can be adversely criticised as springing from the author's own philosophic concepts, rather than arising from the necessities of the legendary and human story. His metaphysical ideas are unwelcome, I think, not because they are obscure, but because they are too clearly defined (in the recitative) and superimposed. Tristan and Isolde become the mouthpieces of a second-hand Eastern conception of philosophy. The roots of the *Tristan* legend, as modern researches prove,[2] are to be found in Celtic mythology, and some suggestion of that Other-world (whose entrance was figured as a sword-bridge) would not have been out of place. Great love, by means of its transcendent quality, overleaps time and space and, as the great dramatic poets represent, walks hand-in-hand with Death. The star-crossed lovers' desire for an ideal world, where " music and moonlight and feeling are one," is only natural. Yet it seems to spoil the

[1] Translation by A. Forman, 1891, p. 44.
[2] G. Schoepperle in *Tristan and Isolt* (1913) traces it to an Irish love story.

dramatic action that Tristan, when discovered with Isolde, should merely turn to her and, like a professor of philosophy, go on with his metaphysical argument :

> The dreary day,
> Its latest dawn, etc.

He makes no attempt to excuse or glorify his action but, even before he is wounded, asks Isolde if she will follow him to the wonder-realms of Night.   Marke is, according to Wagner's theory, an inhabitant of the false and cruel Day.   But from the point of view of rational judgment, he is a wronged man and his attitude of dignified sorrow is to be admired.

Fortunately, to lovers of music, Wagner's music is greater than his philosophy.   His wonderful melodies can be used here to drown the critical faculty.   The dramatic recitative can be looked upon as the scaffolding which upholds a marvellous creation of pillared stone and arched roof ; it can be ignored· as much as possible.

The Prelude at the beginning of Act III gives a musical résumé of the various " motives " which are used throughout the drama and also in the third Act.   At orchestral concerts the Prelude and Liebestod are often played together and make an artistic whole.   At the beginning, the music suggests the repose of holy Night, broken only by the notes of the hunters' horns heard in the distance.   Into this peace breaks in the Day motive like an approaching storm.   Combined with this is the Torch motive.   In the second Act, the Torch burns at the entrance to Tristan's and Isolde's Retreat. Reversed, it is a symbol of Death and Everlasting Day. Isolde's Magic then leads up to a motive which is often styled the Nirvana motive, which represents the bliss which is caused by the final freeing from earthly ties, and the consequent entrance into the realm of Knowledge, Love and Eternal Life.

Dramatically speaking, there is more action and life in the third Act.   The incidents have been simplified to the utmost.   Wagner has not confused issues by introducing a second Isolde, nor the story of the black and white sail.   In Wagner's first version the sail is mentioned only as " a sail of bliss," which may be an indirect reference to the white sail. The death-scene in the Opera follows straight on Tristan's wounding by Melot and there is not the series of adventures we find in Gottfried's episodic story.

When the Act opens, the wounded Tristan is seen lying on a couch in the castle-garden of Kareol, built on a rocky cliff. He is attended by his faithful servant Kurwenal. The whole Act seems to us nearer to Mother Earth than the second Act. Even Tristan's reluctance to come back to the hated " Day " seems natural for a sick man. In recovering from a swoon, it is the return to life which is painful.

The scene is opened by a solo on the herdsman's pipe. This gives Wagner an opportunity for a most exquisite musical lyric, which, recurring again later on, makes the sick man review his past life. The recitative also affords us a glimpse of the feudal Tristan, as a leader of men, subject in his place to his lord. Tristan asks Kurwenal whose are the flocks he sees. Kurwenal replies that they are his own (Tristan's) and that his servants have kept them together for him. Tristan replies in surprise :

> " Flocks of mine ? "

Kurwenal :

> " Master, I meant it.
> There the house,
> Land and herds,
> Thy folk, in faith
> To the lord they loved,
> As best they could,
> Abode and land have kept,
> Which whole my hero
> For gift and guerdon,
> To folk and followers gave,
> When all he left behind,
> A land afar to find." [1]

Kurwenal now tells him he has sent for Isolde to come and heal him. Tristan feels she is coming to restore him to the " Day." Gradually the thought of her makes him long for

[1] Translation by A. Forman.

earthly life and overcomes his desire for boundless night and Nirvana :

> What deep and hungry pain
> Urged me once more
> To seek the shore
> Of day with stress, unturning ? [1]

Kurwenal and he look eagerly for the ship.   Again the herdsman's pipe is heard and it makes Tristan reminiscent. To him it seems that the fever which runs in his veins is caused not so much by his wound but by the magic drink he had drunk in the past :

> The drink ! the drink !
> With its fearful bane,
> It festered my blood
> From heart to brain.
>
> .   .   .
>
> Nowhere, ah nowhere,
> Rest I may ;
> I back from Night,
> Am hurled to Day.[2]

Once again the recurring idea in Wagner's philosophy is put into Tristan's mouth.

Now Isolde's ship is sighted and, with eager eyes, the two watch it making its way towards the harbour.   Tristan sends Kurwenal down to greet Isolde.   In a mad frenzy of joy he raises himself up and tears the bandages from his wounds.   On hearing his beloved's voice, he rises, staggers to meet her, falls into her arms and then sinks lifeless to the ground.   He has attained to his desire in Death.   He expresses this in the cryptic lines, translated thus :

> How hear I the light !
> The torch—at last !
> Behold it quenched
> To her !   To her ! [3]

---

[1] Translation by A. Forman.
[2] Translation by A. Forman, Act III, p. 63.
[3] *Ibid.*, p. 69.

Isolde, in a wild abandonment of grief, falls in a swoon on Tristan's body. The shepherd gives warning of another ship. King Marke and his followers are approaching. The king, who has learned from the repentant Brangäne the story of the love-drink, has come to pardon the lovers and surrender Isolde to Tristan. But Kurwenal, thinking they are still hostile, kills the treacherous Melot, and falls wounded over Tristan's dead body.

Marke addresses Isolde, telling her he has come with the intention of mating her to Tristan, in whom he now can find no blame.

But Isolde's thoughts are far from mortal happenings. Slowly, as in a trance, she rises and tells those around her she hears immortal melodies calling her and is surrounded by an ocean of bliss, whose waves threaten to submerge her. She must follow her lover into the realm of Eternity ; their souls must be blended in the World-Soul in endless bliss.

Conclusion

It may be gathered by the study of these three Operas, the *Parsifal*, *Lohengrin* and the *Tristan*, that the Legend had value for the creative artist in Wagner as myth and dramatic story. Not only this, but in his treatment he shows he has a definite interpretation to embody. This interpretation he expounds fully in his theoretic treatises, *Art Work of the Future* (1850), *Opera and Drama* (1852). The actual wording of these may be expressed in the terms of an outmoded philosophy or psychology. Nevertheless, they are of considerable interest to the student of his work as a conscious artist.

In these he informs us how suitable were legends and, in particular, Arthurian legends, for his artistic purposes. He comprehended that they were part of the great religious heritage of the European nation and of the world. By means of his genius, expressed in music, he was able to call up these associations which are deep-rooted in the human mind, not only of the individual but of the race-mind. Sigmund Freud, in his theories and interpretation of dreams, shows how symbols of myth are buried far down in the subconscious. Music, of all the arts, has power to reach the subconscious by means of association. Wagner himself, in his theoretic treatise, *Opera and Drama*, tells how he consciously used this power of association to call up " remembrance." When a particular musical phrase accompanies a certain dramatic act—he says—it becomes associated with it. Again and again it can be introduced, blending with other phrases and bringing the same quality of emotion with it, through association. Thus, complex emotional schemes can be built up and the appropriate emotional atmosphere skilfully suggested.

Wagner names this psychological state " remembrance," but it might be termed rather " recollection " in the sense of the French " receuillement," gathering the mind together, a term used in manuals of devotion, as the preliminary to meditation. It is akin to the state of reverie. In this receptive and passive state, when the critical and rational faculty is lulled, the myth and the symbol, with their appropriate imagery, rise unchecked from the depths of the mind. A certain emotional atmosphere which surrounds the myth and the symbol can be created by music. It has also the power of inducing transition from one mood to another, when different and even contrary moods can be evoked, the one blending into the other. Wagner prided himself in this art of transition. In a letter to Madame Wesendock, he writes : " My subtlest and deepest art I now might call the art of Transmutation, for my whole artistic woof consists of such transitions : I have taken a dislike to the abrupt and harsh ; often it is unavoidable and needful, but even then it should not enter without the ' Stimmung ' being so definitely prepared for a sudden change, as of itself to summon it. My greatest masterpiece in this art of subtlest and most gradual transition is assuredly the big scene in the second Act of *Tristan and Isolde*. The commencement of this scene offers the most overbrimming life in its most passionate emotions, its close the devoutest, most consecrate desire of death. Those are the piers, now see, . . . how I've spanned them, how it all leads over from the one abutment to the other ! . . . Well, as Art has to bring to understanding those extreme grand emotions of Life which remain unknown to the generality of mankind (except in rare epochs of War or Revolution), so this understanding is only to be compassed through the most definite and cogent motivation of transitions ; and my whole artistic work consists in nothing but evoking the needful, willing mood of receptivity through such a motivation." [1]

The drama of *Lohengrin* is one which exemplifies well the emotions which the mythical story evokes and which are expressed by the music. There is the wonder and astonishment called out by the advent of the strange knight of the Grail from Monsälvisch who comes in answer to Elsa's prayer. There are heard the strains of the mystical Grail music, borne from a land beyond mortal ken, and seeming to contain harmonies almost too ethereal for mortal ears.

And in a way, which is almost too subtle for the kindred art of words, the higher strains are blended with a more earthly music. This is shown when there is introduced the " doubt " motive into melodies of Elsa's love and surrender to her champion and husband.

On the more rationalistic level Wagner felt the greatness of those heroes and their deeds, Parsifal, Tristan and Lohengrin. The manner in which he did so is expressed best in his own words :

" I turned for the selection of my material once for all from the domain of history to that of legend. . . . All the details necessary for the description and preservation of the conventionally historic, which a fixed and limited historical epoch demands in order to make the action clearly intelligible, could be here omitted. And by this means the poetry, and especially the music, were freed from the necessity of a method of treatment entirely foreign to them and particularly impossible as far as music was concerned. The legend, in whatever age or nation it may be placed, has the advantage that it comprehends only the purely human portion of the age or nation, and presents this portion in a form peculiar to it, thoroughly concentrated, and therefore easily intelligible.

" This legendary character gives a great advantage to the poetic arrangement of the subject for the reason already

[1] From the *Letters of Wagner*, translated by W. Ellis, 1905, p. 184.

mentioned, that, while the simple process of the action renders unnecessary any painstaking for the purpose of explanation of the course of the story, the greatest possible portion of the poem can be devoted to the portrayal of the inner motives of the action, those inmost motives of the soul which, indeed, the action points out to us as necessary, through the fact that we ourselves feel in our hearts a sympathy with them." [1]

Wagner, then, realised his personages as representative men of heroic mould, whose experiences and emotions were of general interest and import. But he also dramatised them as individuals, for these stories gave him a simplified series of dramatic incidents, in which fundamental emotions were aroused. It must be remembered that the story in music, or rather in the mixed form of art, which is the Opera, cannot hold the same place as in narrative or in dramatic literature. In spite of Wagner's theories to the contrary, it must take to the musical expression a secondary place. This does not imply, of course, that the story is without importance, because a knowledge of the story and recitative of *Tristan*, for example, is necessary to those who would appreciate fully even the orchestral rendering of the " Prelude " and " Liebestod," which is so often given by the instruments alone at concerts. Also, Wagner, as a musician, is greater than as a dramatist, even although he shows ability in the choice of his dramatic plot and incidents. Yet the stories of Wagner's Operas have become, throughout Europe, the best known popular versions.

Wagner was not content with making his heroes representative. He had a definite philosophic theory by which he tried to interpret the emotions and actions of his characters. This philosophy had in it many of the elements of the religion of Buddha and the fatalistic East. In this, the material world is interpreted as Illusion, and the ideal world the escape from this Illusion, the only Reality. Thus Night and Death as forms of escape from Reality represent Nirvana, a bliss greatly to be desired. Day is all that is

[1] From W. J. Henderson, *Richard Wagner, his Life and Works*, 1923, p. 185.

negative and harsh, but Night and Death restores lover to lover. Tristan's emotions are interpreted in the music (so Wagner himself informed his audience) according to these ideas. Again, the doctrine of Reincarnation comes into his treatment and interpretation both in the *Parsifal*, especially in the story of Kundry, as well as in the *Tristan*.[1] In relation to the chain of destiny, Tristan is made to remark, " It was I myself that made it," referring probably to a former incarnation.

It is an important question to be determined in relation to our argument : How far is Wagner justified in introducing this philosophy into his conception of Tristan and the Grail ? Does it detract from his value as an artist or does it add to his worth ? Is there any principle to be applied as an acid test to distinguish the true metal from the false, the permanent from the passing ?

It may be stated that philosophy is superfluous where it does not spring from the roots of the legend or the emotions and actions of the characters in the story.   When, for example, the longing for another and better life seems natural (as it seems to be in Act III, when Tristan has been at the gates of death) this desire can be suggested by the words and music and action, with great potency to the audience, who can experience it through their sympathy with the character in this set of circumstances.   But when this longing for death (as in Act II) is an emotion which is imposed on the characters by the dramatist and interpreted by a rigid scheme of philosophy, alien to the characters, then it is artistically faulty.   The artist has ceased by creative contemplation to project himself into his characters and interpret their emotions. He rather tries to make his characters and their feelings fit into his own philosophical scheme.   In Wagner's case this seems to have been chosen because of his own temperamental bias.   In short, the artist has ceased to be objective.   This stricture applies especially to the dramatist.   Except in the case of *The Tempest*, which may have a considerable auto-biographic element, Shakespeare obeys this law of objectivity in his dramas.   Very seldom can we point to a statement

[1] For study of Kundry see above, pp. 171-72.

made by one of Shakespeare's characters and say, " Thus spoke Shakespeare, the man." But not so with Wagner. His own interpretations and philosophy are easy to discover in his dramas, even if they had not been so fully demonstrated and taught in his own critical works.

CHAPTER XIII

TRISTAN : SOURCES AND MALORY

SOME knowledge of the origins and development of the earlier Tristan legend is required before any just or valuable critical judgment can be made on the modern poems and plays on this subject. Stress has only been laid in this section on those versions and traditions which have influenced modern European literature.

The true sources of this legend, as of all legends, lie buried in the oral traditions. For example, such a report, which circulated concerning King Mark that he had ass's ears,[1] points to the fact that the tale of Tristan at one time belonged to a group of transformation myths when men were changed into animals and vice versa. This may go still further back, to a time when men worshipped gods in the form of animals. A modern recension of such a tale, which caused considerable interest on its appearance, is David Garnett's *Lady into Fox*.[2]

The old idea that the extant texts were compiled from episodic poems is now untenable. Later critics, including Bédier, Schoepperle and Bruce, have all shown that these texts depend on an earlier lost biographical poem, embodying an important body of tradition. On the details of this hypothetical poem there is not, of course, full agreement. Bédier tries to reconstruct it in his edition of *Tristan*,[3] choosing the incidents and forms he considers most primitive. A later critic, Gertrude Schoepperle,[4] criticises this reconstruction. She herself thinks that Eilhart von Oberg, in his version, embodies the earliest tradition and that his work

[1] Probably of Breton origin. [2] 1928.

[3] *Le roman de Tristan*, ed. J. Bedier, 1902-1905 (Soc. Anc. Textes fr.)

[4] G. Schoepperle, *Tristan and Isolt : a Study of the Sources of the Romance*, 2 vols, 1913.

corresponds most to this " estoire " as she calls this foundation poem. She finds the nucleus of the Tristan story in the tale of the king who, sitting at a window one day, observed a swallow with a golden hair in his beak. He thereupon resolved that he would marry no one but the owner of such golden locks.

The extant texts—most of them fragmentary—can be classified under Beroul and Thomas, respectively. The one group may be called the Beroul-Eilhart group, and this is named by Golther the minstrel group. The other is named the Thomas-Gottfried von Strassburg group. For the study of the sources, the Beroul-Eilhart von Oberg group is the most important. Gottfried von Strassburg, on the other hand, has had the greater influence on modern literature, especially on German literature.

For modern traditions and literature it is not the earlier texts which are of the most importance. The two main groups which have influenced European literature are, firstly, the group of Gottfried von Strassburg (including his continuators), and secondly, the manuscripts of the prose romance. Through modern German translations (the poet Herz and others) and through the influence of Wagner's Operas, the works of Gottfried and his followers have become known throughout Europe and have formed the material for poets.

On the other hand, as Vinaver [1] has shown in his masterly study, the prose romance (especially as contained in MS. 103, 334 and 99) has decided for Malory, in the main part, his choice of incident and form.

It will reward us well, therefore, in setting out on our study of modern presentations of Tristan, to concentrate on one or two of the most important incidents in Gottfried's narration. These incidents have been chosen for their intrinsic value, and also because they will be valuable for comparison all through this study of Tristan. They have been modernised in a graphic translation by the poet Herz, who keeps the *naïveté* of the original. Dr Weston also supplies

[1] E. Vinaver, *Le Roman de Tristan et Iseult dans l'Œuvre de Thomas Malory*, 1925.

a rendering of the tale in English, which has literary value.[1] The importance of good translations in disseminating tradition is often underrated.   Poets often use these rather than the original documents, the language of which is obscure, and which are difficult to obtain.

Gottfried von Strassburg gives in his version a straight-forward tale of the youth of Tristan, a narrative which has something of the salt strength and freshness of the sea about it.   Gottfried relates the sad events accompanying Tristan's birth, the death of his father and, as a consequence of his own birth, the death of his mother, sister of King Mark of Cornwall. He was indeed, from the first, a child of misfortune and sorrow ; the poet derives his hero's name from the French " triste," sad.

The Marshal Rual, who lived also in Parmenie (located by some in the north of England, the ancient Bernicia), adopted the orphan.   Tristan was abducted by Norwegian sailors, who thought they would gain a large ransom for so well-favoured and clever a youth.   However, the ship was overtaken by a storm and the sailors began to think Divine wrath was pursuing them, because of their sins.   So they made for land when they could, and put Tristan ashore with a little food.   The forsaken Tristan, after praying to God for help, wandered on till he met two pilgrims, old men, who directed him towards a city, which turned out to be Tintagel, where his uncle Mark held his court.

A vivid picture is given, in Gottfried, of the hunters of Mark's court riding out with hounds, coming upon this fair boy of noble bearing.   He was well up in hunting-lore and knew a better fashion of treating and cooking venison than Mark's men.   He told them, on their wondering enquiry, that his name was Tristan, that he came from the land of Parmenie and (as he himself believed) that he was the son of a merchant.   He then made them ride back to the city, two by two, and he himself greeted King Mark, who came out to meet them, with a wondrous sweet melody from his horn.   Mark was strangely drawn to the unknown youth

[1] The Story of Tristan and Iseult, rendered into English from the German by J. L. Weston, 1899.

(who was, of course, his nephew) and made him master of the hunt.

Later, when Rual, his adopted uncle, appeared, a ragged old man who had been searching for his lost foster-child, King Mark learned, to his extreme joy, that Tristan was his nephew. Then Tristan and thirty of his companions were knighted with great splendour. Now he must prove his bravery, and he did so by delivering the country from the servitude of Morolt and the tribute of live youths he demanded.

The same story is told in Eilhart von Oberg, with differences. The name of his father and mother are not the same, Tristan is not recognised as Mark's nephew till the dragon-fight, and there are other variants.

Thus in the early tales Tristan is a hero united to Mark by the bonds of kinship and the loyalty of a feudal vassal. These incidents, summarised above, belong to the heroic epic rather than to the romance. In calling it epic, of course, it must be remembered that Tristan is not, like Aeneas, the founder of a country. But the simple and straightforward narration of the hero's exploits and the naïve admiration they draw out among his fellows belongs to an active and heroic age. And here and there, as in a palimpsest there appear indications of a more ancient writing below, so here we have signs of a more ancient tradition as origin. There linger yet reminiscences of Celtic magic and fairy-tale. We catch a glimpse of an earlier Tristan, who can sing to the harp and understand all languages, even of the birds. Marie de France depicts such a Tristan in her lay, especially in *Chèvrefeuille*.[1] The fight with Morolt, now rationalised into a knight, is evidently a transformed account of the early legendary fights of heroes. These, in early Irish tales, took place with the Fomorians, a huge, misshapen, violent and cruel people, representing the powers of evil.

In Malory there is no record of this eager trusting youth and his love and feudal loyalty to King Mark. There is a reference to the fight with Morolt, who has become Sir Marhaus, but the story of the fight is toned down to suit a more refined audience : " And then Arthur made Sir Tristram Knight of

[1] The best edition of Marie's lays is edited by K. Warnke, 1900.

the Table Round, with great nobley and great feast as might be thought. For Sir Marhaus was slain afore by the hands of Sir Tristram in an island ; and that was well known at that time in the court of Arthur, for this Marhaus was a worthy knight. And for evil deeds that he did unto the country of Cornwall, Sir Tristram and he fought. And they fought so long, tracing and traversing, till they fell bleeding to the earth ; for they were so sore wounded that they might not stand for bleeding. And Sir Tristram, by fortune, recovered, and Sir Marhaus died through the stroke on the head." [1]

There remains one reference, in Malory, to the mythical Tristan with his magical powers of music. When Tristan went mad and fled to the forest, his harp was his only comfort. A damosel took pity on him and brought him food and drink, but he refused it and rode away from her. She, thereupon, asked the help of the lady of the castle, to whom Tristan had at one time taught harping. " So this lady and damosel brought him meat and drink, but he ate little thereof. Then upon a night he put his horse from him, and then he unlaced his armour, and then Sir Tristram would go into the wilderness and brast down the trees and boughs ; and otherwhile when he found the harp that the lady sent him, then would he harp and play thereupon and weep together. And sometime when Sir Tristram was in the wood that the lady wist not where he was, then would she sit her down and play upon that harp ; then would Sir Tristram come to that harp, and hearken thereto, and sometimes he would harp himself." [2]

Another incident in the youth of Tristan affords us a good example of how the vigour of a dramatic story has been weakened in the later versions. We will take first the version of Gottfried von Strassburg, with some reference to the earlier versions of Eilhart von Oberg, who differs considerably.

Tristan, after his fierce and long combat with Morolt in the island, suffered terribly with his poisoned wound. No one could cure him or even come near him, the stench was so horrible. In his despair he remembered his enemy Morolt's

---

[1] Malory's *Morte Darthur*, " Everyman " Edition, vol. i., p. 380.
[2] *Ibid.*, p. 326.

words, uttered in mocking, " No one will be able to heal the poisoned wound except my sister Iseult." Tristan resolved to go and seek Queen Iseult even though it meant going to death. He set sail with Kurvenal and eight men. Near land, Tristan left them and set out in a rudderless boat, with only his harp for a companion. He sent forth from his harp most tragic and melting notes which reached the ears of the men of Dublin, for it was to the shore of Ireland he was drifting. They rescued him, and seeing his condition, brought him to Queen Iseult (mother of the future Queen of Cornwall) who healed him of his wound by her wonderful skill. She then begged him to stay at her court and teach her daughter Iseult something of the skill he himself had in languages and music. At last the disguised minstrel managed to leave, on the excuse of having left a pining wife at home. There is in Gottfried no word of any love arising between Tantris, as he is called, and the Princess Iseult. Eilhart von Oberg gives the same story in what is considered an earlier version.[1] Tristan, according to his rendering, set out from Cornwall in an open boat, at the mercy of the winds and waves and with no companions but his harp. On this he played, giving expression to all his woe, pain and despair. He drifted in time to Dublin to the coast of Ireland and was healed at the court of the Queen and Princess Iseult. The spirit of unknown adventure and dependence on Fate is even more marked in Eilhart's version.

But there is little of adventure and the unknown, either in the prose romance or in Malory. Malory writes of the incident thus. After the fight with Marhaus, he relates that the severity of Tristram's wound threatened his life and no leeches or surgeons could do any good. " Then came there a lady that was a right wise lady, and she said plainly unto King Mark, and to Sir Tristram, and to all his barons, that he should never be whole but if Sir Tristram went in the same country that the venom came from, and in that country should he be holpen or else never." [2] Tristram set sail and

---

[1] See Schoepperle (G.), *Tristan and Isolt : a Study of the Sources of the Romance*, 1913.

[2] Malory's *Morte Darthur*, "Everyman" Edition, vol. i., pp. 249 and 250.

came to Isoud's court. He gave his name as Tramtrist and was put in Princess Isoud's charge for his healing. " And when she had searched him she found at the bottom of his wound that therein was poison, and so she healed him within a while ; and therefore Tramtrist cast great love to La Beale Isoud, for she was at the time the fairest maid and lady of the world. And there Tramtrist learned her to harp and she began to have a great fantasy unto him." [1]

Again, in the older romances, Tantris was still an unknown minstrel when he left the court at the first visit. He then returned the second time on his definite mission to seek Princess Iseult's hand for King Mark, his uncle. He undertook to kill a dragon which was ravaging Ireland and was rescued in an unconscious state by the Queen Iseult and her daughter, who still took him for their old friend Tantris, the minstrel. It was not until the bath-scene that Princess Isoud discovered that Tristram was her uncle Morolt's murderer. She found out this by noting that the missing piece of Tristram's sword corresponded to the piece found in Morolt's skull, which she, his niece, had kept, vowing revenge. She was on the point of slaying him when Tristram made himself and his true purpose known. Malory weaves the two incidents together in a confusing manner, calling Tristan sometimes Tramtrist and sometimes Tristram. He tells the incident of finding the sword dramatically, but in his version, it was the Queen and not the Princess who made the discovery that Tantris, *alias* Tristram, was the slayer of Sir Marhaus (Morolt). The Queen desired to kill him. " When Isoud (the younger) heard her (the Queen) say so (that Tristram was a traitor) she was passing sore abashed, for passing well she loved Tramtrist and full well she knew the cruelness of her mother, the queen." [2] Malory and the writers of MS. 103 have used some of the same materials, threads and colour as the older romances, but have woven them into a different design to suit the general nature of their own more complicated, if less vigorous, work of art.

The third scene, the drinking of the magic philtre with its

[1] Malory's *Morte Darthur*, "Everyman" Edition, vol. i., pp. 249 and 250.
[2] *Ibid.*, p. 255.

contents of bliss and woe, has been made famous in modern times by Wagner, who has taken it from Gottfried von Strassburg. Some of the facts of Tristan's former life are brought in in the conversation between Tristan and Isolde, in the first Act of the Opera. Wagner follows Gottfried in the main, but he heightens the drama in making Isolde think that she is offering Tristan a poisoned cup, which she herself drinks at the same time. Gottfried only makes it a flask of wine. Both, however, stress the conflict between loyalty to a feudal lord and passionate love, which raged in Tristan's mind, as the ship neared the shore.

In all poems on the story of Tristan, epic, dramatic or episodic, the treatment of the philtre-scene strikes the keynote of the age and outlook, as well as tests the author's dramatic power. To the modern mind, the philtre is the outward symbol of sudden passionate and fatal love, which is so over-powering that it possesses the force of a Nemesis, driving its victim on to destruction. It represents to the modern mind an inward force as the witches do on the lonely heath in the Play of *Macbeth*. These are outward symbols of the evil forces which were already stirring in Macbeth's own mind. Shakespeare combines the outward and the inward in perfect harmony so that no one in reading *Macbeth* would say that he was compelled by an outward Fate to commit the murder, and was therefore guiltless.

In the Tristan legend, however, emphasis has, throughout the ages, been laid now on one side, now on the other ; at one time on the outward magical philtre, which lessens the human guilt, at another on the strength of the natural human love, which makes the philtre superfluous.

Gottfried takes the story of the philtre quite simply, as he probably found it in his sources. Yet he describes the conflict in Tristan's mind graphically enough to make us feel that at the beginning, at any rate, Tristan accuses himself of being a traitor. In that feudal and religious society, the betrayal of feudal loyalty by the sin of adultery was considered an offence against God and was too serious to be condoned lightly. It was only by laying stress on the outward and magical compulsion of the philtre that the lovers' innocence could be upheld.

For Malory, on the contrary, there was no tragic conflict in the story, and the philtre was really superfluous in his story. In the conventions of the chivalric society which he pictures, each knight must have a liege lady and she must be high in station above her admirer and preferably be married. Isoud fulfilled these conditions and was therefore, in the conventional sense, Tristram's lady. He was vowed to her service. King Mark, according to the chivalric code, was merely an interloper who broke into this ideal romantic love. The question of the physical relations of Tristram and Isoud is calmly ignored.

" Ye should never think," said Sir Percivale to Mark (and here Malory amplifies his source), " that so noble a knight as Sir Tristram is, that he would do himself so great a villeiny to hold his uncle's wife ; howbeit, he may love your queen sinless, because she is called one of the fairest ladies of the world." [1]

In order to prevent our having any sympathy with King Mark as injured husband, the prose romances had already blackened his character. In the prose romance, Mark yielded to his barons in sending Tristram on his dangerous errand and finally, at the end of his nephew's adventures, stabbed him treacherously in the back, overcome with jealousy. " Also that traitor slew the noble knight Sir Tristram as he sat harping afore his lady La Beale Isoud, with a trenchant glaive." [2] In the first episode, at the outset of Tristam's career, Mark, according to Malory, is the initiator himself of the plan to send Tristram to Ireland, to seek a bride for the king. If, as the scholar Vinaver [3] believes, MS. 103 B.N. was one of Malory's chief sources, then he does not always follow them blindly. For example, in the prose romance, Tristram falls in love with Isoud because of his rivalry to Palamides. Malory makes Tristram's emotion a more natural one. He first feels the onset of love, when he is disguised

---

[1] From Malory, " Everyman " Edition, vol. ii., p. 55.
[2] Malory, Book XIX, chap. xi. *Cf.* Tennyson :
   " Mark's way," said Mark and clove him thro' the brain.
                     (" The Last Tournament.")
[3] See Vinaver, *Malory.*

as the harper Tramtrist : " Tramtrist cast great love to La Beale Isoud, for she was the fairest maiden and lady of the world."

Because of the conventions of the chivalric code, the story of the magic philtre was not at all necessary to Malory, though he gives some account of it. No longer is Tristram's love for Isoud a love produced by a magic draught, and told to the accompaniment of the wild lawless sea. It is a court-bred and polite sentiment. La Beale Isoud is Tristram's lady, and on one occasion in the tale, he refuses to yield up her shield when another knight asks him. But on the other hand, in Malory, there appears often a warmer and more spontaneous element than is found in the manuscripts of the prose romances, his source. Malory the man shines through Malory the translator and abbreviator. For instance, there is true human sentiment in the parting between Isoud and Tristram :

" And thereupon Isoud fell down in a swoon, and so lay a great while. And when she might speak she said ' My Lord, Sir Tristram, blessed be God ye have your life, and now I am sure ye shall be discovered by this little brachet, for she will never leave you. And also I am sure . . . as soon as my lord, King Mark, do know you, he will banish you out of the country of Cornwall, or else he will destroy you ; for God's sake my own lord, grant King Mark his will and then draw you unto the court of King Arthur, for there are ye beloved, and ever when I may, I shall send unto you : and when ye list ye may come to me, and at all times early and late I will be at your commandment, to live as poor a life as ever did queen or lady.' " [1]

Another character and set of incidents are treated in various ways by both Gottfried and Malory and poets throughout the ages up to modern times. These concern the second Iseult, " Iseult of the White Hands." There is the story of her marriage to Tristan in the later part of his life, and her curious and pathetic fate as wife, and yet no wife. There is, linked with this, the story of Tristan's death and his wife's jealous lie which caused his death. Unhappily,

[1] Malory's *Morte Darthur*, " Everyman " Edition, vol. i., p. 331.

Gottfried did not finish his story, so the incidents given by
Dr Weston, and quoted here, are taken from his continuators,
Ulrich von Türheim and Heinrich von Freiburg. The
former gives the meeting of the two Iseults.

The story can be summarised as follows :—Tristan, who
had gone to help the Duke of Arundel in war, met his son
Kahedîn and his daughter Iseult of the White Hands. Her
name and beauty called up old memories and he was strangely
torn between two desires :

" And he said in his heart ' Yea God how the name doth
lead me astray ! truth and falsehood betray alike mine eyes
and my soul. " Iseult " rings laughing in mine ear at all
times, yet know I not who Iseult may be—mine eyes behold
her and yet they see her not. Iseult is far from me and yet
is she near. . . . I have found Iseult yet not the fair-haired
Iseult who was so kindly cruel. The Iseult who vexeth thus
my heart is she of Arundel, not Iseult the fair : she, alas !
mine eyes behold not. And yet she whom I now behold, and
who is sealed with her name, her I must ever honour and love,
for the sake of the dear name, that so oft hath given me joy
and gladness unspeakable.' " [1]

This is a complicated situation even for the modern
psychologist and novelist !

Finally, Tristan yielded to the Iseult who was present
and married her. On their wedding-night, however, he
caught sight of the ring on his finger that his former love
had given him. In consequence, Iseult of the White Hands
remained a wife only in name, for the rest of her life.

Malory follows the tradition as to Isoud's marriage. By
the code of chivalry it is to La Beale Isoud (Iseult), Queen
of Cornwall, that Sir Tristram owes his allegiance. He
therefore must defend his marriage to the beau-ideal of
chivalrous love, Lancelot. He does so on the score that it is
one of form only. Sir Tristram [2] brings his wife Isoud to
the court of King Arthur but there are no emotional scenes
between them, such as modern poets, Hardy and Laurence
Binyon, delight to give.

[1] See J. L. Weston, *Gottfried von Strassburg*, vol. ii., p. 144.
[2] Form of name in Malory.

It is important in the study of the modern literature to realise the different traditions of Tristan's death. The tragic death of Tristan is related by Heinrich von Freiberg and may be given shortly.

Tristan had been smitten through with a poisoned spear, and Iseult his wife could not cure him with all her gentle arts. So Tristan sent the faithful Kurwenal to ask Iseult, the Queen of Cornwall, to help in his dire extremity. He sent her back her ring as a token. He said that he lay sorely wounded and would surely die unless she could come at once to his aid. If she came, let her put up a white sail on the returning ship; if not, let there be put up a black one.

Thus Tristan lay on his couch, waiting for life or death. He told Iseult to watch for the ship. His jealous wife had learned who was approaching and what sign had been arranged to herald her rival's approach. Eagerly the sick man lifted up his head and asked Iseult if a ship was in sight. When she replied that she spied one, he demanded what kind of a sail it bore. " Black as night," she replied. While the lie was yet in her mouth, Tristan sank back and died. His last words were " God keep thee, my love Iseult, for I shall look on thee no more." They were not addressed to Iseult of the White Hands.

Iseult of Cornwall arrived, only to hear the fatal news. " She spake no words but laid down on the bier beside her lover, put her arms round him and sighed once, and her soul departed from her body." King Mark now arrived to hear from Kurwenal that Tristan and Iseult had wronged him through no will of their own, but through the overwhelming effect of the love-potion. The King thus accorded them his forgiveness. The tragedy ends in a note of peace, sounding through the sorrow.

Malory does not give this, the most dramatic version, but the account of King Mark's treachery in giving Tristram a stab in the back, in the presence of his wife, Isoud of Cornwall. The MS. 103 B.N. refers to both stories and this Malory probably used. Death as the final triumph and escape of the lovers from a perplexing and suffering life on earth had no place in Malory's creed. His ideal of love and of happiness was a calmer and a more worldly one.   Death was thus to him a mistake and an end of any possible fulfilment of earthly love.

These chosen incidents and the comparison with Malory, will be sufficient to show that in spirit, choice of material and treatment, Gottfried and Malory differ very much indeed. To read Malory after Gottfried is to enter another atmosphere altogether.   In spite of the glamour of Malory's style, the picture of Tristan is, compared to these earlier romances, a lifeless and conventional one.   In Malory's sources [1] the great hunter of the woods and the hero of fierce unlawful love had already been tamed and become " a gentle knight pricking on the plaine " who had perforce to ride on endless quests of chivalry.

Malory's version of Tristan (Tristram) may be compared to a finely worked tapestry, where beauty of design and colour rather than vigour and reality are the artistic merits. In this array of figures on horseback in gorgeous and cumbrous trappings, Tristram is but one knight among many —a rival to Lancelot.   Tristram's passion for Isoud appears and reappears like a scarlet thread in the design, but it is not the main *motif*.   The central scene is not the passionate scene of the magic philtre but the elaborate ceremony in which Tristram is received as a knight in Arthur's court.

---

[1] Vinaver holds that Malory used a MS. approximate to MS. 103 B.N. (also 334 and 99 B.N.).   See his *Malory*.   Also Löseth (T.), *Le Roman en Prose de Tristan*, 1891.

CHAPTER XIV

TRISTAN : TENNYSON AND SWINBURNE

BEFORE considering the versions in English literature based on Gottfried's story, the *Idyll* in which Tennyson treated of Tristan "The Last Tournament," may now be considered. It will be found that Tennyson is the chief representative in the nineteenth and twentieth centuries of the Malory version, as adapted from the prose romance. "The Last Tournament," published in 1872, is one of the latest of the *Idylls of the King*. Tennyson found in his source a conventional enough Tristram to be fitted in with his other chivalric tales and his general plan. His Tristram [1] is not the sea-faring hero of the epic, strong and vigorous, torn between loyalty to his feudal lord and a fatal and passionate love. The poet substitutes a moralising half-scornful, world-weary knight who thinks the best way to regain the favour of his lady-love is to excite her jealousy of Guinevere and then to placate her by clasping a necklace around her neck. The reunion is an ignoble scene. Isolt's [1] mind is so full of hatred of Mark that, like a noxious weed, it has smothered her once noble love for Tristram. The talk of the lovers is not elevating. It is of former pleasures in the grotto and of Mark's weaknesses, his crafts and " legs of crane." And a curious *revanche* ! Tristram seems to have become the advocate of free love—not a love free to expend itself passionately on one chosen object, but free to wander from one to another. Tennyson here wishes to depict the general slackening of the ideal of love in the court, an ideal which was his own idea of marriage sanctity rather than the ideal of chivalry.

The chivalric ideal· was a romantic one rather than a moral one. The knight must have some one to inspire his heroic deeds and he must worship the lady-love chosen for

[1] Tennyson makes use of this form of name.

this and be faithful to her in spirit. Often, however, she was far removed from him in station and he had lighter loves for his less lofty moments. Tristan is not a typical chivalric hero, his love is too primitive and passionate. He belongs to the earlier heroic rather than the chivalric age. So the poet's choice of Tristan to expound a Victorian poet's moral ideals is unfortunate.

For excuse, it must be said that Tennyson was a student of Malory. He had not the heroic conception of Tristram on which to work. He found in Malory a Tristram who was just one of Arthur's knights, a rival to Lancelot in knightly prowess and love, a rival who must not be shown to eclipse Lancelot, the romantic lover. In Malory, King Mark is also vilified. Tennyson had but to heap a few extra scornful insults upon him. The " horses' ears " of the early fairy-tale have become curiously " cranes' legs."

Tennyson devised an incident—the tale of the jewels—and made Tristram the chief figure. This ingenious story does not add much to the dramatic significance of Tristram. It serves as a centre round which to paint a scene, which shows the failure and degeneration of Arthur's court through the sin of Lancelot. All the poet's art is used. He has suborned Nature to add her testimony to declare how a high ideal has been ruined by unlawful love. Every leaf that breaks off a bough and falls to the earth sighs in sympathy for the moral hopes frustrated. The languorous, half-mocking spirit is skilfully impersonated by Dagonet the Fool, who dances in and out " like a withered leaf before the hall." Lancelot, the arbiter of the tournament sits aloft in Arthur's dragon-chair, but does not bestir himself even to prevent the laws of the tournament being broken.

The tournament is sarcastically called " The Tournament of the Dead Innocence." The ladies wear white in irony. Within, is heard the mocking laughter of the fool, and without, the coarser laughter of the brutal world which has never professed any ideals. Tristram visits Isolt and is slain treacherously by his uncle, the King.[1] The deed only adds to the general futility and meanness of everything.

[1] This is one of the traditions of the prose romances (MS. 103 B.N.).

There are fine passages of description, of a falling wave, flowery meadows. But these have not much dramatic relation to the story. One of these shows that Tennyson has not realised Tristram as a wanderer or seafarer. Queen Isolt looks out of her casement at Tintagel and in the beauty of the sea forgets her lover :

> " Here in the never-ended afternoon,
>   O sweeter than all memories of thee,
>   Deeper than any yearnings after thee
>   Seemed these far-rolling westward smiling seas
>   Watched from this tower."

A musical description ! But surely the sight of the sea would have made Isolt remember Tristram, at least the Tristan [1] of the older legend. The unknown Tristan was brought first, to her shores in a drifting boat, a sick man and then, a second time with definite purpose, as King Mark's messenger. The love-drama had taken place to the sound of the wild, lawless waves. It was the sea which had borne her lover away to his simple white-handed bride, Iseult. Swinburne recognised and immortalised the salient fact of this legend. But to Tennyson, as to Malory, Tristram is a knight of the green wood " arrayed all in finest green."

Wagner [2] had produced his *Tristan* Opera at Munich seven years before Tennyson published " The Last Tournament " in his third instalment of the *Idylls of the King*, but the actual plan of these had been conceived much earlier. Thus Wagner seems to have had no direct influence on the poet. But the dissemination of his Operas throughout Europe must have aroused interest in the public mind in his version, summarised on the programmes, often in a translation. Scholars also had been slowly preparing the ground for the more creative products. Sir Walter Scott had edited and concluded *Sir Tristrem* in 1804. In 1835, Frances Michel had also edited the romance of Tristan, giving excerpts from Béroul and Thomas. It remained for Swinburne to add his great poetical contribution in *Tristram of Lyonesse* in 1882

[1] In Tennyson, Tristram.
[2] For the *Tristan* Opera, see Chap. XI., p. 159.

in order to make this form of the story familiar in literary form.

In studying *Tristram of Lyonesse* [1] and in trying to determine its literary and historical value, we must always keep in mind the poet's purpose as clearly stated by himself. Much of the derogatory criticism of this poem is discounted if the true aim of the poet is realised.

Swinburne writes that in undertaking to " rehandle the deathless legend of Tristram," his aim was " simply to present that story not diluted and debased, as it has been in our own time by other hands, but undefaced by improvement, and undeformed by transformation, as it was known to the age of Dante, wherever the chronicles of romance found hearing from Ercildoune to Florence ; and not in the epic or romantic form of sustained and continuous narrative, but mainly through a succession of dramatic scenes of pictures with descriptive settings or backgrounds."

Let us first examine his claim to have set forth the story as known in chronicles of romance from Ercildoune [2] to Florence. Lafourcade, in *La Jeunesse de Swinburne*, supplies and comments on data which fortunately enables us to trace the early stages of the poet's effort through imitation, and also the poet's knowledge and use of his sources.

The first canto of " Queen Yseult " was published in 1857 in the *Undergraduate Papers*. Afterwards, five other cantos were found among a number of College papers, making six complete cantos in all.[3] An introduction by the poet himself gives the plan and scope of the unfinished work, originally meant to be an epic in ten cantos. This preliminary sketch also supplies us with a knowledge of Swinburne's reading at the time. As his biographer [4] points out, it included the old

[1] " Tristan " is the form of the name adopted in this section when the general Tristan legend is referred to. Otherwise, the form of name which the author of the poem or play under discussion adopts, is used.

[2] Thomas of Ercildoune, the Rhymer, has been confused with Thomas the twelfth century French poet.

[3] Now published in the Bonchurch Edition, ed. Sir E. Gosse and T. J. Wise, vol. i. See also Introductory Note.

[4] Lafourcade, in *La Jeunesse de Swinburne*, 1928, vol. ii., chap. 3, gives these interesting points and study of the poet's Pre-Raphaelite period.

romances of Béroul and Thomas, parts of which were given in Michel's text, which Swinburne knew.[1] From the names employed of Tristram's father and mother, Roland and Blancheflour and other details, it can be deduced that Swinburne also was acquainted with Sir Walter Scott's *Sir Tristrem*. In the early poem the influence of Malory is not so much seen as in the later, and his version of the story is rejected as inferior. " Queen Yseult " was written in 1857 immediately after Swinburne had met William Morris at the Pre-Raphaelite gathering in Church Street at Oxford and had heard him read " The Defence of Guenevere." Like Morris in this poem, Swinburne strives to regain the simplicity and *naïveté* of the mediæval romances and ballads. " Queen Yseult " is directly modelled either on Morris's " Blanche " or the " Willow," which are also written in a trochaic metre of three lines with triple rhymes, and he copies the effect which Morris uses so often of the monotone.[2] Morris at the time generously praised it, considering it superior to his own. Swinburne himself did not, in his later years, think highly of these youthful efforts nor did he include them in *Poems and Ballads*. The metrical form is evidently crippling to a poet who was to show himself master of such a range of complicated metres. In Swinburne's poem the hero and heroine are cut out in the accustomed Pre-Raphaelite pattern ; the heroine possesses gold corn-ripe hair, an arrow hand, wears an embroidered blue robe and so on. Like Aubrey Beardsley's illustrations of Malory's *Morte Darthur* the composition[3] is stronger in design than in likeness to life. For example, the description of the " Lady Yseult aux Blanches Mains " (the

---

[1] " Tristan recueil de ce qui reste des poemes, etc.," 1835-7. Swinburne cites this work in a critical note to *Ballads of the English Border*.

[2] A verse from the " Willow " and " The Red Cliff " will exemplify this :

> 'Twas in church on Palm Sunday
> Listening what the priest did say
> Of the kiss that did betray

(quoted, Lafourcade, vol. ii., p. 47).

[3] Composition is used in two senses. Artists speak also of " composing " a picture.

second Yseult) in Canto Five may be taken, which describes
Tristram's wife entering the bridal chamber :

> And the singing maidens there
> Led the bride with tresses bare,
> Singing bridal songs of her.
>
> Purple flowers, blue and red,
> On the rushes round the bed,
> Strewed they for her feet to tread.
>
> But about the bed they set
> Long white blossoms white and wet,
> Crowns the fairest they could get.
>
> Her blue robe along the hem
> Coloured like a lily's stem,
> She put off and gave to them,
>
> And she bade the fairest girl
> All her soft hair comb and curl
> With a comb of jet and pearl.
>
> By the mirrored steel she stood
> Thinking gently as she could
> Sweet new thoughts of womanhood.

These lines suggest the ballad rather than the epic. The
poem continues with an innocent frankness of detail also
copied from the older romances. The more passionate
element is excluded. In *Tristram of Lyonesse* this passion in
the young wife who is spurned is turned into bitterness, which
makes for itself the excuse of righteous wrath. But in the
earlier poem the gentle maiden shows no resentment, though
it must be remembered the poem is unfinished.

As far as the narrative is concerned, in the six completed
cantos there is simplicity and directness of action. In
Canto One the story of Roland and Blancheflour, his death,
the birth of Tristram and his mother's death, the youth of
Tristram, his appearance at court and his fight with Moronde [1]
are told dramatically. The tale is not overweighted with

---

[1] Swinburne's form of " Morgan," probably from *Sir Tristrem*.
" Morolt " according to Gottfried von Strassburg.

wealth of simile and ornament as in the more elaborate later poem.

Adaptation of tradition is shown in the incident in which Yseult (Mark's wife) sends Tristram leaves of melilote as a sign to come to her. He had sent to beseech her to have pity on his love-longing. This is her answer, those leaves of sweet-smelling clover :

> But when snows were thick about
> Yseult sent for Tristram out
> Soft dry leaves of melilote.
>
> That was for a sign to stand
> That he came to take her hand
> In the happy garden land.
>
> So that when his love had got
> Those dry leaves of melilote
> He the pain remembered not.
>
> But he saw not where to go
> Lest his feet some man should know,
> For the ways were marred with snow.
>
> So his bitter doubt he wrote,
> And she sent him for his doubt
> The same leaves of melilote.

She comes to meet him through the snow and with bare and bleeding feet carries him on her back through the court to her own chamber, where the floor is strewn with rushes. Thus the danger of detection through the discovery of footsteps is obviated. The incident corresponds no doubt with that in the early romances in which Tristan sent to the Queen the piece of bark which floated down the stream which ran through Iseult's chamber. The snow is probably a reminiscence of the flour spread by Mark's dwarf between the two beds of the lovers. Swinburne may have changed the incident partly to bring in the tuneful word " melilote " in which he evidently delighted.

When Swinburne came to write his poem in 1882, he used the same sources as in 1857, with one important difference.

In 1882 he was much more under the influence of Malory. It is true that in the main essentials of the story he had rejected his version, but in his description of *Joyous Gard* and Tristram's fight with Palamede, traces of the knowledge of that great prose stylist are found. For Swinburne, a past-master himself in the art of words, could not have failed to appreciate and fall under the glamour of Malory's style, which like a fairy-like mist enhances much which broad daylight would reveal as commonplace.

But the poet's scholarly instincts and wide knowledge of early French romance told him that the older tales of Béroul and Thomas (and *Sir Tristrem*) contained finer material for his poem than Malory. Also, writing as he did after Tennyson, he was fully conscious that he had a rival to surpass. His wider scholarship here stood him in good stead.

Lafourcade points out that Swinburne used *Sir Tristrem* as a source in his early Tristan poem. In his later *Tristram of Lyonesse* its influence makes itself felt. The *Sir Tristrem* is a translation of the French Thomas, who was confused with " Thomas of Ercildoune, the Rhymer," to whom the poem was wrongly ascribed. It differs in certain details from Thomas. For instance, it mentions the curious circumstance that Tristram's faithful dog Hodain also drank the love-potion, a detail to be found again in the Italian romances.[1] It is written in an irregular rhymed stanza of four lines, the first and the third, the second and the fourth, rhyming. Swinburne made use of it, but transformed its dry clipped style into a lyrical form, enriched by simile and enchanting to the ear, with its full-throated melody.

For example, in *Sir Tristrem* the lines run :

> They rowed, those knights so true,
> Tristrem, an oar took he
> E'en as his turn fell due,
> Nor one against the three
> From toil would shrink,
> Ysonde the maiden free
> Bade Brengwain give them drink.

---

[1] In *Tristano Riccardiano*. See E. G. Gardner, *The Arthurian Legend in Italian Literature*, 1930, p. 70.

In lieu of these bare cold facts, Swinburne describes glowingly the manly Tristram at the oar and how Iseult looked upon him:

> Then Tristram girt him for an oarsman's place
> And took his oar and smote, and toiled with might
> In the east wind's full face and the strong sea's spite
> Labouring ; and all the rowers rowed hard, but he
> More mightily than any wearier three.
> And Iseult watched him rowing with sinless eyes
> That loved him but in holy girlish wise
> For noble joy in his fair manliness
> And trust and tender wonder ; none the less
> She thought if God had given her grace to be
> Man, and make war on danger of earth and sea,
> Even such a man she would be ; for his stroke
> Was mightiest as the mightier water broke,
> And in sheer measure like strong music drave
> Clean through the wet weight of the wallowing wave ;
> And, as a tune before a great king played
> For triumph was the tune their strong strokes made,
> And sped the ship through with smooth strife of oars
> Over the mid seas's grey foam-paven floors,
> For all the loud breach of the waves at will.
> So for an hour they fought the storm out still.[1]

And so on, simile after simile succeeds the other as wave succeeds wave, till the inward eye and the ear are sated with magnificence. In the same elaborate style, the poet describes how Tristram naturally became thirsty when the storm abated, and asked drink from Iseult. Iseult went downstairs and spied the fatal flask in Brangwain's bosom. From a loving desire not to waken the sleeping maid, "half-dead with fear and pain" of the past storm, Iseult took it by stealth away. Then she returned to the deck and innocently gave Tristram to drink and drank it herself. Thus Swinburne translates the seven bald lines of the ballad into a hundred or more.

Yet, as in *Sir Tristrem* and Thomas, Swinburne follows the primary conception of Tristan as a sea-hero. Tennyson makes him a knight of the woods, following Malory.

---

[1] Swinburne, *Collected Poems* (Heinemann), vol. iv., p. 34.

This latter conception also appears in early tradition, though less stressed than the sea-hero one. It is found in an old thirteenth-century poem " Donnei des Amanz " when Tristan is found imitating the song of the birds. One of the chief differences between the version of Thomas and that of Béroul is that in Béroul the Tristan story is connected with Arthur. Swinburne follows him in this (and, of course, Malory) and describes the court and tournaments in all their splendour. The lovers, Tristram and Iseult, also discuss the beauty of Guinevere, and relate the story of Merlin and Nimue. King Arthur is pictured by the poet thus :

> King Arthur, yet unwarred upon by fate,
> Held high in hall at Camelot, like one
> Whose lordly life was as the mounting sun
> That climbs and pauses on the point of noon,
> Sovereign : how royal ran the tourney's tune
> Through Tristram's three days' triumph, spear to spear.[1]

Swinburne's description of the grotto reminds us rather of Thomas than Béroul. In Thomas, as in Swinburne, Nature smiles on the lovers and the beauties of the scene are painted in glowing colours. In Béroul, the lovers are in real danger of their lives and take refuge in a cave, where they have to bear the hardships of rough weather, fortified only by their love.

Thus the lovers' dwelling is described by Swinburne :

> There was a bower, beyond man's eye more fair
> Than ever summer dews and sunniest air
> Fed full with rest and radiance till the boughs
> Had wrought a roof as for a holier house
> Than aught save love might breathe in : . . .
>
> .   .   .   .
>
> And thither, ere sweet night had slain sweet day,
> Iseult and Tristram took their wandering way,
> And rested, and refreshed their hearts with cheer
> In hunters' fashion of the woods ; and here
> More sweet it seemed, while this might be, to dwell
> And take of all world's weariness farewell . . .
> Than reign of all world's lordship queen and king.[2]

---

[1] *Collected Poems* (Heinemann), vol. iv., p. 95.
[2] *Ibid.*, pp. 47 and 48.

Béroul's description appeals more to the heart, Thomas, and after him Swinburne, to the eye and ear. Swinburne follows Béroul in his dramatic description of Tristram's escape to the chapel and his plunge into the sea. This gives the poet an opportunity of using all the wealth of words at his command to describe Tristram swimming, a sport the poet himself rejoiced in in his youth. A second description, to be compared with it, is given when Tristram has his last encounter with the sea, before he meets the enemy who is to give him his death-wound (Canto VIII).[1]

Swinburne follows closely his source Thomas, in the story of Tristram's last days and the incident of the black and white sail. Tristram's famous henchman is called Ganhardine, no doubt a poetical form of Käherdin,[2] Iseult's brother, mentioned in Thomas.

The character of the second Iseult, who resembles at first the lily maid Elaine, who died of loving Lancelot, is strongly yet subtly drawn. Her sweet and innocent love for Tristram becomes soured, as hope gradually dies out, and turns to bitter and revengeful hate. Hate, to Swinburne, was no negative quality but as positive as love. It blows like a bleak, devastating wind through what was once the fair garden of Iseult's soul, withering all the opening flowers. She is no hesitating liar, lying out of a jealous spasm and then repenting. Outwardly, she is as gentle and yielding as ever, but inwardly, she nurses with firm resolution the desire for revenge, what she considers a just revenge :

> And as a soil that cleaves in twain for drouth
> [She] thirsted for judgment given of God's own mouth
> Against them, till the strength of dark desire
> Was in her as a flame of hell's own fire.
> Nor seemed the wrath which held her spirit in stress
> Aught else or worse than passionate holiness,
> Nor the ardent hate, which called on judgment's rod,
> More hateful than the righteousness of God.[3]

When the dying Tristram asks her as a last behest to tell

---

[1] *Collected Poems* (Heinemann), vol. iv., p. 126.
[2] Kahedîn in Gottfried.
[3] *Collected Poems* (Heinemann), vol. iv., p. 107.

him whether a ship is coming towards him on the sea, and what colour its sail is, she is strong enough to hide the bitterness that is consuming her, and promises to obey.

> Then seemed her face a pale funereal flame,
> That burns down slow by midnight, as she said ;
> " Speak, and albeit thy bidding spake me dead,
> God's love renounce me, if it were not done." [1]

On beholding the ship, with its white sail, riding the breast of the waves, she replies unhesitatingly that the sail is black. The lie performs its fatal work :

> And fain he would have sprung upright, and seen,
> And spoken ; but strong death struck sheer between,
> And darkness closed as iron round his head,
> And smitten through the heart lay Tristram, dead.[2]

Out of the ship which, alas ! has arrived too late, steps Iseult, led by Ganhardine. She hears the wailing, and instinctively realises it is for Tristram her lover.

Swinburne, when he likes to, can use words sparingly, with swift dramatic effect. The reader could almost wish the poem had ended here.

These passages are sufficient to show how Swinburne uses his sources. In the main he follows the facts without change, but he often simplifies incident and suppresses names and details which would spoil the harmony and beauty of his description. Wagner employs the same device in his Operas, but for a different reason, for the sake of dramatic unity. For example, the early life and exploits of Tristram given in the somewhat conflicting versions of Thomas and Béroul, are summed up by Swinburne in a flowing description, which just mentions enough facts to justify Iseult's youthful admiration of her hero. Tristram's prowess as a harper and a fighter, set on fire maidens' hearts in secret and his youth " gave his fame flower-like fragrance and soft growth." Again, no detail of Tristram's fight with the dragon and dreadful wound is told, which wound was the real cause why he set out in a boat with only his harp as company. Finally

---

[1] *Collected Poems* (Heinemann), vol. iv., p. 106.   [2] *Ibid.*, p. 147.

his little bark drifted on to Ireland's shore.   All is generalised in our modern poet :

> And in mid change of time and fight and song
> Chance cast him westward on the low sweet strand
> Where songs are sung of the old green Irish land
> And the sky loves it, and the sea loves best,
> And as a bird is taken to man's breast
> The sweet-souled land where sorrow sweetest sings
> Is wrapt round with them as with hands and wings
> And takes to the sea's heart as a flower.[1]

No one with any sense of poetic rhythm and metre could deny that Swinburne in this poem has enriched by his descriptive power the story of Tristan.   But the question of the valuation of his poem as a whole and its definite contribution to the Tristan legend is a more difficult one.

This poem has many adverse critics, the chief of whom is Edmund Gosse.   In his life of Swinburne, he pronounces the poem a failure.   Others, including Sturge Moore, complain that Swinburne cannot tell a story.   In a fine essay in the *Criterion*,[2] Sturge Moore writes :   " There is a wind which blows and blows the tale out of the mind."   One of the weakest points in the tale, he continues, is the nightly substitution of Brangwain.

But in judging any work of Art, it is only fair to consider the original purpose of its creator.   Swinburne does not claim to write a unified drama or to tell a story.   To repeat his own words, he rehandled the legend " not in the epic or romantic form of sustained and continuous narrative, but mainly through a succession of dramatic scenes or pictures with descriptive settings or backgrounds."   The incidents for the scenes, such as the substitution of Brangwain for Iseult on the marriage night, he takes as he found them. The relations of Mark and Iseult are left purposely vague. We have to afford the poet a " poetic licence " on this account which is not given in prose.

---

[1] *Collected Poems* (Heinemann), vol. iv., p. 17.

[2] *Criterion*, vol. i. : T. Sturge Moore, " The Story of Tristram and Isolt in Modern Poetry."

It must be admitted that Swinburne has fulfilled the aim he set before him. It might have been a greater triumph still, if he could have created a swiftly moving drama like *Atalanta*, with one central theme. But he did not set this task before himself, and we cannot judge his work on this basis.

True it is that the poem of Tristram and Iseult is not perfect, but can any long poem be perfect ? [1] Often Swinburne does not leave enough to the imagination. For example, in describing Iseult, he is not content to give a general description but enumerates nearly all the parts of her body. Some poets give us one apt simile which, like a flash of lightning in the night, lights up the darkened country behind it. But Swinburne's similes are often heaped up one on the other till the reader is somewhat dazed, and pleased to let the active mind be lulled to sleep by euphonious sound.

Sometimes these quick-changing similes are used with fine effect, as when he speaks in the Prelude of Lovers, whose lives are " inlaid with hopes and fears, spun fine as fire and jewelled thick with tears." These are really four telescoped similes. At other times, simile follows simile, and we are left with enchanting musical sound in our ears but with blurred images in our mind.

Again, the description of the lovers and their amorous joys (in Canto II) becomes wearisome. Like the babes in the wood they become buried, but it is under words, not leaves.

But if there are some passages which are over-luscious, on the other hand there are many perfect descriptive and dramatic passages. One may be referred to here in Canto II,[2] one which combines both elements, the scene where King Mark, " a swart lean man, but kinglike," " close-mouthed " and " gaunt-cheeked " receives his new bride, Iseult. The castle built on its summit of jagged rocks, "a wave-walled palace with its eastern gate, full of the sunrise," is pictured in a vivid and clear manner.

What seem often a greater weakness of the poem than over-luxuriance are the passages of reflection and moralising.

---

[1] See A. C. Bradley, *Oxford Essays on Poetry*, 1909, especially pp. 191 and 192.

[2] *Collected Poems* (Heinemann), vol. iv., p. 41.

Swinburne is at no time a deep or subtle thinker. Also, his pantheistic philosophy and impersonal view of Fate and the gods has been adequately given in the Prelude in fine poetical expression. As the Prelude is in the form of an Invocation or Epitaph, the personal expression of the poet's philosophy or belief is fitting as it is fitting in Shelley's *Adonais*. But the long appeal to Fate at the beginning of Canto IX is too long drawn out and a needless repetition. It does not add either to the lyrical or dramatic excellence of the poem.

Iseult's appeal to God is also, in my opinion, an error of judgment on the part of the poet. For he has taken a hero and heroine, representative of no especial age or nation, but belonging to an early and vigorous epoch. He has drawn them in large outlines, as the first man or woman might be drawn, magnificent in their bodily perfection and youthful prowess, against a background of sea and sun and sky. They had drunk a magic draught and had been, in spite of barriers of circumstance, drawn irresistibly to each other. So far, so good. But with Iseult's appeal to God, the factor of morality is brought in and the limiting time-element. What laws of morality are the lovers subject to, that of the early Celtic age of the fifth or sixth century, or that of the feudal and religious conception of the twelfth century? Iseult, in her passionate, unlawful but self-forgetting love, is nobler than the God she appeals to, with His fixed relentless condemnation of it. Surely this is Swinburne's revolt against the narrow conception of his own day, not Iseult's!

Swinburne has prefaced his poem by a magnificent Prelude. In it he has enumerated a zodiac of famous women-lovers, in which each is depicted as a star in the firmament, ruling over her especial month. The history of each is told in a pregnant phrase or two, of Juliet, Dido, Cleopatra, Guinevere and others. Dido's betrayal by Æneas is aptly phrased :

> . . . —and for June,
> Flares like an angered and storm-reddening moon
> Her signal sphere, whose Carthaginian pyre,
> Shadowed her traitor's flying sail with fire.[1]

---

[1] *Collected Poems* (Heinemann), vol. iv., p. 8.

Iseult, the poet's chosen heroine, reigns aloft amidst her compeers.

This Invocation to Lovers ranks as one of the most beautiful English poems on the subject of Love, and may be compared with Shelley's *Epipsychidion*. It shines resplendent with fire and light, and ranges from the trumpet-tones of Milton to the ethereal music of Shelley. In the description of the Valley of the Shades where the dead lovers wander, there are touches reminiscent of the pitying humanity of Virgil in the sixth book of the *Æneid*, when he also visits these nether regions. Yet it is not a mere pastiche, it is characteristically Swinburnian, full of splendid images and of volume, swift and sure. The poet had learned from the Greeks to personify the forces of Nature, giving them body and motion. The image of the Sun-god, who reigns supreme, is a Titanic figure :

> These are the signs wherethrough the year sees move,
> Full of the sun, the sun-god which is love,
> A fiery body, blood-red from the heart,
> Outward, with fire-white wings made wide apart,
> That close not and unclose not, but upright
> Steered without wind by their own light and might
> Sweep through the flameless fire of air that rings
> From heaven to heaven with thunder of wheels and wings
> And antiphones of motion-moulded rhyme
> Through spaces out of space and timeless time.[1]

The Invocation to the Lovers is also an epitaph and, as in Shelley's *Adonais*, the poet gives expression to his pantheistic philosophy. Swinburne can promise his lovers no individual existence in the future, no fuller life where their aspirations will be fulfilled :

> They have the night, who had like us the day,
> We, whom day binds, shall have the night as they,
> We from the fetters of the light unbound,
> Healed of our wound of living, shall sleep sound.[2]

The most they can hope for is to be resolved into the elements and be at peace. One gift alone the poet can make them ; he can blow the " living breath between dead lips and immortalize in words these lives."

[1] *Collected Poems* (Heinemann), vol. iv., p. 9.   [2] *Ibid.*, p. 11.

CHAPTER XV

TRISTAN : OTHER MODERN VERSIONS.

THE story of Tristan has been put into dramatic form by a number of modern poets of the twentieth century. The first group of these, including Laurence Binyon, Comyns Carr and Arthur Symons, show the influence of the Gottfried tradition, probably through Wagner, in the incidents chosen, but these evidently hold themselves free to modify tradition as they desire. Thomas Hardy and John Masefield, in the second group, use tradition even more freely, incorporating an incident according to any precedent they can find, if it happens to suit their dramatic purpose. If they cannot find one, they invent it. The question in how far these modern authors are justified in the liberties they take, is one which must be answered separately in each individual case.

Laurence Binyon's poem, " Tristram's End," [1] an Ode, takes for its subject the death of Tristan according to the Gottfried traditions.[2] It is not, however, an Ode in the most precise sense. Its form is irregular, being divided into three parts, the second of which is a dialogue (between Tristram [3] and Isoult) in eight-lined stanzas with alternating rhymes.[4] The first and third parts are in lines of irregular length, with iambic stressing and rhyming irregularly. The poem has the emotional appeal of the lyric rather than the stately effect of the Ode or the impersonality of the Narrative poem.

In " Tristram's End " the final and dramatic scenes of Tristan's death are narrated. The poem shows real poetic power. Sometimes, however, like a spider's web over-weighted with heavy drops of shining morning dew, the web

[1] *Odes*, by Laurence Binyon, 1913.
[2] That is, according to the successors of Gottfried.
[3] This is the form of the name in Binyon.
[4] For quotation, see below, pp. 221-23.

of fact the poet has spun, breaks under the stress of his passionate mysticism.

When Tristram's wife, Isoult,[1] has told him the lie concerning the colour of the sail, the sick man manages, with the false strength of despair, to struggle to the outer door and to gaze on the ocean.   Then he sees a towering ship, with a shining sail approaching.   He hears the mariner's cries and can espy a blue cloak :

> . . . and now
> Like magic brought to his divining ears,
> A voice, that empties all the earth and sky,
> Comes clear across the water, " It is I." [2]

It is the voice of Isoult.   Overcome with joy, Tristram sinks on his knees, but she is far below, where the spray dashes upon the rock-hewn steps.   She is overcome with a pity like despair :

> How shall her strength avail
> To conquer that steep stair,
> Dark, terrible, and ignorant as Time,
> Up which her feet must climb
> To Tristram ?   His outstretching arms are fain
> To help her, yet are helpless ; and his pain
> Is hers, and her pain Tristram's : with long sighs
> She mounts, then halts again,
> Till she have drawn strength from his love-dimmed eyes :
> But when that wasted face anew she sees,
> Despair anew subdues her knees :
> She fails, yet still she mounts by sad degrees,
> With all her soul into her gaze upcast,
> Until at last, at last . . .
> What tears are like the wondering tears
> Of that entranced embrace,
> When out of desolate and divided years
> Face meets belovèd face ?
> What cry most exquisite of grief or bliss
> The too full heart shall tell,
> When the new-recovered kiss
> Is the kiss of last farewell ? [3]

---

[1] This is the form of the name in Binyon.
[2] " Tristram's End " in *Odes*, 1913, p. 13.   [3] *Odes*, p. 12.

In a passionate dialogue the lovers review past events—
Tristram's appearance at Isoult's window in Ireland with
his harp, the early love, and Tristram's vow to King Mark
to bring him a bride, which he could not keep and the
breaking of which rent his heart.   But in spite of the suffering,
the lovers regret nothing, nor would they accept one pain
the less.

The emotional strain of the reunion is too much for the
sick man and he dies.   Isoult can no longer endure this
dark world and also expires.

The ascent of Isoult up the rock staircase, unattended,
and the vigil of both all night on the rocky platform, certainly
seems improbable, as Mr Sturge Moore [1] points out.   But
the lyrical emotion of the poem may carry the reader beyond
cold logic and make him forget the seeming impossibility.

The treatment of death by the poet is a noble one.   In
its presence, Tristram's wife forgets her ignoble jealousy
which brought forth the lie that like a swift-poisoned arrow
has caused her husband's death.   She accepts the fact that
Death has decided to whom Tristram belongs and she will
give them both a lordly burial, conveying the dead bodies to
Mark's court :

> " Put out your torches, for the dawn grows clear.
> And set me out within the hall a bier,
> And wedding robes, the costliest that are
> In all my house, prepare,
> And lay upon the silks these princely dead,
> And bid the sailors take that funeral bed
> And set it in the ship, and put to sea,
> And north to Cornwall steer,
> Farewell, my lord, thy home is far from here,
> Farewell, my great love, dead and doubly dear !
> Carry him hence, proud queen, for he is thine,
> Not mine, not mine, not mine ! " [2]

Mark comes to the realisation that the lovers have been

---

[1] See interesting discussion by Mr Sturge Moore on his essay on
Tristan and Iseult in *Criterion*, vol. i.

[2] *Odes*, p. 25.

starcrossed rather than treacherous. Now all conflict is passed :

> " O Tristram, no more shalt thou need to hide
> Thy thought from my thought, sitting at my side,
> Nor need to wrestle sore
> With thy great love and with thy fixèd oath,
> Even now death leaves thee loyal unto both
> Even as thou would'st have been, for evermore." [1]

Like most modern writers, Binyon also rejects the idea of love being caused by magic. When the lovers are discussing their past love and Isoult reminds Tristan of the charmèd cup, he replies :

> " Or ever that draught we drank,
> Thy heart, Isoult, was mine,
> My heart was thine. I thank
> God's grace, no wizard wine,
> No stealth of a drop distilled
> By a spell in the night, no art,
> No charm, could have ever filled
> With aught but thee my heart." [2]

This poem rises at times to heights of strong feeling and imaginative expression, but it lacks proportion. It leaves that impression on the mind, which a torso, representing heroic figures, makes to the eye. If the lyric beauty could have been combined with epic breadth and architectonic skill, this would have been one of the finest modern poems on Tristan.

Both Swinburne and Binyon presuppose a cognisance of the story according to the Thomas and Gottfried traditions. The two dramas written by Arthur Comyns Carr and Arthur Symons, though they also adhere to the same set of traditions in the main, reconstruct the story more completely.

Comyns Carr, in his *Tristram and Iseult*,[3] chooses his scenes so as to make a dramatic whole of the story of Tristan. His play is divided into four Acts and he makes the climax fall in the last Act, when Andred, one of Mark's barons, kills Tristram. This incident is, of course, contrary to any of the accepted versions.

Tradition is altered not always advisedly. For example,

[1] *Odes*, p. 28.   [2] *Odes*, p. 19.   [3] Published 1906.

Mark has been made jealous of Tristram from the first and desirous of getting rid of him though pretending otherwise. This is a fundamental change because, in the older versions, the tragic conflict was between Tristram's passionate charm-compelled love for Iseult and his feudal loyalty to Mark. The hypocrisy of Mark in Carr's play lessens Tristram's guilt and weakens the tragic issue.

The potion scene on the ship in Act III shows in a marked degree the influence of Wagner. The lovers believe they are drinking death only to find they are at the beginning of a more intense life.

The last Act (Act IV) is the real climax, and the romantic and tragic elements are well sustained. The lovers are met together for a short and blissful period, as has been their custom for some time past. But an evil shadow has been cast on the lovers' paradise by Ogrin the Dwarf, who has betrayed their meeting-place to King Mark and Andred, their enemy. The lovers anticipate death and romanticise the idea. Thus it does not come, a swift treacherous stabbing in the dark, as in Thomas Hardy's play. The following excerpt illustrates the manner of treatment by the dramatist and the style.

Tristram speaks :

> " Iseult.   My Queen Iseult,
>   The end draws very near : In that pale dawn
>   We thought 'twas death we drank and so it was :
>   For love like ours, that swallows up all life
>   Dwells on the verge of death.   The earth's poor day
>   Cannot contain it, and the boundless night
>   Where every path is set with golden stars,
>   But leads us onward to that larger world
>   Whereof death holds the key."

On the whole, the play has certain poetical merits as a romantic drama, but the poet misses the deeper implications of tragedy.

The play of Arthur Symons, *Tristan and Iseult*,[1] is a more subtly-conceived drama and a study of the interplay of motive. In the first Act, the subject-matter is taken from the narrative

[1] Published 1917.

of Tristan's life, at the time of his second visit to Ireland. This, it will be remembered, portrays the finding of the splinter in Tristan's sword, which fact goes to prove that he is the slayer of Princess Iseult's uncle Morold.[1] This discovery causes Tristan to disclose that he represents Mark's messenger, sent to win the Princess Iseult's hand for the old king. In spite of Iseult's reluctance, she is forced by her ambitious parents to accompany Tristan to Mark's court to be his bride.

Act II contains the great dramatic scene of the play, the drinking of the potion. The actual events and outward circumstances follow more or less the Gottfried and Opera traditions. The conversation of Tristan and Iseult before they drink the love-potion, in which Tristan is the loyal servant of Mark and therefore answers Iseult's laments in a sympathetic but restrained manner, is after Gottfried. Mark is an old man. Thus the youth of both tends to make the sudden passionate love which arises between the two, natural. This lessens the mere magic of the love-drink.

The similes, drawn from Nature and the sea, add to the vigour and dramatic effect. The old tale also breathes the keen salt air of the ocean, though there is something modern in the self-conscious dwelling on the affinity between Nature and man in moments of high passion and exaltation.

(Tristan) :

> " I do not think that I am yet awake.
> What is it that has bound me with these chains
> That burn like shining fire about my soul ? "

(Iseult of Ireland) :

> " What is it that has set me free ?   I feel
> As if a boundless joy had given me wings :
> I am as universal as the sun.
> Look, Tristan, there is nothing here but light :
> Light in the sky, light in the hollow sea,
> The encircling and caressing light of the air :
> Light eats into my flesh and drinks me up :
> I am a cup for the immense thirst of light,
> I cannot see you, Tristan, for the light." [2]

---

[1] Form of name in Symons, Morolt.
[2] A. Symons, *Tristan and Iseult*, 1917, p. 49.

And yet, for Tristan, the old loyalties have not altogether died. He is torn in two, as in the older heroic tale :

> " I have drunk,
> A poison that no man has ever tasted,
> For it has withered honour in my heart
> There was a king for whom I would have died."

Their passion seems to partake of the nature of the limitless ocean, but events move on relentlessly : the shore of Cornwall approaches and Tristan must lead Iseult by the hand and present her to his feudal sovereign.

In outward circumstances, the third Act differs little from the one of the " discovery scene " in Gottfried, in which Tristan and Iseult are betrayed and discovered by King Mark. In this case it is Melot the fool who betrays them.

But the spirit and treatment of the scene is wholly different. The contrast of the two characters, Tristan and Iseult, their separate reactions to the same event, that of discovery by King Mark, is modern in its conception. In the old epic, the emotions of the heroine are not analysed, she plays a passive rather than an active part until she has to decide whether she will leave her kingdom and go to the rescue of her dying lover. But here, in Symon's play, her attitude is firm and uncompromising, rather that of a modern heroine, pleading for the rights of free and passionate love against legal bonds. When she is discovered with Tristan, she shows courage and dignity. In vain Tristan reminds her that he has robbed her of worldly glory and reputation.

She exclaims proudly :

> " Now I am glad, utterly glad, at last,
> The first time wholly since the day of days,
> We drank down love together.   I have my will
> I have always willed that he [Mark] should take us thus." [1]

She carries the war right into the enemy's camp, tells Mark that it is he who has betrayed love by forcing her into a marriage, for the sake of reconciling the enmities of two lands.

[1] A. Symons, *op. cit.*, p. 76.

Mark is not degraded as in Malory. He truly loves Iseult. His dignified reply to this reproach is merely that he requires her as a Queen for his kingdom, even if there can no longer be love between them.

Tristan, on the other hand, is overcome by the thought of his own treachery and can make no defence. He is torn by conflict : his love for Iseult has lost its triumphing quality. When Mark asks for his sword and breaks it and throws it contemptuously away, Tristan submits without a protest to this greatest of all humiliations. He seems to admit that Mark is right. The very nobility in Tristan, his quick sensitiveness to the ideal of honour, seems to weaken his actions and his character. Yet, in some ways, it makes him more lovable, if less heroic. He, at any rate, does not take refuge in the thought that the magic draught excuses him altogether.

(Tristan) :

> " I have been conquered and all's vain, Iseult,
> If you have loved me, be a little sorry
> And you, my King, forgive me."

His emotions are more complex than those of the old heroic warrior.

The last Act follows in the main the usual tradition of the black and white sail, and Iseult's lie. A slight change is made in the story. Iseult believes at first that a man doctor is coming to heal Tristan, but she is undeceived by the talk of her maids. This alteration makes no vital difference to the drama. What is really of import is the careful drawing of the character of the second Iseult, who has already been introduced by the dramatist, contrary to tradition, in the first Act, and made the cousin of Princess Iseult. She is pictured here, in contrast to her energetic full-blooded revengeful cousin, peacefully embroidering a piece of tapestry, " a knight in armour." In the last Act, she is not so content. She is overcome by a very natural jealousy. Tristan, in his delirium, has forgotten all their past life together and all his wife's loving service. He remembers only his first love, Iseult, the Queen of Cornwall.

(Tristan) :

    " I have been lying in my grave, I think,
      These years and she is coming to waken me." [1]

In an agony of jealousy the wife lies concerning the colour
of the sail seen on the horizon. Very swift is her remorse at
Tristan's death, caused by that lie.
    (Iseult of Brittany) :

      " Too late, too late ; I told him that the sail was black
        Was black, I killed him.   It was I killed him." [2]

Iseult, her rival, arriving from the ship, sweeps her aside,
with majestic mien.
    (Iseult of Ireland) :

      " Comfort yourself, Iseult of Brittany,
        And hide yourself, and weep, if you will weep,
        Because it had to be, and leave me here.
        You have done nothing in this mighty death." [2]

In the sorrow of the latter is all the disillusionment of the
world-weary soul :

      " He was the glory of the world ;
        All the world's dust, for Tristan can be dead,
        The dust was once a fire and burned the stars :
        Now what a little ashes holds the fire
        That was blown out too early.   There is nothing
        Left in the world, and I am out of place.
        Could you not wait for me until I came, Tristan ? " [2]
                                (She dies.)

Mark now arrives, and when he hears the story of the philtre
and realises the tragedy, he is full of resigned sorrow at the
havoc wrought through blind ignorance.   " Had I but known,
had I but known ! " is his cry.   He commands that the two
be borne back to Tintagel and buried among kings.
    Like a dark-pinioned bird, there hovers over the whole
play a dark mysterious Fate, which creates the beauty as well
as the sorrow of the human scene.   Even in the first Act,

     [1] A. Symons, *op. cit.*, p. 102.   [2] *Ibid.*, p. 106.

Iseult seems to challenge Fate, when she asks why she should fear love :

> " Why, how should the free soul
> Fear any power in the firmament ?
> For there are women who have never feared
> The face of steel, or face of any man
> Or blood or battle or the foam of the sea,
> When the wind wrings out the sails and washes them." [1]

Arthur Symons, in this play, keeps close to the old traditions and yet imparts a certain modern atmosphere to it. The greatest weakness is a certain lack of spontaneity and grace, and a too self-conscious style. The play is perhaps written rather for the study than the stage. On the whole it is a noble and convincing piece of work.

Two authoresses, under the name of Michael Field,[2] have composed two plays on Tristan, *The Tragedy of Pardon* and *Tristan de Leonois*,[3] which, in the incidents chosen, follow the Thomas-Gottfried tradition. But, as Sturge Moore remarks,[4] the author of a modern drama is judged more critically than a mediæval writer of narrative. More verisimilitude is demanded of the former. A drama, in order to fulfil the artistic conditions of its genre, requires closer construction than the narrative-story, and if the subject-matter be traditional, a wise choice of incidents. This both these dramas lack, for such awkward events as the substitution of Brangaena (Brangwain) and the quibble of the " Trial by Ordeal " and the discovery by Mark of the lovers with the sword between them, are given.

In the *Tragedy of Pardon*, the character of Mark shows uncertain handling. He refuses to face facts and his repeated forgiveness appears as cowardice rather than the fruit of a noble character. There is a condoning of moral fault which is due to lack of moral standard. Thus, when he discovers

---

[1] A. Symons, *op. cit.*, p. 18.
[2] Katherine H. Bradley and Edith E. Cooper.
[3] *Tragedy of Pardon*, 1911, and *Tristan de Leonois*, " The Accuser," 1911.
[4] In *Criterion*, vol. i., 1922-3, p. 172, " The Story of Tristram and Isolt in Modern Poetry."

the lovers asleep, he sends his companions away and soliloquises thus :

> " My heart is cold with joy—the naked sword,
> They in their beauty and seclusion : round them
> Noon's fervid hour ; both guileless, innocent.
> O Easter day, how can my heart arise
> To greet a joy like this ! " [1]

He departs and sends Kurvenal to announce that he will reinstate his queen and restore Tristan also to his former position of trust and honour.

Though these plays are lacking in dramatic construction and strong character-drawing, there are passages of poetical beauty. When the occasion is a great one, as in Act I of the *Tragedy of Pardon*, the potion-scene, and also in the last Act which deals with the death of Tristan, the verse rises in certain lines to poetical heights and occasional telling phrasing, which unfortunately is not sustained.

Thus, in the first Act, when Brangaena exclaims on the havoc the contents of the goblet have wrought, Tristan exclaims in the triumph of newly-awakened passion :

> " I have no sorrow,
> No shame to call upon.   The whirr of pinions
> Strong as the elements, is all I hear
> When mortal voice condemns me." [2]

But the encounter of Iseult of Cornwall and Iseult of Arundel (as she is here called) at Tristan's death-bed lacks dignity. The meeting between the two Iseults at the death-bed of Tristan is one which requires a master hand, for each loved Tristan in her own manner. Unfortunately, the supreme touch is here lacking.   Mark, however, rises to dignity at the very end, when, as the lovers lie dead before him, he is informed of all.
(Mark) :

> " Open your heart to me ; and have no fear
> I make no claim on anything.   My palace
> Strong on Tintagel's rock, fades twice a year
> Before my sight : I have seen all things pass."

---

[1] *Tragedy of Pardon*, p. 78.   [2] *Op. cit.*, p. 11.

(Iseult of Arundel) :

> " Take her away ! "

(Mark) :

> " But they must lie together.
> I dare not sever them in death, I dare not.
> Here let them rest.
> I bade Brangaena tell you
> As she has poured into my ears the tale
> How they drank wine together, wine her mother
> Had steeped in wizard passion of her prayers :
> The hands that bore the draught were hands of Fate :
> These the appointed lips, these, these ! " [1]

He commands them to be buried in royal tombs and that there should be planted on their graves an intertwining rose and vine.

In *Tristan de Leonois* the magic element prevails to the extent of losing itself in phantasy. Contrary to the modern fashion of rationalising the power of the fatal cup, its influence is emphasised. The drama, in three Acts, chooses the three incidents of Tristan's appearing in disguise as a fool at the court of Mark, Iseult's journey to the dying Tristan, Iseult's death and the appearance of her spirit to Tristan. The last two circumstances are, of course, the author's own invention. The heroine evidently dies on board ship between the second and third Acts, but the reader is not told when or how and wonders why : in the last Act her spirit appears with the cup she has rescued from the bottom of the sea. She mockingly commands her lover to follow her to the land of shades. Her character, even when living, seems dæmonic, and her last appeal, in broken-up lines, frenzied. The play illustrates the fact that true originality in the handling of a legendary story is not shown by mere ingenuity or novelty of detail.

A much stronger and more masterly handling is shown in the drama of Thomas Hardy. He, along with John Masefield, has been bold in modifying and mingling different traditions. Hardy's *Famous Tragedy of the Queen of Cornwall*,[2] a play in

---

[1] *Op. cit.*, pp. 123, 124.

[2] Thomas Hardy, *The Famous Tragedy of the Queen of Cornwall at Tintagel in Lyonnesse*, 1923.

one Act of twenty-two scenes, is original and audacious in its seeming simplicity.   In some respects, Hardy, in his change of tradition, is a startling innovator.   And yet, in spite of it he seems, in comparing his work with the Old-French epic of Béroul, very near to the original story in such a scene—for example, as that of the lovers in the cave, suffering all the hardships of Nature.   His characters are simple, straightforward, primitive people who feel strongly and act and do not stop to analyse their feelings.   Even those of the twelfth-century Thomas seem courtly and sophisticated by contrast. Hardy's personages love or hate directly and passionately. The story of the potion is followed as it stands, the drinking of it is the cause and moral excuse of the passion of the lovers and all their consequent actions.   As in Gottfried, even the Deity is juggled with.   Or is this a touch of the Hardyesque irony ?   The chorus remarks that Queen Iseult of Cornwall ought to thank God for covering up her tracks !

The form of the play is worthy of attention.   There is a chorus, as in the Greek play, which gives a kind of moral judgment and criticism of the chief actors, and relates past history and events.   But the sentiment expressed has not the fineness and subtlety of the chorus of Euripides.   The tragedy of Hardy might be called a kind of historical-morality play. The scenery and surroundings are so simple that it can easily be imagined as played on a movable platform with wheels, as the old miracle and morality plays were performed.   A rough rhythmic blank verse interspersed with lyrics, ascends in moments of tense emotion to heights of great beauty and often descends to a mere jog-trot.   The chorus of (dead) Cornish men and women who chant, is in the form of irregular paragraphs, interspersed with rhymes.

A summary of the main events, some of which are told to us briefly by the chorus, will show the traditions followed and those refashioned or transgressed.

Tristram [1] and Iseult are represented to us as already lovers having spent happy months, shut up in Joyous Gard. This passionate love has been caused by the magic of the potion.

[1] This is the form of name in Hardy.

When the play opens, Tristram had returned to his wife, in Brittany, Iseult the White-Palmed. He was believed to be dying of a poisoned wound, and in utter despair Iseult his wife had sent for her hated rival, Queen Iseult of Cornwall. A white sail was to be hoisted if the vessel carried Iseult, and a black sail if the reverse. Meanwhile Tristram's wife had let her jealousy conquer her fear and she had told a lie, telling her husband the sail was black. The sick man, on hearing the news, had fallen back in a swound. Iseult his wife, in distraction had rushed down to Queen Iseult's ship, which had just arrived, and told the Queen Tristram was dead. Queen Iseult, on hearing the dread news, had fallen back in a dead faint and was borne back to Cornwall amid fierce storm and tempest, without ever putting a foot in Brittany.

When the first scene opens, Queen Iseult has just arrived on the shore of Cornwall. She is followed by King Mark, who has been hunting all the time of her absence. He hears rumours of her journey, but the Queen informs him that she has not set a foot in Brittany, which, of course, is literally true. Mark, however, is very suspicious but his suspicions are somewhat allayed when he hears that Tristram is dead. Queen Iseult really believes it to be true and is full of grief and woe.

Tristram, however, has only fallen into a deep swoon and recovers. He follows Iseult's ship to Cornwall and he, in his turn, is pursued by his wife Iseult the " Whitepalmed," as Hardy calls her. Disguised as a minstrel, he seeks an audience with Queen Iseult, unsuspected by King Mark who is carousing with his knights. Sir Andret, however, perceives something strangely familiar about the minstrel and proceeds to act the spy.

The disguised harper has an interview with the Queen to whom he reveals his identity, and he revives memories of their old love. He sings to her a love-lyric to the accompaniment of his harp. They arrange a more secret meeting-place.

Meanwhile Iseult, the wife of Tristram, has arrived. She beseeches Tristram to come back with her, reminding him of all the faithful, wifely love and service she has given him. At first, her husband repulses her roughly, then, in a more gentle humour, seems to yield. But the jealous Queen is watching them from the balcony, and calls Tristram and his wife to come to her. Iseult the White-Palmed, overcome by the presence of her hated rival, faints, and her namesake tells her chamberwomen scornfully to look after her.

We now come to the last scene, full of stirring drama. Tristram and Iseult have met to renew their love. At first, Iseult shows jealousy of Tristram's wife, but he calms her and harps to her a love-song. But they are surrounded by enemies. Sir Andret has conveyed his suspicions to King Mark. Half drunk, he slips away from his revelling courtiers and creeps up behind Tristram. When Tristram asks Iseult where King Mark is, he answers in a thick voice :

> " He's in his own house, where he ought to be,
> Aye, here, where thou'lt not be much longer, man."

and runs Tristram through with his dagger. Tristram, with reproaches on his lips at Mark's ingratitude to himself as the saviour of Cornwall, falls dead. Iseult stabs King Mark and then rushes to the cliff and throws herself over it. The faithful dog Hudain follows her in her violent death.

Iseult of the White Hands and Brangwain are alone left to bewail the holocaust. The chorus joins in the lamentation.

If we compare even this short summary with the scenes given from Gottfried von Strassburg, or with Malory, we can see the plot has been materially altered. Hardy keeps to the tradition of the prose romances and Malory in utterly vilifying King Mark. He is not even excused, as in Arthur Symon's play, by ignorance of the fact that the lovers have drunk the love-potion. An interesting reference is made in Hardy's play to Tristram, " Gloom-born in his mother's death and reared mid vows of poison by a later spouse," which is found in Malory. Readers of Malory will also be familiar with the tournament with Sir Palomides, which is mentioned, and also with the reference to Tristram's healing at the hand of the King of France's daughter. The drinking of the love-potion is taken just as it is found in the traditional story, a cause and an excuse for what follows. Tristram, as in Béroul and Malory, is connected with the court of King Arthur, and a letter from Mark to King Arthur is intercepted. But there is no hint of the later refinements of King Arthur's court.

Apart from similarities, such as those mentioned above, the modern poet has taken great liberties with tradition. Two traditions connected with Tristram's death are used : (1) the story of the black and white sail, and (2) the story of the death of Tristram due to King Mark's treacherous stabbing in the back. The first is usually connected with Thomas (though reference to it is found in the prose romances) and the second with the prose romances and Malory who has taken it from there.[1] Hardy makes Tristram's wife herself send for Queen Iseult, altogether against the facts in the older version. The old tale of Tristan, disguised as a minstrel, which comes in Gottfried at an earlier period of Tristan's life, is skilfully made use of in the latest scenes of Tristan's life.

Yet in spite of this drastic remodelling, the true and permanent essence of the tale is not lost. Hardy writes in his Prologue :

> " I saw these times I represent,
> Watched, gauged them, as they came and went,
> Being ageless, deathless."

and in his representation, this element is retained. It is difficult to analyse in its various constituents. The truth lies in the fact that in spite of change in surroundings, manners of society and inventions, the primitive emotions, such as love and hate, have an unchanging element in them which continue to move us throughout the ages.

Thomas Hardy has hewn his material from the old quarry itself, and in moulding it, it has not lost its pristine vigour. As in the Scottish National War Memorial of Edinburgh on the Castle Rock, the original rough rock appears. But it causes no shock to the observer, for the artist, in designing the material, has built his whole building round the original material and harmonised each detail with this.

The verse of the dramatist, rhymed and unrhymed, has the same flavour of the soil about it. It keeps close to the natural vigour of the speech of men inhabiting the sea-girt castle of

---

[1] In Book XIX. See " Everyman " Edition of Malory, vol. ii., p. 344.

Tintagel, men in contact with the elements of Nature, the sun, the wind, and the rain. These primitive sons of the earth feel strongly, act decidedly for good or evil, weal or woe. The author's style is unequal. There are phrases which are reminiscent of Shakespeare in his later tragedies, where he takes everyday things and dips them in boiling lead, remoulding them in the intense heat and passion of the tragedy. Such is Macbeth's " peep through the blanket of the dark to cry ' Hold, Hold ! ' " [1] A like phrase in Hardy is Brangwain's " Here's more of this same stuff of death ! " when she discovers the dead bodies of Queen Iseult and King Mark.

This concentrated and abrupt style is apt in less tense moments to become unmusical and prosaic. As, for example, when Iseult Whitepalmed (as Hardy calls her) pleads to Tristram :

> " But you don't *mean* you'll live away from me,
> Leave me, and henceforth be unknown to me,
> Oh you don't surely ?   I could not help coming ;
> Don't send me away—do not, do not do so ! "

And the irregular verse of the chorus is often too compressed and bald. When Iseult, Tristram's wife, faints, this is the comment of the chorus :

> " Fluttering with fear,
> Out-tasked her strength has she !
> Loss of her Dear
> Threatening too clear,
> Gone to this length has she !
> Strain too severe ! "

These faults are redeemed by the love scenes, especially the lyrics, and will remain in the memory when the other scenes in the play have been forgotten.

John Masefield's play *Tristan and Isolt* combines successfully many traditions. It is written for the stage and has been performed by the Lena Ashwell players (1927) ; the action is swift and moves steadily to the death of the lovers in the woods. The tragedy is one of outer events and the cruelty of circumstance, rather than one of inner emotional conflict.

---

[1] *Macbeth*, Act I, Scene 5.

One event follows on another and expectation is kept alive, even in this well-known story. Some may deem that the dramatist is too daring in his changes of tradition. He constructs altogether a new building from the stones, taken from the ruins of older traditions. His style is a curious blending of the prosaic and the poetical, between unrhymed verse and prose, which is a special art of Masefield's. It accomplishes a good imitation of real life and conversation, where only in moments of high tension and strong emotion do simple people rise, often unconsciously, to dramatic utterance. Masefield took his traditions where he found them and improvised names and incidents where he desired.

The forms of the names in this play are Welsh—Marc, Kai, Bedwyr ; these have characteristics of the personages found in the *Mabinogion*. Kay, for example, is surly and full of tricks and prepares a trap for Tristan. Masefield in comic scenes, worthy of Shakespeare in *Henry IV*, dramatises an incident found in the " Triads." Tristan is called upon to keep swine, and Kai and Bedwyr try to outwit him but do not succeed. These comic scenes are worked into the main plot. Marc is so annoyed with Tristan for neglecting to look after his own princedom and wasting his time with the pigs, that he orders him out of the country.

Arthur is also brought in as a Romano-British general. In the histories, he is made to belong to the British side and fights against the Romans.

A short analysis of the first Act will be sufficient to show the general groundwork of the play and the chief characters. When the play opens, Kolbein, a Scandinavian pirate, who has also a fief in Ireland, arrives in Cornwall and demands his tribute of thirty young men from its king, King Marc, whose kingdom is subject to him. Dinan now comes in to introduce Tristan. He announces to the astonished Marc that the latter is his nephew, who has been brought up by him (Dinan) as his son, for safety. In reality, he is the son of Olwen, Marc's sister, who was rescued from the pirate Kolbein and married by Tallorc. Kolbein now appears on the stage and again demands the human tribute. It is refused. Tristan, in defiance, offers to fight him. At first

Kolbein declines, for Tristan reminds him too much of his mother, Olwen, whom Kolbein had loved in his own rough way. He finally consents, saying it is " wisdom against man's youth." Youth wins and Kolbein is mortally wounded, though Tristan is also hurt. Before the pirate dies, he proposes that Marc should marry his daughter Isolt in Ireland, and the two countries Cornwall and Ireland be united. Tristan is to be sent to woo her. Thus the stage is set for tragedy.

The rest of the play is taken from a number of different traditional incidents changed and woven together in an ingenious manner. For instance, the " magic wine," otherwise the famous love-potion, is drunk twice by the lovers, once on the ship which carries Isolt [1] as a bride to Cornwall and once on Marc's wedding night.

As Tristan is shown to be attracted to Isolt the first time he sees her, the love-drink is rather superfluous. Brangwen [1] also drinks it, as she plays the awkward part of being a substitute for the Queen. Unfortunately, through nervousness, she spills it after she has drunk it herself, so that only the grounds which contain the sleeping-draught are left for King Marc. Thus Marc falls into a drugged sleep, while in Brangwen awakes an unrequited passion for Marc the King. This whole scene is an attempt to make the very awkward traditional incident of the substitution of Brangwen have verisimilitude. Brangwen's passion for King Marc does not seem to serve much purpose, except that she offers later on to go and give him decent burial, when Isolt refuses and flees to Tristan in the woods, in a late repentance for her cruelty.

These changes might be permitted, but what really weakens the effect and beauty of the play is the sudden change of mind in Isolt. Masefield follows Béroul and Thomas in the scene, when Marc discovers the lovers, sleeping in the grotto. The King, it will be remembered, is so overcome with their loveliness and innocence, that, leaving his glove beside them, he steals away without harming them. [2]

[1] Thus written in the play.

[2] In Thomas's version Mark places his glove in the aperture which serves as a window, and thus it prevents the rays of the sun from disturbing the lovers' repose.

But in Masefield's play the effect this has on Isolt is quite unprecedented. She is so overcome with Marc's generosity that she goes back to her husband. Not only this, but she is unnecessarily cruel to Tristan, who runs wild and mad in the woods. After Marc's death in battle, Isolt refuses to give her husband decent burial and flees to Tristan. They both die together in the woods in a scene of pathos rather than high tragedy.

Isolt laments :

" He has gone from me for ever from this shell,
This broken body that my cruelty killed.
I will come with you, Tristan ; stay but a moment
We two will journey together whatever ways
Bodiless spirits travel in the heaven
Of being set free. You were more beautiful, Tristan,
Than the young stag, tossing tines near the holly thicket.
You were dearer to me than anything else on earth.
Take pity upon me, darling, though I took none.

(She stabs herself.)
Tristan, my captain, my love : my only love.

(She dies.)

In criticising the play as a whole, it may be remarked that the historical background of the play is well drawn in. In the foreground, the various characters move naturally and events follow each other in quick succession. There is no great character-drawing or tragic climax. Tristan stands out as a man of action, quick-witted, humorous, capable of loyalty to his companions, who love him. He has been drawn aside from his duty and career by his passion for Isolt, and it is an era when war matters more than love. Isolt certainly does not reward him for it by faithfulness. His pitiful death in the woods is a fitting end to his life, laid waste by what seems an infatuation rather than a high passion.

As regards his handling of traditions, Masefield is very bold and ingenious, but he does not quite succeed in the very difficult task of adapting these to the historical setting. For example, the sword which is laid between the lovers and which is mentioned in the grotto scene, and taken from the

Gottfried tradition, is a curious survival from ancient Norse mythology. Sigurd laid his sword between himself and Brunhild to separate them, for in the likeness of Gunnar and in his behalf he was wooing Brunhild. Thus he was enabled to be loyal to his friend. But in the Tristan and Isolde story, as Tristan and Isolde were already lovers, the sword has lost its significance.

Two poems which have in essence more of the narrative element in them than the dramatic, call for comment. The one is Matthew Arnold's " Tristram and Iseult," [1] in which the poet's fancy plays around the figure of the second Iseult. The anomalous position of Iseult seems to have intrigued modern poets and dramatists and sometimes she has distracted attention from the central figure. Wagner, on this account, was perhaps wise to leave her out of his Opera altogether. Swinburne makes her resentful and passionate. In Comyns Carr's play she appears in a vision to the Queen of Cornwall, but this fantastic element is unconvincing.

Matthew Arnold breaks with tradition altogether in giving her children. She is happy, but not conversant with the deeper joy. " Joy has not found her yet nor ever will."

The poet draws a charming and delicately etched-in picture of her, relating to her children the Breton romance of Merlin and Vivian. After she has put them to bed,

> She'll light her silver lamp, which fishermen
> Dragging their nets through the rough waves, afar,
> Along this iron coast, know like a star,
> And take her broidery frame, and there she'll sit
> Hour after hour, her gold curls sweeping it,
> Lifting her soft-bent head only to mind
> Her children, or to listen to the wind.
> And when the clock peals midnight, she will move
> Her work away, and let her fingers rove
> Across the shaggy brows of Tristram's hound
> Who lies guarding her feet, along the ground :
> Or else she will fall musing, her blue eyes
> Fix'd, her slight hands clasp'd on her lap ; then rise,

---

[1] *Collected Works*, 1909.

And at her prie-dieu kneel, until she have told
Her rosary beads of ebony tipped with gold,
Then to her soft sleep : and tomorrow'll be
To-day's exact repeated effigy.[1]

She is a heroine of the twilight as the warm-blooded Iseult of Cornwall is of the sunlight. The verse in which she is enshrined, like a saint in an illuminated border, partakes of the same passionless quality. The rich glow has faded, but the figure shines with soft radiance in the fading light.

E. A. Robinson in his *Tristram* (1928) also changes tradition and dispenses with the magical altogether. Not only this, but substituting a version of his own, he misses out or waters down the dramatic part of the Tristan which has so much of the primitive element in it. Thus he says nothing concerning the magic potion or the last stirring episode of the approaching ship with its black and white sail. Tristram and Isolt are first introduced in his poem on the eve of Isolt's marriage to King Mark. Then, after the marriage, King Mark banishes Tristram, who resorts to Brittany where he meets the other Isolt, whom he marries. Tristram leaves her on a pretext to go to King Arthur's court at Camelot. But here Queen Isolt meets him at Joyous Gard, for her husband has conveniently been imprisoned for some offence against chivalry.

Finally, the Queen returns to Mark and Mark invites Tristram to his court in Cornwall, and gives him a treacherous welcome. The knight and Isolt are stabbed when they are together by Andred, who considers he is doing the King a service. Mark gazes at the dead bodies and pronounces this epitaph, in Andred's hearing :

" I do not know," he said,
" What this is you have done. I am not sure." . . .
His words broke slowly of their own heaviness,
And were like words not spoken to be heard :
" I am not sure that you have not done well.
God knows what you have done. I do not know,
There was no more for them and this is peace." [2]

---

[1] M. Arnold, *Collected Works*, 1909.
[2] *Tristram*, by Edwin Arlington Robinson, 1928, p. 198.

In this strain he continues during a long speech, which demonstrates the poet's tendency to over-elaborate his sentiments which are often apt and just in themselves and which would be more impressive if expressed more shortly. For example, Isolt's question :

> " Are you sure that a world given
> Is always more than a world forsaken ? "

gives the problem of the lovers in a nutshell.   But this treasure is hid in a long speech.   Again, on the eve of Mark's marriage, the despairing lovers, on the parapet below Tintagel, discuss at length the idea of suicide :

Tristram speaks :

> " But to be over-strong now at this hour
> Would only be destruction.   The King's ways
> Are not those of one man against another,
> And you must live and I must live—for you.
> If there were not an army of guards below us
> To bring you back to fruitless ignominy
> There would be an end of this offence,
> To God and the long insult of the marriage." [1]

There are many passages which show a fine sensitiveness and analytic powers, but the general effect of the long speeches is apt to be monotonous.

Perhaps the poet's skill is shown best in the drawing of Isolt of Brittany and the analysis of her feelings towards Tristram, and their response.   The situation is delicately handled and the passage ought to be read as a whole, but here a few extracts must suffice :

> Once by the shore
> They lingered while a summer sun went down
> Beyond the shining sea ; and it was then
> That sorrow's witchcraft, long at work in him,
> Made pity out of sorrow, and of pity
> Made the pale wine of love that is not love,
> Yet steals from love a name.   And while he felt
> Within her candor and her artlessness
> The still white fire of her necessity,

---

[1] *Op. cit.*, p. 44.

> He asked in vain if this were the same fate
> That for so long had played with him so darkly
> —With him and with Isolt, Isolt òf Ireland,
> Isolt of the wild frightened violet eyes
> That once had given him that last look of hers
> Above the moaning call of those cold waves
> On those cold Cornish rocks. This new Isolt,
> This new and white Isolt, was nothing real
> To him until he found her in his arms,
> And scarcely knowing how found her there,
> Kissed her and felt the sting of happy tears—
> On his bewildered lips.

> .   .   .   .

> He knew that while his life was in Cornwall,
> Something of this white fire and loneliness
> In Brittany must be his whereon to lavish
> The comfort of kind lies while he should live.[1]

This method of fine etching in the neutral tints of black and white and grey does not suit so well the delineation of the stormier passion of Tristram and Isolt of Ireland, which requires stronger and more vivid colours. It is an interesting fact that the figure of Iseult [2] of Brittany seems to challenge modern poets, such as Robinson and Matthew Arnold, to exercise a refined craftsmanship.

[1] *Op. cit.*, p. 88.   [2] In Robinson spelt " Isolt."

CHAPTER XVI

THE ARTHURIAN LEGEND IN SATIRE

MALORY had little or nothing of the humorist in him, nor did he possess the critical type of mind. But from the sources [1] at his disposal he took over the character of Dinadan, thus introducing among his romantic characters a sceptic and a satirist. Vinaver, in his study of the sources of Malory, shows how Malory abbreviated his original [2] so much that he blurred the portrait of Dinadan and deleted his most characteristic comments and jokes. And what Malory transcribes is often meaningless without the context. As Vinaver writes : " Malory makes a clean sweep of all Dinadan's mockery and of that peculiar love among knights which expressed itself in a desire to do battle with its object."

In a passage of the prose Tristan, Dinadan tells his friend Agravain who has been hurled to the ground by a strange knight, " My cowardice makes me live and thy prowess has tumbled thee down from thy horse." [3] He thus cries like Falstaff, " What is Honour ? " He questions the whole chivalric conception of duty and valour. And in another passage, he argues that he would rather be the enemy of a knight than a friend, for the chief privilege of a knight's friend seems to be knocked down ! It is thus a love " that torments and kills its servants and punishes them for their folly. May God guard and protect me against such love ! " [4]

The criticism voiced by the Dinadan of the French romances is developed into a philosophic and creative novel in the immortal *Don Quixote*.

True, as regards the Arthurian romances, the actual

[1] See E. Vinaver, *Malory*, Appendix 2, p. 138.
[2] Or a MS. similar to the original.
[3] MS. B.N. fr. 334 r, col. 2.
[4] MS. B.N. r. 334 f. 318 r, col. 1, quoted by Vinaver.

244

references are not many. There is one to the romance of Lancelot.[1] Also there is an interesting one concerning the return of Arthur :

" Have you not read, then," cried Don Quixote, " the Annals and History of Britain, where are recorded the famous deeds of King Arthur, who according to an ancient tradition in that kingdom, never died, but was turned into a raven by enchantment, and shall one day resume his former shape, and recover his kingdom again ? For which reason, since that time, the people of Great Britain dare not offer to kill a raven." [2]

Nevertheless this novel is the most salient commentary that has ever been written on the extravagances of the romances, although in France and England the bombast and absurdity was not carried to such lengths. In the conduct of the hero, in the romance of Cervantes, this absurdity and extravagance is shown in a fantastic chimera, which, like a child's soap-bubble, bursts as it touches the ground of reality. Here, through the medium of a brain crazed with reading chivalric romances, inns become castles ; windmills with long arms, giants ; a flock of sheep, a vast army ; and ridiculous contests, glorious victories for knight-errantry. As in many of these romances, including the Arthurian group, the central conception is of a knight performing services for his chosen lady, overcoming foes in her name and sending captives to her castle, with a desire only for her commendation as reward. In this satirical romance, the stage is set forward with a background of actual Spanish life, which shows the chosen lady, Dulcinea, threshing corn, refusing to read the knight's amorous letter till her task be accomplished and laughing at the knight's crack-brained notions. And this background with its scenes of diurnal happenings shatters by contrast the illusion of the stage on which Don Quixote imagines himself such an heroic figure and shows up its cardboard scenery and its footlights gleaming palely and uncertainly in the revealing daylight.

[1] Book I, chap. 2 (Chandos Classics).
[2] Book I, chap. 13 (Chandos Classics).

But this satirical, though not cruel, book differs from lesser
satire in that it is creative as well as critical.   In Don Quixote
and Sancho, in particular, Cervantes has created living
characters, not mere abstractions.   Once the initial premises
of the definite cause of the madness is allowed, the derangement
of the knight is compounded of so much logicality that the
reader hesitates to condemn him altogether in case he thereby
condemns himself.   As by the consideration of Hamlet's
madness, many a man discovers that he himself is living in a
world of illusion, so in Don Quixote a mirror is held up to
man.   Also, if Cervantes shows up the weaknesses and
absurdities of the romantic world, held suspended between
heaven and earth, he also shows that the chivalric ideal rouses
much that is noble and brave and selfless in a man, even
although in this instance, the execution of it causes the reader
to smile.   Also, at the same time, in his subtlety, the satirist
shows the reverse of the picture in Sancho Panza, the knight's
follower and squire, whose cupidity and materialism and
ignorance leads also to absurd credulities and situations.
Thus, in depicting with all his eloquence and powers of
description and irony the extremes of idealism and materialism,
Cervantes is actually pleading for the Greek ideal of the mean
" to see life steadily and see it whole."

Thus the final effect on the mind is not one of bitterness
and disillusion as in Swift's satire, Gulliver's Travels, but
rather of sorrow that so much good material in the hero has
gone to waste.   So Cervantes seems to tilt at chivalric idealism
only in so far as this idealism contradicts reality.   By the
time of Malory's Morte Darthur [1] and still more of Don Quixote [2]
the forms of chivalry were outworn.   If they have some
value in the symbolic world of poetry, they fade away like
Hamlet's ghost at cock-crow, in the more realistic world of the
novel, the successor of romance.

In the next satiric work, the form is that of the burlesque.
John Hookham Frere (1769-1846) was himself a reader and
admirer of Don Quixote, where, as he himself says,[3] " the knight
himself represents a higher type of burlesque passing into
pure pathos and comedy, while his squire stands at the

---

[1] Published 1485.   [2] Published 1605.   [3] In his Memoirs, p. 166.

opposite pole and submits all his experience to the most vulgar considerations." In order to produce a comic impression, Frere wished to give an example of a romantic theme passing through a prosaic and uneducated mind. To accomplish this he desired it to be believed, or at least imagined, that the poem *The Monks and the Giants*[1] was written by William and Robert Whistlecraft, harness and collar maker, under which pseudonym the first two cantos were published in 1817. It deceived at the time a few people, but the evident erudition betrayed the fact that the authorship was not that of an illiterate tradesman.

Frere chose for his metre " ottava rima " with the last rhyming couplet which can be used to give a lash with its tail to increase the humorous effect. His burlesque poem shows especially the influence of Pulci's *Morgante Maggiore*,[2] from which he has taken his central incident of the war between the monks and the giants with the idea of the bell as a weapon of war. This he links up with Arthur's court. Here (Canto I) at the usual feast at Carlisle the usual mis-shapen damsel appears to seek the aid of the knights for the monks' feud with the giants. But the description of the humorous verse-maker is different from the customary romantic one and the effect of the verse on the ear and mind is dissimilar to that of Spenser's stanza, for example. With a certain realistic force, the rabble at King Arthur's court is thus described :

> All sorts of people there were seen together,
> All sorts of characters, all sorts of dresses ;
> The fool with fox's tail and peacock's feather,
> Pilgrims and penitents and grave burgesses ;
> The country people with their coats of leather,
> Vintners and victuallers with cans and messes ;
> Grooms, archers, varlets, falconers and yeomen,
> Damsels and waiting maids, and waiting-women.

---

[1] Ed. with Notes, and Introduction on the Italian medley poets and their English imitators, including Byron, by R. D. Waller (Ward Bequest), 1926. Complete known edition, 1821.

[2] See R. D. Waller's Introduction to above edition.

The characters of Lancelot, Gawain and Tristan are sketched in the terse epigrammatic style reminiscent of Dryden's *Absalom and Achitophel,* and lead us to suspect some topical reference, although this was denied by the author :

> His memory was the magazine and hoard
> Where claims and grievances from year to year,
> And confidences and complaints were stored,
> From dame and knight, from damsel, boor and peer :
> Lov'd by his friends and trusted by his Lord,
> A generous courtier, secret and sincere,
> Adviser-general to the whole community
> He served his friend but watched his opportunity.

This description seems far more applicable to some statesman of the author's own generation than to the Gawain of the romances. Frere is of interest to students of English literature mainly through the influence of his poem, and especially its verse-form, on Byron's " Don Juan " which is written in the same " ottava rima." But as far as Arthurian legend is concerned, Frere's poem is a mere *jeu d'esprit,* a skit on some of the surface characteristics of the romances, such as their dependence on a former source (Frere, for example, invents a " Morgan's Chronicle "), their diffuseness and inconsequence, and their over-refinement. The idealisation of the romances is emphasised by presenting a contrast in style and treatment. But the satire does not strike at the fundamental aspects of romance.

Mark Twain's *A Yankee at the Court of King Arthur* is a farce in prose. The situation conceived is a good one for the purpose, an irreverent and commercially-minded American visiting Arthur's court. The contrast between the two worlds follows logically and is carried out ingeniously. There is some political satire and the hero introduces some of the products of a machine age amidst the paraphernalia of the mediæval, with bizarre results. Various circumstances and details of the life of the Middle Ages [1] are shown up as ridiculous in rather an obvious manner—the heaviness and the

---

[1] The novel is purported to be in the sixth century, but the trappings apply equally to mediæval times in general.

uncomfortableness of the armour, the vagueness of the romantic quests and the objectlessness of the fighting.   The inconvenience and convenience of being able to use the enchanter's wand at an awkward moment is commented [1] on, but much less subtly treated than in the famous scene of the " windmills " in *Don Quixote*.

The satire is not deeply conceived and consists mostly of what Meredith in his *Essay on Comedy* calls " shooting a burglar and then hurling a pistol after him."   The scene in which the hero, an intruder from a more scientific age, makes use of his knowledge of the coming eclipse to stage a rival performance to that of Merlin, with his more old-fashioned magic,[2] is good fooling.

[1] *Op. cit.*, chap. 20.   [2] *Op. cit.*, chap. 6.

CHAPTER XVII

SUMMARY AND CONCLUSION

IN this concluding chapter it may be well to try to sum up the value of myth in general, and of Arthurian myth in particular, to modern literature.

The value of myth in poetry, it is hardly necessary to question. Myth is to be taken here, unless defined otherwise, in the sense of a story or drama in which the gods appear. It often implies ritualistic practice. There are different kinds of myth and mythological stories—Ætiological myth, which tries to explain the causes of things such as the creation of the heavens and the earth, the so-called Cosmological myth. Two varieties of the Ætiological myth are, the Cultus myth, purposing to explain the origin of ritual practices, and the Foundation myth, describing the origin of society and of particular cities and nations. These myths, themselves, are of the essence of poetry and drama. The Foundation myth, when it takes a developed literary form, may become the nucleus of the epic, as in the *Æneid*, where the gods appear to aid the hero. Ritual itself becomes often the starting-place of the drama, as the history of mediæval drama shows.

Classical myth has influenced English poetry more than any other. When pagan ritual ceased to represent a living faith, it left behind it a heritage of myths and legends, which have enriched English literature in such poets as Spenser, Milton, Tennyson, Swinburne and Robert Bridges.

All through the present study, myth as representing two kinds of truth, factual and ideal [1] truth, has been illustrated in Arthurian story. And for exemplifying this, a brief reference to the myths Plato used or rather of the purpose

[1] " Ideal " used here in the Platonic sense.

for which he employed them, will be helpful. Plato's myths may be termed " Philosophic myths," and the term myth is used with a somewhat different signification from that used elsewhere in this treatise. In some ways these myths approximate to allegory, that is, they are stories or incidents deliberately manufactured to represent " ideal " truths. But as J. A. Stewart, in his *Myths of Plato*, is careful to point out, they are not mere allegories ; they are attempts to body forth truths which cannot be proved logically, they are " Dreams expressive of Transcendental Feeling, told in such a manner and in such a context that the telling of them regulates, for the service of conduct and science, the feeling expressed," [1] and this writer continues : " I hold that it is in Transcendental Feeling, manifested normally as Faith in the Value of Life and ecstatically as sense of Timeless Being, not in Thought proceeding by way of speculative construction, that Consciousness comes nearest to the object of Metaphysics, Ultimate Reality." [2]

This is a philosophic way of saying that Plato's myths are poems rather than logical expositions, if the definition of poetry be one which lays emphasis on the fact of the emergence and regulation of Transcendental Feeling. But it is manifest that Plato's myths contain the two kinds of truth, the factual and the ideal. In these myths is bodied forth the ideal form of Beauty, " That which was and is and shall be." And if they lack the traditional roots which can be traced in evolutionary myths, yet Plato often refers to these beliefs and traditions in Greek life, even although he himself logically may have outgrown them. For example, in the " Phædrus myth " in his division of human souls into nine classes ranging from the true lover to the tyrant, he refers to the Pythagorean Orphics, where the soul descends through the Heavenly Spheres to her incarnation on Earth.

Myth, then, has a value of its own to Plato, both as a philosopher and a poet, in conveying truth not through the logical faculty alone, but subconsciously through what J. A. Stewart calls " the dream world-consciousness," what is often

[1] J. A. Stewart, *The Myths of Plato*, 1905, p. 42.
[2] *Ibid.*, p. 43.

called the subconscious.[1] The myth is one means by which this is evoked, in which man realises his oneness with Universal Nature. The same critic expresses it thus :—" It is good, Plato will have us believe, to appeal sometimes from the world of the senses and scientific understanding, which is too much with us, to this deep-lying part of human nature, as to an oracle. The responses of the oracle are not given in articulate language which the scientific understanding can interpret ; they come as dreams, and must be received as dreams, without thought of doctrinal interpretation. Their ultimate meaning is the ' feeling ' which fills us in beholding them ; and when we wake from them, we see our daily concerns and all things temporal with purged eyes." [2] . . . " It is such moods of feeling in his cultivated reader that Plato induces, satisfies, and regulates, by Myths which set forth God, Soul and Cosmos, in vision."

And conversely, the poet who experiences this communion, though it may be intermittently, desires to communicate it to his fellow-beings. Consequently he must find a vehicle which expresses the dual nature of his vision, the eternal realising itself, through the temporal. And one channel of expression is the myth.

That the artist and poet find in the myth an appropriate form to embody this revelation, is exemplified also in the autobiographical confessions of Wagner. Even although it is expressed in what is considered now an outmoded psychology, this testimony of experience, if taken as genuine, is of value.

Throughout his letters and especially in the Wesendonck Correspondence, Wagner speaks of his experience and inspiration as an artist. He belongs, like all artists, to the deeply intuitive type of man and the first approach to his subject

[1] It is only fair to state Professor A. E. Taylor's view, who perhaps does not give quite such a high place to the value of myth in Plato as J. A. Stewart. In *Platonism and its Influence* (p. 93), he writes : " Plato has taken care to warn us against literalism by the caution that the details of his myths are no more than ' likely stories,' and it is notable that when he comes to the construction of a theology in the ' Laws ' the great doctrines of Providence, immortality and judgment to come are set forth without the trappings of mythology."

[2] From J. A. Stewart, *The Myths of Plato*, 1905, p. 21.

was a unified vision of the whole. In this whole lay concealed the germ of the parts, as the branches of a tree are contained in the root. When he came to work out the separate parts at a lower level, in the limiting conditions of artistic form, it seemed to him as if he were returning to his first experience in which he had seemed to transcend time and space. Wagner describes it thus :

" The supreme marvel must be, tho', if that foreknown essential Something should enter at last the poet's own experience. His Idea then will take great part in this experience's shaping : the purer and higher that, the more unworldlike and incomparable this ; it will purge his will, his æsthetic interest will become a moral one, and to the highest poetic idea will link itself the highest moral consciousness.

" . . . That phenomenon I have observed the most surprisingly in my own case. With my poetic conceptions, I have been so far ahead of my experiences, that I may consider my moral development as almost exclusively induced and brought about by those conceptions ; Flying Dutchman, Tannhäuser, Lohengrin, Nibelüngs, Wodan, all existed earlier in my head than my experience." [1]

Whether we agree with Wagner's interpretation of Art or not, it is evident that he shared a common experience with creative artists. He interpreted it according to Schopenhauer and Eastern philosophers such as Buddha. He agreed, by virtue of his experience with Schopenhauer's statement, that it was the privilege and duty of the work of Art to represent for us the eternal essence of things by means of prototypes. The human mind should rise above the conditions of time, place, cause and tendency, and thus come to the contemplation of eternal ideas.

It has been shown that Wagner found expression for his experience through the medium of myth and legend—of Arthurian legends in particular. He was not an original philosopher and his philosophy and theories often seem

[1] *Richard Wagner to Mathilde Wesendonck*, translated by W. A. Ellis, 1905, p. 96.

superimposed on his art rather than springing from it. But his experience as such and his mode of embodying it in his Operas, is of interest in the present argument.

The modern critic, J. Middleton Murry, in his essay on " The Nature of Poetry," [1] has discovered the same underlying experience in his analysis of the working of Shakespeare's mind, especially as exemplified in " The Phœnix and the Turtle," a poem ascribed to him.

" The artist," he says, " is the man who communicates his intuition of an ultimate reality, intuitions which have in themselves no shape or form or likeness, through symbols chosen in the world of common experience." And again, in the same essay, when he comments on Shakespeare, whom he takes as the most typical universal poet, he writes, " There is a poetry that may almost be called absolute. The ' Phœnix and the Turtle ' belongs to this kind of poetry. It is the direct embodiment, through symbols which are necessarily dark, of a pure, comprehensive and self-satisfying experience, which we may call, if we please, an immediate intuition into the hidden nature of things. It is inevitable that such poetry should be obscure, mystical, and strictly unintelligible : it is too abstract for our comprehension, too essential, too little mediated." Of course, as far as Art is concerned, it is only when the artist can interpret it through a suitable medium that it has value for the human race. Also the use of rhythm and metre, and sometimes rhyme, in poetry, and rhythm in prose, aids the poet to induce and regulate this transcendental emotion. Fortunately, perhaps, the exact manner in which he accomplishes this can never be analysed. It remains the mystery of poetry. The reader only knows when it is communicated as in the lines in *The Tempest* :

> These our actors,
> As I foretold you, were all spirits and
> Are melted into air ; into thin air ;
> And, like the baseless fabric of this vision,
> The cloud-capp'd towers, the gorgeous palaces,

---

[1] In *Discoveries*, 1930 (Traveller's Library), pp. 38-42.

> The solemn temples, the great globe itself,
> Yea, all which it inherit, shall dissolve
> And like this insubstantial pageant faded,
> Leave not a rack behind.[1]

It will be allowed, then, from these quoted examples of Plato, Wagner and Shakespeare, and their interpreters, that poets of a certain temperament share this intuitive experience. And these poets evidently find in the myth a kind of half-way house between the unified vision and the time-and-space-conditioned realities of the world, from which the poet has to choose his facts. Poets such as Wordsworth, on the other hand, sharing this experience as testified in his famous lines in " Tintern Abbey," [2] have given interpretation to it through Nature.

If the origin of the nature of myth be considered, it will be understood why it provides so suitable a medium. For myth, with its connection with religious ritual, has its roots deep down in the subconscious. The order of succession of the poet's experience, according to his own testimony, seems to be from transcendental vision to detailed expression. It is his mission and art, by awakening of images in a logical sequence,[3] word-association and rhythmic lines, to enable his reader to catch glimpses of the same vision.

If then, in order to share his inspiration, the poet can appeal to a myth or legend which is already part of the traditions of the race, if the creator has some notion of the associations he may call up, his task is made easier. It is the part of the original poet to combine by subtle art the familiar and the new, heightening the consciousness of his reader till the more passive agent will partake also of the creative vision, a vision interpreted through the medium of

---

[1] *The Tempest*, Act IV, Scene I.

[2] Beginning—

> " And I have felt
> A presence that disturbs me with the joy of elevated thoughts."

[3] Some of the modern experiments in poetry and prose, such as T. S. Eliot and James Joyce, leave out the logic of sequence altogether, using words almost like notes in a musical composition. See above, criticism on *The Waste Land*, pp. 146 ff.

the poet's own personality. Like a familiar landscape at sunset, it is the same known country, but recreated by the fiery rays of the sun.

Thus the mythic and legendary traditions of a race supply valuable material which may be transformed by the genius of a poet, dramatist or prose-writer. This was accomplished by the Greek dramatists, Sophocles, Æschylus and Euripides, from the mythic and legendary lore of the Greek people. Dante had all the religious traditions of the Mediæval Ages behind him.[1] Milton addressed a Protestant people who were versed in Scripture. Of course, as Professor Grierson points out,[2] many of these traditions began as religious belief and thus had the force of authority behind them. It is possible that the story of the Garden of Eden was believed in literally by Milton [3] and was not regarded as a myth. But the point to be stressed here is that there was for the writer in former times this wealth of traditional material from which to draw.

The modern poet, in these later times, has a more difficult task. If he uses classical myth, as Robert Bridges does in his earlier work, his poetry can only be appreciated by those who have had the benefit of a literary education. Thus the poet tends more and more to write for a selected audience.

He has another choice before him. He may discard myth and elaborate similes from the classics, such as those with which Milton enriched his poetry, and go straight to Nature or Science for his comparisons. It is of interest in this connection to note the similes in " The Testament of Beauty," a later poem by Robert Bridges. Perhaps, because it is of a philosophic nature, reference to classical myth is rare, though Plato's allegory in the *Phædrus*, of the chariot of the soul driven by a charioteer and two horses, is worked out in detail.

[1] J. A. Stewart, in *The Myths of Plato*, pp. 357 *seq.*, shows Dante's debt also to Plato's Cosmology.

[2] In *Background of English Literature : Essays*, 1925.

[3] Another interpretation of course was the allegorical which approaches the mythical. It is interesting to find Dean Inge writing on Colet (*d.* 1519) thus : " Colet showed the effect of his Greek studies when he taught that the Mosaic account of the Creation was intended to convey a moral lesson, not a scientific one ; Moses," he said, " wrote after the manner of a popular poet." From *Platonic Tradition in English Religious Thought*, p. 37.

Other similes are from Nature, as that of the long discourse on the ways of bees.[1]   One or two are taken from the scientific inventions, as the one on the subject of the engine-room :

> " I felt the domination of Nature's secret urge,
> and happy escape therein ;   as when in boyhood once
> from the rattling workshops of a great factory
> conducted into the engine-room I stood in face
> of the quiet driving power, that fast in nether cave
> seated, set all the floors a-quiver, a thousand looms
> throbbing and jennies dancing ;   and I felt at heart a
> kinship with it and sympathy, as children wil
> with amicable monsters." [2]

W. B. Yeats is another example of a modern poet who has made a distinct break in his poetic style, and who abandons mythological references in his later work.   His earlier poems are of more importance in this study, as by them, as well as by his prose essays, he has renewed and created interest in his national myths and legends.   He is one of a group of poets and scholars connected with the recent Renaissance of Irish literature and drama.   The history of this Revival is illuminating.   It shows among other things the connection between traditionary lore and more sophisticated culture, and how the one acts and reacts on the other.   It also forms an interesting comparison with the history of the development of the Arthurian legend, especially in regard to the Welsh sources and the *Mabinogion*.

In 1902 and 1904, Lady Gregory published two books of importance in the history of this epoch—*Cuchulain of Muirthemne : the Story of the Men of the Red Branch of Ulster*, and *Gods and Fighting Men : the Story of the Tuatha Danaan and of the Fianna of Ireland*.   These stories were freely translated, sometimes in new combinations, from manuscripts of the eleventh and twelfth centuries.[3]   They give in popular

---

[1] This is too long to quote.   It will be found in Book II, ll. 365-447, *Testament of Beauty*, 1929.

[2] *Ibid.*, Book I, ll. 44-52.

[3] For all information, see prefaces and notes of Lady Gregory's two books mentioned above.   The prefaces are by W. B. Yeats.

form and with literary charm the myths and legends of the
earlier cycles of the Tuatha Danaan and of Finn and also
the stories surrounding Cuchulain. Alfred Nutt, in *Ossian
and the Ossianic Literature*, [1] ascribes the Fenian cycle to
an early race once occupying both Ireland and Scotland.
He declares that the Fenian cycle has not been forgotten
by the Scotch or Irish, [2] and in the latter country has found
its way into the written literature, and thus has secured a
more stable existence. " The Fenian cycle," he concludes,
" is non-Aryan folk-literature, partially subjected to Aryan
treatment." The Cuchulain cycle is considered by Nutt
and other scholars to be later and refers to more definite
historical episodes, though a great deal of mythology is
inextricably intertwined. It found favour with the court poets
before the Fenian cycle and is thus a more literary product.

This revival of interest in the folk-tales of Ireland is part
of an Irish national movement felt in the domain of literature
and politics. In literature, it has been connected with such
names as Edward Hyde, J. M. Synge the Irish Dramatist,
and W. B. Yeats. It was engineered by an educated section
of the community but it had traditional lore and sanction
behind it. W. B. Yeats summarises its chief aims when he
writes, " We had in Ireland imaginative stories, which the
uneducated classes knew and even sang, and might we not
make those stories current among the educated classes,
rediscovering for the work's sake what I have called ' the
applied arts of literature,' that is, the association of literature
with music, speech and dance ? and at last, it might be, so
deepen the political passion of the nation that all, artist and
poet, craftsman and day-labourer would accept a common
design ? " [3] A great many of the poems of W. B. Yeats were
inspired by his personal contact with the men and women of
Ireland in country places, who could neither read nor write,
but who recited ancient tales to him from memory. The
poet hopes that by the teaching of the Irish language in schools
the children of these men and women may become acquainted

[1] No. 3 of " Popular Studies in Mythology, Romance and Folk-Lore."
[2] This refers, of course, to the early nineteenth century.
[3] *Autobiographies*, 1926, p. 240.

with these legends. Meanwhile Lady Gregory has made them available in her literary translation. Thus the tradition will be continuous.

In some ways, the interest in Irish legend aroused by Lady Gregory's translations corresponds to that awakened by Lady Charlotte Guest's translation of the *Mabinogion*. The former books are more of one piece, in neither of them is there the sudden cleavage which appears in the Welsh book, between the more primitive stories and the redactions influenced by the French. The Fenian cycle is a story of gods and heroes in far-off prehistoric times, when gods and men inhabit the land as equals. They are hunters and move about in the woods, the homes of bird and beast. There is the same love of colour in dress and accoutrements as in the *Mabinogion*, but the actors seem closer to Nature and there are eloquent descriptions of her loveliness.

Cuchulain is a book of heroes and heroines. They are visited and helped by the gods, and magic transformations take place from human to animal form and back again. There is more distance, however, between gods and men than in the earlier saga. The heroines are fit companions for the men, the noble Emer for Cuchulain, and Deirdre, with her tragic gift of foreseeing the disasters she cannot prevent, is a worthy mate for Naois.

The Irish epic differs also from the Arthurian romances in having a definite patriotic appeal and a definite topography. In some ways this limitation is a strength. Though in the English chronicles and romances Arthur is a British king, and though certain places claim to be connected with Arthur, the south-west and west of England, Brittany and the Border district of Scotland,[1] yet the romances cannot be specifically termed English, French or Scottish. The places such as Camelot and the land of Lyonesse, for example, are hard to identify with exactitude. Perhaps this vagueness leaves more to the imagination as placing them in the land of fairie.

[1] For Arthur's claims in Scotland, see *Merlin*, ed. H. B. Wheatley (Early Eng. Text Soc.), 1869-1899, essay by J. S. Stuart Glennie on "Arthurian Localities." Also John Veitch, *History and Poetry of the Scottish Border*, 1878.

Still, there is no doubt that, if legends are connected with a certain locality, and if a writer awakens interest in it by the quality of his work, then in return, the locality with its associations helps to keep the fame of the writer alive. This has proved true in the case of Thomas Hardy and his *Wessex*, a partly real and partly imaginary topography. Thus the poetry and prose of W. B. Yeats, though he does not deal directly with the traditionary legends, has helped to create a love for the legends and literature of Ireland. And conversely, those who love Ireland welcome W. B. Yeats as a national poet.

Another recent poet who has stirred up fresh interest in the legends of his native province is Mistral (1830-1914). He also was the centre of a movement whose object was to restore the native language and literature. Seven of these poets in 1854 founded the society of the " Félibrige " near Avignon, and by their poetic and prose work aided this revival. Mistral's earlier and simpler poem " Mirèio," [1] written in the Provençal dialect, is held together by a simple tragic tale of a poor girl and her rich lover. In this rustic epic of great charm the poet has related many customs and legends belonging to his native province. It is interesting to note that part of the Joseph of Arimathea legend, connected with the Grail, has become attached to the stories of Saint Martha, and is told by Mistral in this poem. Saint Martha is a favourite saint in Provence.

In summing up the value of myth and legend, the statement may be made that these have a permanent value for poetry and will continue to have. Though new movements in art and literature often seem to break away from the past altogether, and sometimes claim to do so, yet, when enough time has elapsed for the student of literature to get the true perspective, this break is not so complete as it seems at the time to the ardent iconoclasts. [2]

One of the main reasons for the immortality of the myth and legend is so simple that it is apt to be overlooked. There

---

[1] It has been translated into French and called " Mireille."

[2] Such an extreme theory is found in F. R. Leavis's *New Bearings in English Poetry*, 1923.

dwells in man, and especially in the poet, the eternal child. Thus to those, in whom the memories of childhood are not altogether extinguished, there is always an appeal in a legend or fairy story, especially if the outward form matches the inward simplicity and beauty.

Other reasons have been given throughout this study and exemplified. The modern findings of psychology and the modern studies in comparative mythology have testified that there are in the race-consciousness and in the individual, subconscious symbols and pictures which appear and re-appear in stories of all lands,[1] such as the lake, the dragon, the serpent, which seem fundamental to the human mind. Thus on this level there is a vast store of associations which the artist in colour, sound or words can arouse and make use of in his art. It has been exemplified how, in a society, province or nation, the traditions of legendary lore form a storehouse from which the literary artist can draw. If he himself belongs to the society, province or nation, he will share in a special manner in this heritage and become its mouthpiece for others. Thus in the novels of Sir Walter Scott is seen the flowering of generations of Scottish tradition.

Another fact which makes for permanence is that a well-told story, legendary or otherwise, will always be of interest. A legendary story often has the advantage of dealing with types representing a particular nation. Though legendary matter has proved suitable for narrative and artistic telling in prose, as in James Stephen's *Deirdre*, the novel with its more realistic setting has not shown itself adaptable.[2] The poetic drama and lyric have been more potent to convey the original spirit of these stories.

It has also been made clear that the philosophic poet who wishes to expound the deeper truths of existence to mankind often finds in the myth and legend a medium through which he can communicate in some degree his spiritual vision.

---

[1] Another theory to explain the similarity of fairy tales in all lands is that of the migration of the peoples, but this does not explain the similarity in all cases.

[2] See also Grail section (Powys's *Glastonbury Legend*), pp. 154 ff.

On the other hand, the modern poet (including the prose-writer) will probably use the traditional legends less, because as standardised education spreads, these have become less and less a race-heritage, told to the children at their mothers' or nurses' knees. They are treasured more at the present day by the peasant in parts remote from urban centres. And as the means of communication and civilisation advance, these rural inhabitants lose their individual traditions and characteristics. Thus any myths and legends which survive will be a literary heritage rather than a race one.

We are now in a position to ask and answer in general terms. What special characteristics in legend will make for survival in literature? How far do the Arthurian legends possess the special characteristics?

The answer to this question has underlain the analyses of the separate legends. Very briefly it may be summarised thus.

Many of these Arthurian legends will survive merely as fairy stories. As long as there are children in the human race and poets who have not lost the fresh and innocent imagination of early youth, these will be told and appreciated. The story of Merlin and his enchantments, the story of Arthur and the sword embedded in the stone at Westminster, will take high rank in English fairy lore.

Also, such a tale as that of Tristan, with its tragic conflict, is likely to remain one of the world's great love stories. It holds, I think, more promise of permanence than the Lancelot story which has come to maturity in a certain period, embodying specific conventions, as the chivalric period did. Malory's classic has probably given to this story in its particular entourage, its most characteristic expression in English literature.

From our consideration of myths as symbols it can be stated that that type of myth will have the greatest vitality and meaning for modern poetry, which has within it the seed of philosophic truth which exists for all periods. This kind of myth might be termed a root-myth, for, like a bulb, it holds within itself the nucleus of mighty forces, capable of a magic flowering under suitable conditions. The myth and legend of Prometheus is a good example of this, for it embodies the idea of the eternal struggle between man and Fate, and the seeming cruelty and irrationality of Destiny. This myth has been chosen by poets and dramatists from Greek times onwards to our own, including Shelley and Robert Bridges. It has been demonstrated here,[1] that of all legends, the Grail legend satisfies mostly this criterion, but unfortunately, owing partly to Malory's inferior version being chosen, and partly to unsuitable modern conditions, it has not fulfilled its promise nor been adequately represented in English literature. Even unsuccessful attempts at treatment such as Powys's *Glastonbury Legend*[1] and experiments such as T. S. Eliot's *Waste Land*[1] show that the nucleus of spiritual energy remains and may yet be liberated in an artistic form worthy of the subject.

In comparison with classic legend, used in simile and allusion, Arthurian legend has never been so much utilised by the learned. Also, as compared with Irish legends, it is not so deeply associated with certain places and peoples. Nevertheless the Arthurian legend is likely to hold in some measure its place in English literature as embodying romantic ideals and aspirations.

[1] See above, Chap. X., pp. 146 ff. and 150 ff.

APPENDIX A

CHRONOLOGICAL [1] SUMMARY OF ORIGINAL POEMS, PLAYS AND PROSE WORKS AFTER 1485 WHICH HAVE ARTHURIAN SUBJECTS.

EDITIONS OF MALORY NOT INCLUDED.

Translations and editions of texts which have had a literary influence, such as the *Mabinogion*, are included.

When work is a drama, the fact is stated

Lytel Tretys of the Byrth and Prophecies of Merlin (first ed.)	1510
WARNER, W., Albion's England	1586
HUGHES, T., Misfortunes of Arthur (drama, acted) .	1588
SPENSER's Faerie Queene, Books I-III	1590-6
MICHAEL DRAYTON, Polyolbion	1612
HEYWOOD, T., Life of Merlin	1641
DRYDEN, JOHN, King Arthur (drama, acted) . .	1691
BLACKMORE, SIR RICHARD, Prince Arthur . .	1695
King Arthur	1697
PERCY, Reliques	1765
WARTON, W., Grave of King Arthur . . .	1777
Myvrian Archaiology (Collection of Welsh poems) .	1801-7
Sir Tristrem, ed. Sir Walter Scott . . .	1804
SCOTT, SIR WALTER, Bridal of Triermain . .	1813
PEACOCK, T. L., Misfortunes of Elphin . .	1829
WORDSWORTH, W., Egyptian Maid . . .	1830
TENNYSON, ALFRED, Lady of Shalott. In 1832 volume of poems	1832
Sir Launcelot and Queen Guinevere : Sir Galahad : and the Morte d'Arthur. In 1842 volumes .	1842

---

[1] For poems, the date of the first volume of poems in which the special poem is printed, is given. For plays, unless stated, the date of publication.

264

Sir Gawayne, ed. Sir F. Madden . . . 1847
WAGNER, RICHARD, Lohengrin (opera) . . 1848
LYTTON, EDWARD BULWER, King Arthur . . . 1848
Mabinogion, ed. Lady Charlotte Guest . . . 1838-49
SWINBURNE, ALGERNON, Queen Yseult and Arthurian
    Fragments 1857
ARNOLD, MATTHEW, Tristram and Iseult (poetical drama) 1857
TENNYSON, ALFRED, Idylls of the King. First publication,
    including Enid, Vivien, Elaine and Guinevere . 1859
WAGNER, RICHARD, Tristan (opera) 1859
HAWKER, R. S., Quest of the Sangreal 1863
WESTWOOD, THOMAS, Quest of the Sancgreall . . 1868
Four Ancient Books of Wales, ed. W. F. Skene . . 1868
TENNYSON, ALFRED, Idylls of the King. Second publica-
    tion, including " The Coming of Arthur," " The
    Holy Grail," " Pelleas and Etarre," and the
    " Passing of Arthur " 1869
    Third publication, " Last Tournament " . . 1871
    Republished a year later with " Gareth and Lynette " 1872
LOWELL, JAMES RUSSELL, Sir Launfal, in Poems . . 1880
WAGNER, RICHARD, Parsifal (opera) 1882
SWINBURNE, ALGERNON, Tristram of Lyonesse . . 1882
TENNYSON, ALFRED, Idylls of the King. Third publica-
    tion, Balin and Balan 1885
    Merlin and the Gleam 1889
HOVEY, RICHARD, Launcelot and Guinevere (drama) . 1891
CARR, J. COMYNS, King Arthur (drama) . . . 1895
SWINBURNE, ALGERNON, The Tale of Balin . . . 1896
DAVIDSON, JOHN, The Last Ballad 1898
THOMAS. Le Roman de Tristan, ed. J. Bedier . . 1902
CARR, COMYNS, Tristram and Iseult (drama) . . 1906
FIELD, MICHAEL, Tragedy of Pardon (drama). Tristan
    de Léonois (drama) 1911
BINYON, LAURENCE, " Tristram's End " in Odes, 1913 . 1913
SYMONS, ARTHUR, Tristan and Iseult (drama) . . 1917
BINYON, LAURENCE, Arthur (drama) 1923
HARDY, THOMAS, The Famous Tragedy of the Queen of
    Cornwall at Tintagel in Lyonesse (drama) . . 1923
MASEFIELD, JOHN, " Sir Bors " in Collected Poems . 1923
ELIOT, T. S., The Waste Land, in Poems, 1909-25 . 1925
BOTTOMLEY, GORDON, Merlin's Grave in " Scenes and
    Plays " . . . . 1925 (approx.)

MASEFIELD, JOHN, Tristan and Isolt (drama) . . 1927
    Midsummer Night and other Tales in Verse.
    Includes " The Birth of Arthur," " Badon Hill,"
    " Midsummer Night," " The Fight on the Wall,"
    " The Death of Lancelot," etc. . . . 1928
POWYS, J. COWPER, A Glastonbury Romance . . 1933

APPENDIX B

THE ARTHURIAN LEGEND IN THE DECORATIVE ARTS

BIBLIOGRAPHICAL NOTE

This is a study in itself, but illustrates the popularity of the Arthurian Legend in the Mediæval Ages and in the nineteenth century, and thus casts an interesting sidelight on the literature.

References will be found in Loomis, *Illustrations of Mediæval Romance in Tiles from Chertsey Abbey* (University of Illinois Studies in Language and Literature, II., pt. 2), which contains a bibliography on Tristan romances in the Decorative Arts.

See also *Bildteppiche und Decken des Mittelalters*, ed. Marie Schuette, Leipzig, 1927. This volume, a copy of which is in the Library of the College of Art, Edinburgh, reproduces fourteenth century tapestries found in the monastery at Wienhausen. Among other subjects is the story of Tristan, probably from Gottfried von Strassburg, with his horse, dog and dragon, also a drawing of Iseult, all rather like the drawings of small children, but stronger in colour.

For the restoration of the Pre-Raphaelite Drawings by Professor Tristram, see *Studio* III, 1936, article by Derek Patmore.

APPENDIX C

LIST OF IMPORTANT REFERENCE BOOKS INCLUDING TEXTS

The texts are listed under the name of the editor and the whole list is alphabetical.

BIBLIOGRAPHICAL NOTE.—A full bibliography up to 1923 will be found in J. D. Bruce, *Evolution of Arthurian Romance*, 1923. This ought to be supplemented by the *Manual of Writings in Middle English*, by J. E. Wells, 1916, with supplements up to date.

In this thesis the translations of the " Everyman " editions (Dent) have been considerably used.

The following are the most important works of reference used :—

ARNOLD, M., The Study of Celtic Literature, 1891.

BAKER, E., History of the English Novel, I, 1924.

BÉDIER, THOMAS, ed. Le Roman de Tristan, 2 vols., 1902-5.
    Les deux poèmes de la Folie Tristan, 1907.

BELLOC, HILAIRE, Tristan et Iseut, 1900.

BROWN, A. C. L., The Round Table before Wace (Harvard Studies and Notes, VII), 1900.

BRUCE, J. D., Evolution of Arthurian Romance from the beginnings down to year 1300 (with bibliography), 1923.

CHAMBERS, E. K., Arthur of Britain (with bibliographical notes), 1927.

CHILD, F. J., ed. Ballads.

FARAL, E., La Légende Arthurienne, includes Geoffrey of Monmouth's Historia, and Vita Merlini, 1929.

FLETCHER, R. H., The Arthurian Material in the Chronicles. (Harvard Studies and Notes, X), 1906.

FOERSTÉR, W., ed. Christian von Troyes. Sämtliche Werke, 1884-99.

FORMAN, A., Parsifal (English Translation), 1899.
    Tristan and Isolde (English Translation), 1891.

GILES, J. A., Six Old English Chronicles, 1841.

GOLTHER, W., Tristan and Isolde (treatise), 1929.

GREGORY, LADY A., Cuchulain of Muirthemne, 1902.
    Gods and Fighting Men, 1904.

GRIERSON, H. J. C., Background of English Literature, 1925.

GUEST, LADY CHARLOTTE, Mabinogion (English Translation), 3 vols., 1838-49.

HALES and FURNIVALL, ed. " Folio MS.," 1867-8.

HENDERSON, W. J., Richard Wagner : his Life and Works, 1923.

KALUZA, M., ed. Le Bel Inconnu, 1890.

LACHMANN, E., ed. Wolfram von Eschenbach, Werke. 1833.

LAFOURCADE, G., La Jeunesse de Swinburne, 1928.

LEAVIS, F. R., New Bearings in English Poetry, 1923.

LICHTENSTEIN, F., ed. Eilhart von Oberge, 1877.

LOTH, H., " Les Mabinogion " (French translation, valuable introduction), 1913.

MADDEN, SIR F., Syr Gawayne : collection of Ancient Romance Poems (Bannatyne Club), 1839.
Layamon's Brut, 1847.
MALORY, THOMAS, Le Morte Darthur, 2 vols., ".Everyman" Edition, 1906.
MAROLD, ed. Gottfried von Strassburg, Tristan, 1906.
MAYNADIER, G. HOWARD, The Wife of Bath's Tale : its Sources and Analogues, 1901.
The Arthur of the English Poets. (This book has been used extensively in thesis), 1906.
MIDDLETON MURRY, JOHN, Discoveries (Essays), 1930.
MOMMSEN, T., Chronica Minora, IV-VII (M. G. H., III, 11) text of Nennius.
MOORE, T. STURGE, The Story of Tristram and Isolt in Modern Poetry (Criterion, vol. i., article), 1922-3.
MORRIS, R., ed. Sir Gawayne and the Green Knight, 1864.
Morte Arthur. Two Early English Romances (Stanzaic and Alliterative Morte), "Everyman" Edition, 1912.
MURET, E., ed. Béroul, Le Roman de Tristan, 1913.
MURRY. See Middleton Murry.
NEILSON, W. A., Origins and Sources of the Courts of Love (Harvard Studies and Notes, VI).
NUTT, ALFRED, Celtic and Mediæval Romance, 1899.
OSBORNE TAYLOR, The Mediæval Mind, 1911.
PARRY, J. J., Vita Merlini (University of Illinois Studies in Language and Literature, x. 3), has translation of the Welsh " Afallenau," 1925.
PAUPHILET, A., Études sur la Queste del Saint Graal, 1921.
Ed., La Quête del Saint Graal (Text), 1923.
RHYS, ARTHUR, Studies in Arthurian Legend, 1891.
LE ROUX DE LINCY, ed. Le Roman de Brut par Wace, 1836-8.
SCHOEPPERLE, G., Tristan and Isolt, a study of the Sources of the Romance, 1913.
SKENE, W. F., Four Ancient Books of Wales, 1909.
SMITH, J. C., ed. Spenser's Faerie Queene, 1909.
SOMMER, H. OSKAR, Vulgate Version of the Arthurian Romances, 1910-12.
SPENCE, LEWIS, Introduction to Mythology, 1921.
STEWART, J. A., The Myths of Plato, 1905.
TAYLOR (OSBORNE). See above, Osborne Taylor.
TENNYSON, ALFRED (LORD), Memoir by his Son, 1899.
TOLKIEN, J. R. R., ed. Sir Gawain and the Green Knight, 1925.

VINAVER, E., Le Roman de Tristan et Iseult dans l'Œuvre de Thomas Malory, 1925.

Malory, 1929.

WAGNER, Letters, translated by W. Ellis, 1905.

WARNKE, ed. Die Lais der Marie de France, 1900.

WESTON, J. L., Parzival (translation of W. von Aeschenbach), 2 vols., 1894.

The Legend of Gawain : studies upon its scope and significance, 1897.

Story of Tristan and Iseult : rendered into English from the German, 2 vols. From Gottfried von Strassburg (Arthurian Romances), 1899.

The Legend of Sir Perceval, 2 vols., 1906-9.

Sir Cleges, Sir Libeaus Desconeus (Arthurian Romances unrepresented in Malory), 1902.

Romance, Vision and Satire (translations), 1912.

From Ritual to Romance, 1920.

WHEATLEY, H. B., ed. Merlin, prose romance (English translation), Early English Text Society, 1899.

INDEX

Titles of published works are printed in italic.

Amour courtois, 1, 4

Anfortas, King, in *Parzival*, 167, 168, 169, 172

" Annales Cambriæ," 16

Arderydd, battle of, 71

Arnold, Matthew, " Tristram and Iseult," 240

Artegal, 73

Arthur, 1, 12, 49, 53
  as chieftain, 53
  as culture hero, 117
  birth of, 74
  death of, 22, 27
  feudal, 20
  historical, 14
  in Chronicles, 14-29
  in eighteenth century, 35-41
  in *Mabinogion*, 120
  in Malory, 28
  in metrical romances (English), 59-64
  in seventeenth century, 34-35
  in sixteenth century, 30-33
  in Tennyson, 137
  in *Tristram of Lyonesse*, 213
  mythical Arthur, 14
  slayer of monsters, 120
  tomb of Arthur, 151
  See below under " Avowynge of Arthur," *also* " Auntres of Arthure," etc.

Arthur, return of, in *Don Quixote*, 245

Arthurian myth, value of, 250, 262

Astolat, maiden of, 92-3

" Auntres of Arthure at the Terne Wathelyn," 63

Avalon, 22, 26, 42, 111, 131. *See also* Glastonbury

" Avowynge of Arthur," 63

Balan. *See* Balin and Balan

Balen. *See under* Swinburne

Balin (Balen) and Balan, in Malory, 159. *See under* Tennyson and Swinburne

Ballads, 11, 12, 35, 96

Beardsley, Aubrey, illustrator of Malory, 208

Bedevere (Bedwyr, Bedivere), 1, 27
  slayer of monsters, 120

Bédier, Joseph, ed. *Tristan*, 12, 191

Béroul, 208, 213, 214, 215, 282
  and Masefield, 238
  Tristan of, 192

Binyon, Laurence, *Arthur*, a play, 49, 107
  " Tristram's End," Ode, 220-223

Black Book of Cærmarthen, 71, 113. *See also under* Skene, W. F., ed.

Borron (Boron), Robert de, ed. " Joseph of Arimathea," 72
  " Merlin," 72
  " Perceval," 72

Bors, Sir, 134

Bottomley, Gordon, " Merlin's Grave," 81-83

" Boy and Mantle," stories of, 36, 37, 121
  in Malory, 121

Brangäne. *See under* Brangwain

Brangwain (Brangäne), 216
  in Wagner, 185

Bredbeddle, Sir, 37

Bridges, Robert, " The Testament of Beauty," 256

Britomart, 73

Brut. See Wace and Layamon

Cabal, the dog of Arthur, 16

Caer Lleon, amusements at, 108

Caliburnus, Arthur's sword, 17

Camlan, battle of, 118

Caradawc (Caradoc or Craddocke), 121

Caradoc of Lancarvon, *Vitæ Gildæ*, 87

" Carle of Carlile." *See under* Gawain Romances

Carlisle, 6, 64
Carr, J. Comyns, 220
  King Arthur, 50
  Tristram and Iseult, 223-224
Caxton, 31
  poem on Merlin, 76
Celtic contes, 3
  fairy-tale, 194
Cervantes, Don Quixote, 244-246
Chadwick, theories on Merlin, 71
Chambers, E. K., 116, 151
  theory on Merlin, 71-72
Chaucer, 8
  " Wife of Bath's Tale," 8
Chivalric love, 4
  ideal, 1, 244
Chivalry, age of, 10
Chrétien de Troies, 3, 5, 8
  and the Mabinogion, 122, 123-4
  and Tennyson, 122
  " Cliges," 4
  " Erec et Enide " (" Geraint and
    Enid "), 4, 122
  " Lancelot " (" Chevalier de la
    Charette "), 4, 5, 87-89, 124
  " Perceval le Gallois " (" Conte del
    Graal "), 4, 64
  " Yvain " (" Le Chevalier au Lion "),
    4, 5
Cistercians and the Grail cult, 157
Coggeshall, Ralph, 151
  Chronicon Anglicanum, 151
Contes, Celtic, 3
Courtly love, 1, 6
Courts of love, 2
Cradock, Sir, 25
Crusades, 173
Cuchulain, 18

Davidson, John, The Last Ballad, 102-
  104
Dinadan, character in Malory, 244
" Dolourous stroke," 160
Don Quixote, 244. See also under Cervantes
" Donnei des Amanz," Tristan in,
  213
Drayton, Michael, Polyolbion, 76
" Dream of Rhonabwy." See under
  Mabinogion
Dryden, Merlin in, 77
  King Arthur, 35, 77
  Prince Arthur, 35

Eildon Hills, connected with Arthur, 42,
  51
Eilhart von Oberg, 194
  version of Tristan, 191, 195-6
" Elaine, Lancelot and," 92. See also
  Tennyson
Eleanor of Aquitaine, 19, 87
Eliot, T. S., " Waste Land," 145,
  263
Elphin. See Peacock
Eucharist and Mass, symbols of, 159
Evans, Evan, Specimens of the Poetry of
  Ancient Welsh Bards, 35
Excalibur (Caliburnus), Arthur's sword,
  17, 18

Fabliaux, 7, 37, 64
Feirefis, King, in Parzival, 169
Field, Michael, Tragedy of Pardon, 229-231
  Tristan de Leonois, 231
Fisher-King, 167
" Folio MS.," 37
Four Ancient Books of Wales. See Skene,
  W. F., ed.
Frere, John Hookham, The Monks and
  the Giants, 246-248
Froissart, Chronicle of, 91

Gaimer, Geoffrey, 72
Galahad, 90, 133, 134, 136, 138
  as Grail-Quester, 64
Ganhardine, form of Käherdin, 214
Garlon, invisible knight, 160
Gawain, 2, 12, 24, 26, 28
  as Grail-Quester, 64
  degradation of, 96
  in J. Hookham Frère, 248
  in the Queste, 133
  in Tennyson, 140
  in Wolfram von Eeschenbach, 128
  solar myth, 64
Gawain Romances, 59-64
  " Avowynge of Arthur," 63
  " Carle of Carlile," 62
  " Golagros and Gawaine," 63
  " Grene Knight," 61
  " Sir Gawain and the Grene Knight,"
    44, 61
  Syr Gawayne, ed. Sir F. Madden, 44·
  " Turke and Gowin," 63
  " Weddynge of Sir Gawen and Dame
    Ragnell," 62

Geoffrey of Monmouth, 1, 7, 8, 12, 14, 15, 70, 74, 88, 116
   connection with "Dream of Rhonabwy," 118
   Historia (History, Chronicle), 18, 24, 29, 30, 31
   Merlin in, 70-72
   Vita Merlini, 70, 71, 151
"Geraint, the Son of Erbin." See under *Mabinogion*
"Geraint, Marriage of," 8
Gerard de Leew, "Chronicle," 36
Gesta Anglorum. *See* William of Malmesbury
Giraldus Cambrensis, 150
   De Principis Instructione, 151
Glastonbury, 26, 88, 96, 111, 151, 152
Godfrey of Bouillon in Lohengrin story, 173
"Golagros and Gawaine," 63
"Gospel of Nicodemus," 152, 153
Gosse, Edmund, criticism of Swinburne, 216
Gottfried von Strassburg, *Tristan*, 178, 192
   and Wagner, 178, 179, 183
   King Mark in, 193
   story of Tristan, 193-4, 195-6
Grail—
   Holy Grail, 48, 87, 128-158, 159
   Galahad, hero of, 90
   Lancelot as hero of, 99
Grail Castle, 168, 170
Grail-concept, 159
Grail legend, 152
   and Cistercians, 157
Gray, Thomas, *The Bard*, 108
Gregory, Lady, *Cuchulain of Muirthemne*, 257-9
   Gods and Fighting Men, 257-9
"Grene Knight." *See* Gawain
Guest, Lady Charlotte, ed. *Mabinogion*, 12, 14, 44, 115
Guinivere (Guinevere, Wenhaver, Gaynor), 2, 3, 25, 28, 37, 45, 48, 50, 52, 89
   rape of, 87-88, 111
   See also Morris, W., and Tennyson

Hardy, Thomas, *Famous Tragedy of the Queen of Cornwall*, 12, 220, 231-236
   Gottfried as source of, 235

Hardy, Thomas, Malory and, 234
   style of, 236
Hawker, R. S., "Quest of the Sangraal," 141-143
   Cornish names in, 141
   Sir Galahad in, 142
Heinrich von Freiberg, continuator of "Tristan," 201, 202
Heywood, Thomas, *Life* of Merlin, 74-76
Holy Grail. *See under* Grail
"Holy Thorn," 154
Hovey, Richard, *Lancelot and Guinevere*, play of, 102
Huchown of the Awle Ryale, authorship of *Morte Arthure*, 22

Idylls of the King, 45
   ideals of marriage in, 47
   moral ideals in, 93, 204
   plan and argument of, 48
   For separate Idylls *see under* Tennyson
"Immortal Hour," 175
Irish epic, topography in, 259
Irish *Imrama*, 151
Irish saga, 117
Iseult (Isolde, Ysolde, Ysolt, Isolt, Isoud)—
   in Gottfried von Strassburg, 196
   in Heinrich von Freiberg, 202
   in Malory, 197, 201
   in Tennyson, 204
Iseult of the White Hands, second Iseult, 200-1, 227, 240, 242
Isle of Man, legendary associations, 63

Jeschuté, character in the *Parzival*, 166, 168
John of Glastonbury, 152, 153
   Chronicle, 152
Joseph of Arimathea, 142, 150, 151, 152, 153
   "Holy Thorn," 154
   "Lyfe of Joseph of Arimathea," 153
Joseph of Arimathea, legend of, in the poet Mistral, 260

Käherdin, brother of Iseult, 214
Kay (Kei), 1, 17, 19, 63
   slayer of monsters, 120
Kentigern, Saint, 71
"Kilhwch and Olwen." See under *Mabinogion*

"King Arthur and the King of Cornwall," 37

"King Arthur's Death," 36, 37

Klingsor, in Wagner, 172

Kondrie. *See under* Kundrie

Kondwiremur, wife of Parzival, 166, 170

Konrad von Wurzburg, "Der Schwanritter," 174

Kundry (Kondrie), character in Grail story, 167, 168, 171, 172

Kurwenal, servant of Tristan, 202
in Wagner, 183

"Lady of the Fountain." See under *Mabinogion*

Lafourcade, biographer of Swinburne, 207, 210

Lancelot, 2, 28, 45, 53, 59
in *Don Quixote*, 245
in John H. Frère, 248
in L. Binyon's *Arthur*, 49, 50, 52
in the *Queste*, 132, 135
in Tennyson, 93, 140

"Lancelot (Sir) du Lake," ballad, 37

Lang, Andrew, 81

"Lanval." *See under* Marie of France

Layamon, *Brut*, 14, 20, 22, 24, 28, 53, 55

"Legend of King Arthur," 36, 37

Legend, value of national, 255-6

Leyden, "Scenes of Infancy," Arthurian references in, 42

Lilly, William, Almanack, 77

Lohengrin. See under Wagner

Lowell, James Russell, "The Vision of Sir Launfal," 144-5
influence of Wolfram's *Parzival* in, 145

"Lyfe of Joseph of Arimathea," 153

Lytton (Lord), Edward Bulwer, 39
King Arthur, 39-41, 64-69

Mabinogion, 12, 14, 17
"Dream of Rhonabwy," 14, 115, 118
"Geraint, the Son of Erbin," 115
"Kilhwch and Olwen," 16, 17, 18, 63, 115, 116, 120
"Lady of the Fountain," 115, 120
"Peredur, the Son of Evrawc," 115
"Taliesin," 116
and Tennyson, 122. *See also under* Guest, Lady Charlotte, ed.

Madden, Sir Frederick, ed. *Syr Gawayne*, 44

Magic philtre, in *Tristan*, 197, 200

Maid of Ascolat, 27

Malory, 1, 2, 6, 8, 10, 27, 28, 29, 37, 38, 44, 48, 59, 61, 78, 79, 90, 115, 128
abduction of Guenevere, 88
and Hardy, 234
and Morris, 96, 100
and the *Queste*, 133, 135

Malory's *Morte Darthur* and Tennyson, 204, 205
and Welsh romances, 120-122
chivalry in, 199, 200
comparison with Gottfried von Strassburg, 193-203
editions of, 29
ideals of chivalry in, 47
King Mark in, 199
Lancelot and Elaine story in, 92
stories of chastity tests in, 121
Tristan in, 191, 194, 195

Manawyddan, connection with Irish god, 120

Map, Walter, 5, 7

Marhaus, Sir, same character as Morolt, 194, 196

Marie of Champagne, 2, 4, 87

Marie of France, 2, 8, 72
"Chèvrefeuille," 3, 194
"Lanval," 3
Tristan in, 194, 195

Mark, King, 191
in Malory, 197, 205

Marke, in Wagner, 180, 182, 185

"Marriage of Geraint," 8

"Marriage of Sir Gawain," 36

Masefield, John, 7, 220
and *Mabinogion*, 237
"Badon Hill," 53
"Birth of Arthur," 55
"Midsummer Night," 51-58, 104-107
"Sailing of Hell Race," 55
"Sir Bors," 13, 159
Tristan and Isolt, 236
use of tradition, 237

Mead, W. E., theories on Merlin, 71

Meleagant, 88

Meliagrance, Sir, 88

Melvas, King of the Summer country, 88, 109

Merlin (Myrddhin), 45, 50, 71, 72
and Lailoken, 71
and Stonehenge, 39

Merlin (Myrddhin), " Avallenau Myrd-
dhin," 113-114
  Caledonian, 81
  imprisonment of, 73
  in eighteenth century, 70
  in Geoffrey of Monmouth, 70, 71
  in Swinburne, 161
  in Welsh poems, 151
  Lytel Tretys of Byrth and Prophecies of,
    76
  Ordinary, 79
  prophecies on, 77
  " Suite " of, 79
Metrical romance, English, 60
Michel, Frances, editor of Tristan
  romance, 206
Mider and Etain, 88
Milton, " Epitaphium Damonis," 33
  Paradise Lost, references in, 33
  Paradise Regained, references in, 33
Minstrel, 6
" Mirabilia," 16
Mistral, poet, 260
" Modern " used as a term, 1, 9
Modred (Mordred, Medraul), 16, 17,
  21, 24, 25, 47
Mont St Michel, monster of, 22
Moore, Mr Sturge, 222
  Essay on Tristan and Iscult, 216, 222,
    229
Moore, Mr, explanation of hunting of
  Twrch Trwyth, 117-118
Mordred, 151. *See above, under* Modred
  in Swinburne, 162
Morolt, 195. *See also under* Marhaus
  (Sir).
  (Morold, Morgan, Maronde), 209
  in Gottfried von Strassburg, 194, 195
  in Wagner, 179
Morris, William, 10, 68, 95
  and Swinburne, 208
  decorative qualities of, 98
  influence of Malory on, 96
  " Defence of Guenevere," 91, 92, 96,
    97, 98, 105
  " King Arthur's Tomb," 96, 98, 99
  " Sir Galahad," 96, 100
Morte Arthure, alliterative, or Thornton,
  22, 24, 27, 28, 59
  authorship of, 22
Morte Arthur, stanzaic, 24, 27, 28
Morte Darthur. *See under* Malory

" Morte d'Arthur." *See also under*
  Tennyson
Mount Badon, 15
Murry, J. Middleton, " The Nature of
  Poetry," 254-5
Myrddin. *See* Merlin, Welsh
Myth, in Plato, 250-252
  use by modern poets, 256-7
  value of, 260
Myvyrian Archaiology, 35

Nennius, 14, 15
  mention of Twrch Trwyth in, 116
Nimiane, 73. *See also under* Vivien
Nimue, 80, 82. *See also under* Vivien

Oral tradition, 11
Ortrud, in *Lohengrin*, 176
Oxford Union, Arthurian frescoes in, 97

Parsifal. *See under* Wagner
Parzival. *See under* Wolfram von
  Aeschenbach
Pauphilet, Albert, ed. the *Queste*, 132, 157
Peacock, Thomas Love, *Misfortunes of
  Elphin*, 108, 111, 112
  style of, 112
  " War-Song of Dinas Vawr," 113
  translation of " Avallenau Myrddhin,"
    113
Pellam, King, 160
Perceval (Percival, Percivale), 134, 142.
  See also Parzival under Wolfram von
  Aeschenbach, and *Parsifal* under
  Wagner
Percy, Bishop, *Reliques of Ancient Poetry*,
  35, 36, 42, 65, 96
Peredur, Welsh, 127
" Peredur, the Son of Evrawc." *See
  under Mabinogion*
Plato, allegory of *Phædrus*, 256
Powys, J. C., *Glastonbury Legend*, 145, 150,
  154, 263
Pre-Raphaelites, 91
  aim of, 95
  and painting, 96
  and Swinburne, 101
  decorative qualities of, 96-7
  romantic attitude of, 97
Pridwen (Prydwen), 17
Prose romance, and Tennyson, 204
Prose romances, Hardy and, 234

Prose Tristan, 244
Pulci, *Morgante Maggiore*, 247

Queste, version of Grail, 49, 128, 132, 134, 157, 159, 171
   miraculous ship in, 134

Raven in Celtic mythology, 118
Red Book of Hergest, 71. See also under *Mabinogion*
Reliques of Ancient Poetry. See Percy, Bishop
Renaissance, form in Arthurian legend in, 8
Ritho (Rhitta, Ryons, Ryence), Welsh King, 23, 73, 120
Robert de Borron, 5, 7
Robinson, E. A., 241
   Isolt of Brittany, portrait of, 242
Robinson, Edwin Arlington, " Merlin," 83-86
Romantic Revival, 10, 31, 91
Ron, Arthur's lance, 17
Rossetti, D. G., 97, 98
Round Table, 21, 37
Rowley, William, " Birth of Merlin," 76
Ryence, King. *See under* Ritho, Welsh King

Sancho, character in *Don Quixote*, 246
Schoepperle, G., critical work on Tristan, 191
Scott, Sir Walter, " Bridal of Trier-main," 42
   Minstrelsy of Scottish Border, 42-43
   Sir Tristrem, editor of, 44
Seithenyn ap Seithyn, in Peacock, 109
Shakespeare, references in, to Arthurian legend, 12
Sir Gawain. *See under* Gawain
Sir Lancelot du Lake. *See* Lancelot du Lake
Sir Tristrem. *See under* Tristrem (Sir)
Skene, W. F., ed. *Four Ancient Books of Wales*, 119
   Black Book of Carmarthen, 119-20
Spenser, 10, 29, 44
   and stories of mantle as chastity test, 121
   Faerie Queene, 30, 31-33, 38, 55
     Merlin in, 73, 74
     Sir Calidore in, 122

Stewart, J. A., *Myths of Plato*, 251
Sturge Moore. *See under* Moore, Sturge
Swan-Knight, 167, 173
Swan, symbolism of, 167, 175
Swinburne, Algernon C., 9, 10, 11
   aim of, 207
   and Malory, 160, 163
   and the Pre-Raphaelites, 101
   and *Sir Tristrem*, 208, 211
   and W. Morris, 208
   Brangwain in, 216
   " Lancelot," 101
   Mark in, 216, 217
   Merlin in, 161
   Mordred in, 162
   philosophy of, 219
   Prelude to *Tristram of Lyonesse*, 218-219
   " Queen Iseult," 101, 207-210
   sources of, 48, 79, 215
   Tale of Balen, 160, 163
   Tristram of Lyonesse, 80, 206-7, 209, 211-19
Symons, Arthur, *Tristan and Iseult*, 225-229

Tennyson, Alfred, Lord, 6, 9, 10, 11, 13, 45, 52, 68, 73
   and Malory, 205
   and Wagner, 206
   Chrétien de Troies and, 122
   comparison with *Mabinogion*, 125-6
   comparison with Swinburne, 163-4
   Gawain in, 68
   " Merlin and the Gleam," 79
   Merlin in, 70
   Earlier poems (Arthurian)—
     " Lady of Shalott," 45, 91-2
     " Morte d'Arthur," 45
     " Sir Launcelot and Queen Guinevere," 45, 94
   Idylls of the King—
     " Balin and Balan," 163-4
     " Coming of Arthur," 45
     " Geraint and Enid," 44, 122-7
     " Guinevere," 49, 93-5
     " Holy Grail," 48, 137, 138-140
     " Lancelot and Elaine," 92-4
     " Last Tournament," 49, 204-6
     " Marriage of Geraint," 122
     " Merlin and Vivien," 79
     " Pelleas and Etarre," 68-9

Thomas, French poet, 208, 210, 211, 213, 214, 215, 232
and Masefield, 238
plays after, 220, 223
" Tristan," 192
Tintagel, 193, 206
Titurel, king in Grail Castle, 170
Tramtrist, other name for Tristan, 197
Trevrezent, hermit in Grail Castle, 168
Triads, Welsh, 17, 73
Tristan (Tristram), 3, 9, 49, 80
and Iseult, 90
death of, 202, 220, 235
in " Donnei des Amanz," 213
in J. Hookham Frère, 248
in Malory, 191-203, 195, 202
in Marie of France, 194
legend of, 13
magic philtre in, 197
modern plays of, 204-243
prose Tristan, 197, 199, 202
sources of, 191-203
See also under Arnold (M.), Binyon (L.), Carr (Comyns), Field (Michael), Hardy (Thomas), Masefield (John), Robinson (E. A.), Swinburne (A.), Symons (A.)
See also under Gottfried von Strassburg. For Tristan opera see under Wagner.
Tristeran (Tristan), 37
Tristram. See under Tristan
Tristrem (Sir), 8, 44, 96, 206
Troynt, name of boar, 16
" Turke and Gowin," 63
Twain, Mark, A Yankee at the Court of King Arthur, 248-9
Twrch Trwyth, hunting of boar, 116-117

Ulrich von Türheim, continuator of Tristan, 201

Ulrich von Zatzikhoven, Lanzelet, 87

Vinaver, E., critical studies on the Tristan, 192, 199
study of Malory, 244
Vita Merlini. See under Geoffrey of Monmouth
Vita of Cadoc, 17
Vivien, in Tennyson, 48, 79. See also under Nimiane and Nimue
" Vulgate Cycle," 73

Wace, Brut, 14, 19, 28
Merlin in, 72
Wagner, Richard, 165-190
and Wolfram von Aeschenbach, 165-172, 173
art of transition in, 186
" Art Work of the Future," 185
" motives " in, 179
opera of Lohengrin, 147, 165, 172-177
analyses of, 175, 187
interpretation of, 177
origin of, 172-173
plot of, 174-5
opera of Parsifal, 129, 165-172
Kundry in, 167, 171-2
opera of Tristran, 177-185
" Opera and Drama," 185
philosophy of, 179, 181, 183-190
value of myth in, 252-254
Wandering Jew, 172
Warner, William, Albion's England, 30, 76
Warton, " Grave of King Arthur," 38
Observations on the Faerie Queene, 38
Wauchier de Denain, continuation of Perceval, 64
Wayland legends, 22
Weston, J. L., 59, 64
From Ritual to Romance, 146
Legend of Sir Perceval, 64
translation of Wolfram von Aeschenbach's Parzival, 128
translation of Tristan, 193
For list of works see Appendix C
Westwood, Thomas, Quest of the Sancgreall, 143-4
Sword of Kingship, 49
" Wife of Bath's Tale." See above, Chaucer
William of Malmesbury, 16, 150
De Antiquitate Glastoniensis Ecclesiae, 150, 151, 152
Gesta Anglorum, 17
Gesta Regum, 150
Wolfram von Aeschenbach, Parzival, 128, 136, 160
story of, 165-171
and Wagner, 131, 165-172, 173
Wordsworth, " Egyptian Maid," 44, 77

Yeats, W. B., national myths and legends in, 257